INTERNET MADE EASY FOR THE OVER 50s

First published in the UK in 2010 by Which? Books
Which? Books are commissioned and published by Which? Ltd, 2 Marylebone Road, London, NW1 4DF
Email: books@which.net

British Library Cataloguing in Publication Data
A catalogue record for this book is available from the British Library

Some of the material in this book has previously been published in Which?, in our Computing magazine and online

ISBN 978 1 84490 075 6

1 3 5 7 9 10 8 6 4 2

The publishers would like to thank Sarah Kidner and the Which? Computing team for their help in the preparation of this book.

Consultant editor: Lynn Wright
Project manager: Kirstie Addis
Designer: Blanche Williams, Harper-Williams
Proofreader: Chris Turner
Indexer: Ben Murphy
Printed and bound by: Charterhouse, Hatfield
Distributed by Littlehampton Book Services Ltd, Faraday Close, Durrington, Worthing, West Sussex BN13 3RB

Essential Velvet is an elemental chlorine-free paper produced at Condat in Périgord, France, using timber from sustainably managed forests. The mill is ISO14001 and EMAS certified.

For a full list of Which? Books, please call 01903 828557, go to www.which.co.uk, or write to Littlehampton Book Services. For other enquiries, call 0800 252 100.

which?

INTERNET MADE EASY FOR THE OVER 50s

Contents

BE SOCIAL

PROTECT YOURSELF

JARGON BUSTER

EDITORIAL NOTE

The instructions in this guide refer mainly to the Windows operating system and Internet Explorer. Where other software or websites are mentioned, instructions refer to the latest version (at the time of going to print). If you have a different version, the steps may vary slightly.

Screenshots are used for illustrative purposes only.

Windows is an American product. All spellings on the screenshots and on the buttons and boxes in the text are therefore spelled in US English. The rest of the text remains in UK English.

All technical words in the book are either discussed in jargon busters within the text and/or can be found in the Jargon Buster section from page 215.

INTRODUCTION

Using the internet can save you time and money, as well as opening up a new world of experiences. The good news is that getting the best from the internet needn't be a stressful experience. With this book you'll find simple, step-by-step instructions and advice for getting the most from staying in touch with loved ones to online shopping, all explained in easy-to-understand terms.

Internet Made Easy for the Over 50s is designed to guide you through everything you need to know to become a competent user of the internet. If you're starting out, the early chapters give clear, jargon-free advice on setting up and getting online. There's also helpful advice on understanding how to use the web and email, and chatting to family online for free. Other chapters take you through finding information, booking a restaurant or theatre tickets, to setting up an online bank account and watching online TV.

And you needn't worry about security. Later chapters help you protect yourself online, avoid internet scams and stop online threats, such as viruses, from causing your computer harm. A helpful jargon buster is on hand at the end to explain some of the more complex terms in plain English. But, if you do have a problem, you can ask the Which? Computing Helpdesk (see page 224). Simply go to www.which.co.uk/computinghelpdesk and input code **INTERNET500310** where it asks for your membership number.

Feel free to work through the book chapter by chapter, dip into a specific chapter, or use the Contents page or index if you need advice on a particular subject. In fact, let's get started now – turn the page and let's Get Online.

GET ONLINE

By reading and following all the steps in this chapter, you will get to grips with:

- **Setting up a broadband connection**
- **Boosting your broadband speeds**
- **Switching broadband provider**

YOUR INTERNET OPTIONS

To connect to the internet, you need a modem (and/or router), a phone line and an account with an internet service provider (ISP). A modem is a small, box-shaped device, connected at one end to your PC and the other to your phone line. Most new computers now come with a built-in modem.

The modem connects via the phone line to another modem at the ISP. The two modems then talk to each other and send information back and forth to your computer.

This used to involve a dial-up connection that used your existing phone line – it was slow and you couldn't use your telephone at the same time. Most people now connect using a broadband connection – it provides a much faster service and you can use the phone and be online at the same time.

There are three types of broadband.

Jargon buster

Mbps

A measure of bandwidth speed, Mbps stands for millions of bits per second or megabits per second. The higher the number of Mbps, the faster the internet connection and quicker you'll be able to view and navigate web pages.

ADSL Broadband

Available to more than 99 per cent of UK households, ADSL (asymmetric digital subscriber line) broadband requires a fixed BT phone line. However, BT is not the only choice of broadband provider – ISPs such as TalkTalk and Tiscali use BT's network and offer their own broadband packages.

Some ISPs also offer local loop unbundling (LLU) ADSL broadband, which sees them install their own equipment in BT exchanges. This allows them to be more competitive with the prices and services they offer, although availability for this is currently limited to just 70 per cent of UK households, usually in urban areas.

Advertised ADSL download speeds typically range from 0.5 to up to 20 megabits per second (Mbps). The speed you'll actually get, however, depends on a number of factors including your distance from the phone exchange and the number of other people using your local BT exchange.

Pros

- Good choice of providers and packages
- Speeds are increasing and prices are dropping

Cons

- Some limitations on speed
- You have to pay a fixed-phone line rental

Who is it for?

Anyone with a fixed BT line who wants a good choice of providers and packages.

Cable broadband

Offered only by Virgin Media at present, it is available to around 50 per cent of UK homes, mostly in urban areas. You don't need a BT line, but you may need to have a Virgin phone line installed.

Cable broadband has potentially faster download speeds than ADSL and can even get as high as 50Mbps. Unlike ADSL broadband, the speed at which you can connect to the internet isn't affected by your physical distance from the exchange. However, don't rely on getting advertised speeds as these are still affected by equipment or traffic at peak times.

Virgin Media offers several cheap 'bundling' deals to cable customers taking two or more of its services (broadband, home phone, digital TV and mobile).

Pros

- Speed isn't affected by distance from exchanges
- Cable fibre quality means the potential speed is higher than ADSL
- Broadband bundles are competitively priced
- If you don't have a fixed line already, a Virgin one is cheaper to install than a BT one

Cons

- Only available to half of UK households
- Only one choice of provider
- Cable broadband has many of the same speed limitations as ADSL broadband

Who is it for?

Price-conscious consumers in search of a cheap deal 'bundle' with digital TV, phone and/or mobile. Or those living a fair distance from a BT exchange but want to achieve fast broadband speeds.

If you are not happy with your existing broadband ISP, find out how easy it is to switch on page 23.

Mobile broadband

Growing in popularity, mobile broadband means the ability to connect to the internet wherever you're using your computer. By plugging a USB modem (dongle) into your computer's USB port, your computer can connect to the internet using a wireless data connection such as a 3G mobile signal.

Pros of mobile broadband

- You can use it wherever there's a 3G mobile signal
- You don't have to pay for fixed phone-line rental
- Some companies offer pay-as-you-go (PAYG) mobile broadband so you don't have to tie yourself in to a lengthy contract

Cons of mobile broadband

- Maximum mobile broadband speeds aren't yet as fast as traditional fixed-line broadband
- The amount of data (such as music, text files, video and films) that you can download from the internet is capped at a fairly low level, and exceeding this can be very expensive
- Like for like, mobile internet access is more expensive than most fixed-line broadband contracts

Who is it for?

Mobile broadband is ideal for anyone who doesn't want to pay for a fixed phone line and for those people who travel for work or leisure.

GET ADSL BROADBAND

If you're not already connected to the internet, follow these steps to get ADSL broadband:

1. Find out if ADSL broadband is available in your area. Use a friend's internet connection to visit the website www.broadbandchecker.co.uk. Type in your postcode to see the options that are available in your area. Alternatively, phone a broadband provider and ask
2. Phone your chosen broadband provider to discuss which package best suits your needs
3. Ask them what speed you can expect to get and if there are any contract conditions – such as a limit on how much you can download. Also check their pricing structure. If your computer doesn't come with a built-in modem, ask whether they will provide a router or modem as part of the deal
4. Once you've signed the contract, your line will be remotely activated so that it can carry ADSL broadband and voice calls at the same time. This may take about a week to be done
5. Once your line has been activated, you'll need to connect your router or modem and configure your computer following instructions on a CD sent to you by the ISP. See page 14 for tips on setting up your computer

Getting broadband if you already have dial-up internet

1. Choose a broadband provider and find out from them how long it will take for broadband activation
2. Cancel your dial-up internet subscription, timing it so you're not left without internet access for long
3. Ask your chosen broadband provider to activate your broadband, then install your modem and configure your computer as normal

TRY THIS

Check what broadband speed your phone line can support before you sign an ISP contract. Go to www.dslchecker.bt.com/adsl and enter your phone number.

What to consider when choosing a broadband provider

- **Cost** Unlike with some dial-up internet services, with broadband you don't pay for the time spent online. Broadband services start from £10 a month up to a maximum of around £35; prices vary according to the connection speed you opt for and how much data you download or upload

- **Start-up costs** You may need to pay up front for broadband line activation (around £25 - £50), though some ISPs waive these fees in return for tying you into a 12-month contract. Some also throw in a free broadband modem or router in exchange for a 12- or 18-month contract, though you may have to return this if you switch provider within that time

- **Speed** Up to 8Mbps is the norm with most ISPs, though several are introducing speeds of up to 16 or 24Mbps in some areas. Virgin Media now offers a broadband speed of up to 50Mbps and is trialling a whopping 200Mbps, while BT plans to roll out a superfast broadband service to 40 per cent of the UK population by 2012. In practice, most people will find speeds of 1 or 2Mbps are adequate for surfing the internet, sending emails and downloading the odd music track. But, if you want to download films, watch TV or play games online, you'll see the benefits of a faster broadband speed

- **Advertised vs actual speed** What you pay for isn't necessarily what you get. Many broadband customers find they get speeds well short of those advertised. Factors such as distance from the BT exchange, demand and internet traffic play a part in reducing broadband speeds

- **Availability** If you live in a rural area, you're more likely to run into difficulties getting a decent broadband service. Those living in urban or highly populated areas have more choice of providers and broadband packages

- **Contracts** Many broadband ISPs insist you sign up for 12 or even 18 months. Some do offer one-month contracts – but you'll usually have to pay for broadband equipment and connection up front. If you want to end a contract early, you normally have to pay a cancellation fee

- **Usage limits** Most ISPs put a limit on how much internet data you can download and upload – anything from 1 to 75 gigabytes (GB) a month. 1GB a month, for example, would let you surf the internet for two hours a day, send and receive 100 emails a week, and download 30 music tracks a week. But downloading or streaming TV or film can really bump up your broadband usage and many ISPs charge for exceeding the limit. Costs for this typically range from around £1–£2 for each extra GB

- **Fair usage policies** If you opt for a home broadband service with no limits, check the ISP's 'fair usage policy'. If you abuse this, it may result in warning letters, restricted broadband speed or, at worst, a cancelled service. You'd have to try pretty hard to exceed most broadband fair usage limits, though. For example, AOL Broadband gives the following examples of excess downloading in a single month: more than 12,000 music tracks, more than 30,000 high-quality photos or around 60 movies

- **Technical help** Check how much it costs to call your ISP's technical helpline. Prices range from free to 10p a minute from a landline. If you run into difficulties, you'll be glad you have a free or low-cost technical helpline

- **Go a bundle** Many ISPs offer big discounts on their broadband services if you take them as part of a bundle with other home phone, TV and mobile services. Some even offer 'free' home broadband if you sign up for other services at the same time. Check to see if there are hidden costs to this so-called 'free' broadband, such as broadband connection fees, download and upload usage restrictions and lengthy broadband contract

TRY THIS

Check your broadband speed at www.speedtest.net or www.thinkbroadband.com – though remember that your broadband speed results may vary by time of day, and accuracy will be affected by anything else you're doing on the computer.

Get Online

Jargon buster

Microfilter
A device that attaches to your telephone socket and enables you to make voice calls and use broadband at the same time via ADSL.

CONNECT YOUR EQUIPMENT

To connect to the internet, you need a modem and usually a router. A modem allows a computer to send information over a telephone line and acts as a bridge between your computer and those at the ISP. A router is a device that splits that connection up so it can be used on more than one computer at home.

Set up your router

Once you've signed up with an ISP, most likely you will be sent a booklet/CD that helps you to set up your internet connection. For a router with in-built modem, it's likely to include these steps:

1. Attach a microfilter to the main phone socket (where the phone line enters the house)
2. All the cables you need should be included in the box with the router. Plug one end of the modem cable into the relevant microfilter socket. Plug the other end into the back of your router
3. Your telephone plugs into the microfilter too. This means that you can be on the phone while also having an active broadband connection
4. Connect your router's power supply and switch it on

Connect your router to the computer

1. Connect your router to your PC or laptop using the ethernet cable, which should come with the supplied router
2. Put one end of the ethernet cable into the socket on the PC and the other end into one of the four identical sockets on the router

Jargon buster

Router
A device that routes data between computers and other devices. It can connect computers to each other or connect them to the internet.

Accessing your router's setup

To configure your router, follow these steps:

1. Start up your computer and open your web browser to access your router settings

2. Enter the address of your router into the browser's address bar. This is a number listed in your manual. In the case of many routers, this number is 192.168.1.1

3. Press **Enter**

4. You will then be asked for login details. Your default username and password will be in your manual

Change your settings

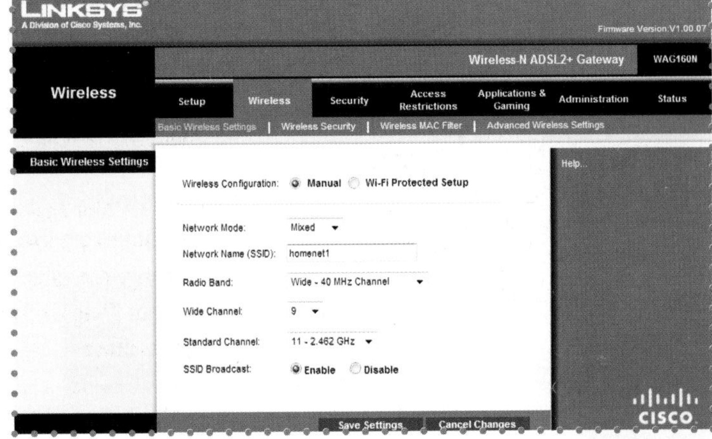

1. You'll see the router set-up page – it looks like a web page. From here you can make changes to the router

2. To change the default password, click the **Administration** tab, enter a password in the password window, confirm it and save

3. For the router to connect to the internet you need to configure the ADSL part of it with the right settings. Click on the Setup tab

4. The router will ask you to enter your ISP user name and password. These should have been provided by your ISP

5. You may be asked to enter details about 'encapsulation' or 'multiplexing'. You don't need to know what these mean. Just ask your ISP what should be in these settings, and the ISP should let you know these details

6. Scroll down and save your changes

7. You should now be able to connect to the internet on the PC connected to the router. If you don't want to connect any PCs wirelessly, then you're done

SET UP WIRELESS BROADBAND

Having set up your broadband connection with cables (see page 14), you can choose to go wireless if your router supports it. This means that your PC doesn't have to be physically connected in order to use broadband.

Set up a wireless network

To set up a wireless (Wi-Fi) network, you'll need a central wireless router plus a wireless adaptor for each of the PCs or devices you want to connect. Many computers, particularly laptops, are already wireless enabled. If not, the easiest method is to plug in a USB adaptor. You can buy one of these small devices from a computer shop.

1. In the router set-up page, click the **Wireless tab**
2. In the **Network Name (SSID)** field change the name of your network to something memorable like 'Home network'

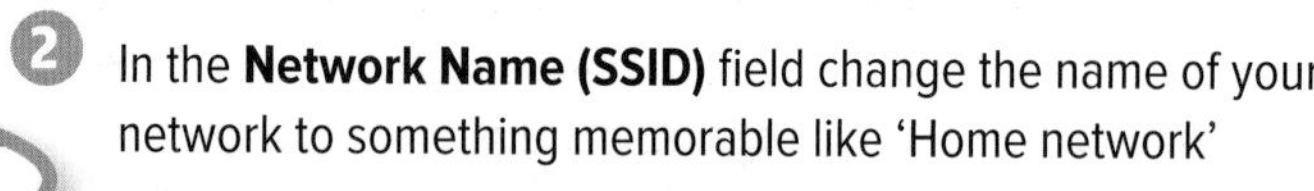

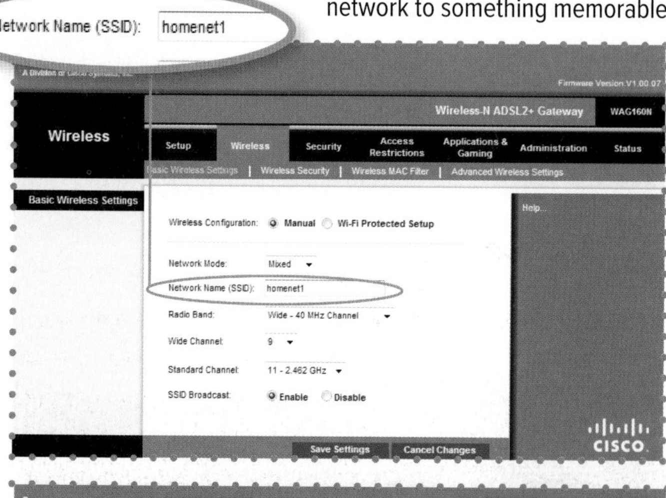

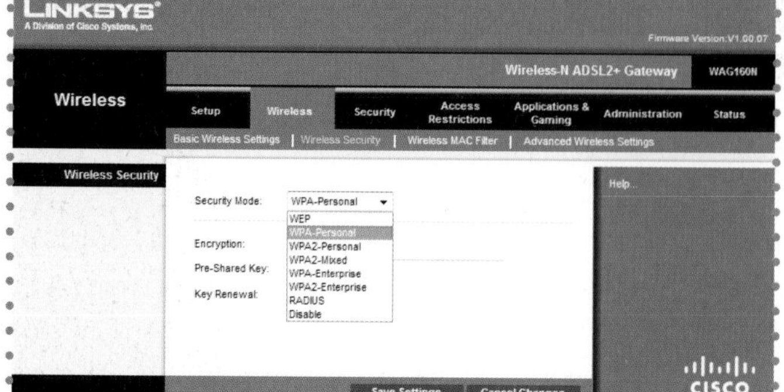

3. Choose the **Wireless Security** option. Here you can turn on security for your wireless network
4. Select **WPA** or **WPA-Personal** from the drop-down menu (the options will differ depending on your router) and enter a pass phrase (this works the same as a password)
5. Save your settings and unplug the ethernet cable

6. Your computer should automatically detect any wireless network within its range. Click on the pop-up message and you will see a list of available wireless networks. On the list should be the network you named earlier, in this case 'Home network'

7. Select your wireless network from the list and connect to it

8. You'll be prompted to enter your security pass phrase. Once you've done this, you'll be connected to your wireless network and can surf the internet

SECURE YOUR WIRELESS NETWORK

While wireless networks are far more convenient than traditional, wired ones, they do come with extra security risks. As wireless-enabled computers will search automatically for any networks within range and can then connect to any network that's open to them, it's vital that you keep your network secure by taking these steps:

- All wireless networks have a name (sometimes called the SSID) that you can change when you set up your router. Make it something that doesn't give any clues to your identity, or to the type of router that you're using

- If you're not planning on connecting new devices to your network, consider turning off the router's broadcast SSID option. This will make it more difficult to find for anyone looking for a network to connect to it

- Change your router passwords to something that's hard for others to guess

- Encrypt your network to make it more secure. Your router instruction manual should show you how

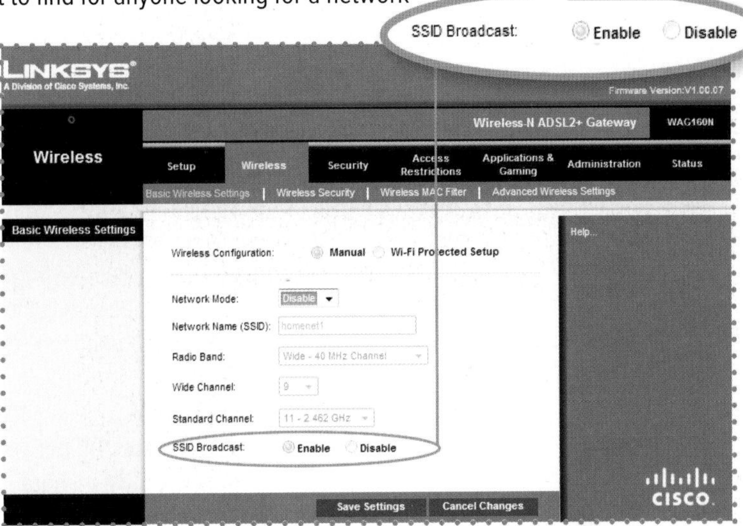

GET MOBILE BROADBAND

Mobile broadband is ideal for anyone who doesn't want to pay for a fixed phone line or who travels a lot for work or leisure. However, if you're a heavy broadband user, you might still be better off looking at a traditional fixed line broadband.

Mobile broadband costs

BT, O2, Orange, 3, T-Mobile, Virgin Mobile and Vodafone all offer mobile broadband services, with prices starting from around £10 a month. There are two main types of mobile broadband tariff – pay-as-you-go (PAYG) and contract.

BE CAREFUL

Contract cancellation fees can be steep so, if you're tied in to a long mobile broadband contract, you won't be able to take advantage of better deals that come onto the market.

Pay-as-you-go (PAYG) mobile broadband

Here, you pay for a specific amount of mobile broadband time rather than paying per megabyte (MB) of mobile broadband data you actually use. Beware, though, that there will probably be a cap on your total mobile broadband use.

You can cancel at any point, so it's easy to change your mind or switch to another provider but you'll have to pay for your mobile broadband dongle upfront, and monthly fees may be higher than on longer contracts.

Pay-monthly mobile broadband contract

With pay-monthly mobile broadband contracts, you must sign up to a direct debit agreement that takes a payment from your bank account on a monthly basis. You may get more for your money with a longer contract – 12, 18 or 24 months – since most longer contract tariffs include a free mobile broadband dongle.

Usage limits for mobile broadband

Usage caps restrict the amount you can download or upload each month. Mobile broadband usage caps are fairly low – typically around 3GB. Monthly costs rise steeply for mobile broadband usage limits higher than 5GB, and costs for exceeding limits can be extortionate. However, 3GB should be plenty for relatively low internet users.

3G mobile broadband availability

The 3G mobile signal covers, at best, 90 per cent of the UK population. It is better in urban areas; in more rural parts it can be patchy. However, in some rural areas that are unable to get fixed-line broadband, you may still be able to get mobile internet access. You can check providers' 3G mobile coverage on 3G maps or 3G postcode checkers on their websites.

Mobile broadband dongles

When you sign up to a mobile broadband service, your provider will send you a small mobile broadband modem – or dongle – to let you connect to the 3G mobile broadband network. Your computer may need to meet certain minimum specifications for mobile broadband to work. Check with the mobile broadband provider before you sign up.

USB dongles

Most dongles are small USB receivers that look at bit like a memory stick. You plug the dongle into one of your computer's USB ports. While you can use this dongle on any of your computers, you can only connect one to the internet at any one time.

TRY THIS

Not sure if mobile broadband's right for you? Consider a pay-as-you-go deal to begin with, and upgrade to a longer contract if you decide you like it.

Mobile broadband Wi-Fi dongles

Mobile provider 3 offers a dongle that lets you connect multiple computers to the mobile internet wirelessly. 3's Wi-Fi broadband dongle – dubbed the 'MiFi' – in effect gives you your own portable router that connects wirelessly to the mobile broadband network. One major advantage is that you can use the MiFi to connect any internet-enabled device such as an iPhone to the internet too.

Mobile broadband speed

Maximum mobile broadband speeds aren't yet as fast as traditional broadband – typically up to 3.6 or up to 7.2Mbps, although some are a little slower. Mobile broadband has similar speed limitations to fixed-line broadband, meaning that the maximum 'up to' speed is a theoretical rather than a practical maximum – you may not actually receive the full advertised speed.

Wireless mobile broadband (Wi-Fi)

At public places like cafes, airports and railway stations you may be able to access the internet via a wireless broadband network or 'hotspot' that's been set up at that location. Some mobile broadband providers allow their customers free access to these Wi-Fi hotspots – check with your ISP.

BE CAREFUL

Be wary of using mobile broadband abroad – charges can be very high.

BOOST YOUR BROADBAND SPEEDS

Does your broadband connection seem sluggish and slow? If so, try these tips for getting the most from your available online speed.

Change your broadband router

If you access the internet via a wireless network, you may get a slower broadband connection than if connected via a router or modem directly. Connecting via ethernet or upgrading your wireless broadband router (routers can differ in performance levels and ease of use) could make a real difference to the speed of your connection.

Try the BT Broadband Accelerator

The BT Broadband Accelerator (formerly known as the BT I-Plate) is a self-install device that can be fitted to your main telephone socket. According to BT, it can help increase your broadband speed by up to 1.5Mbps by reducing interference from your home telephone extension wiring.

The BT Broadband Accelerator is free for BT Total Broadband customers who order it online (though you'll need to pay postage and packing), but non-BT customers can also get the Accelerator for around £7. It doesn't work on Virgin Media cable phone lines.

Secure your wireless broadband network

If your wireless broadband network isn't secure, your neighbours may be logging on to and sharing your broadband connection. This will decrease your own broadband speeds. Secure your network by using the security settings within your router's browser (see page 17).

Spring clean your web browser

Every time you access a web page through your web browser, the browser stores or 'caches' it.

Periodically clearing out your browser's cache will help it to function more efficiently and therefore serve up pages faster. Here's how to do this for the browser you are using:

Internet Explorer 8

1. From the **Tools** menu, click **Internet Options**

2. Select the **General** tab

3. Under Browsing history click **Delete browsing history on exit**. Click **OK** to exit

Firefox

1. From the **Tools** menu, select **Clear Recent History**

2. From the **Time range to clear** drop-down menu, select the desired range – this could be from 'Today' to the just the 'Last Hour'

3. Alternatively, to clear your entire cache, select **Everything**

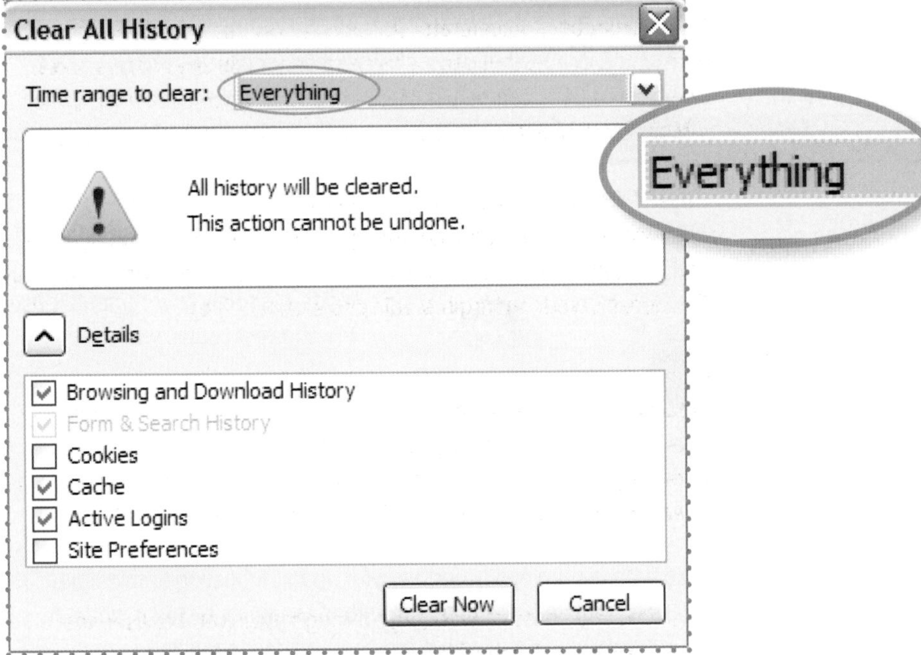

4. Click the down arrow next to **Details** to choose what history elements to clear, then click **Clear Now**

Safari

1. From the Safari menu, select **Empty Cache**

2. When prompted, click **Empty** to confirm that you want to empty the cache

Avoid peak surfing hours

More people attempt to access the internet globally at certain times of day than at others. Peak internet times include when America wakes up (anytime from 1pm onwards UK time) and evenings, which tend to be more congested than during the day or night. If you can avoid going online at these times, you'll find you experience a faster broadband speed.

Avoid excessive online multi-tasking

Internet speeds are likely to seem faster if you only do one thing online at a time. The more you try to do online, the longer each individual task is likely to take. For example, if you're downloading a TV show in the background using BBC iPlayer (see page 99), this may make it slower to surf from one web page to another (see page 30).

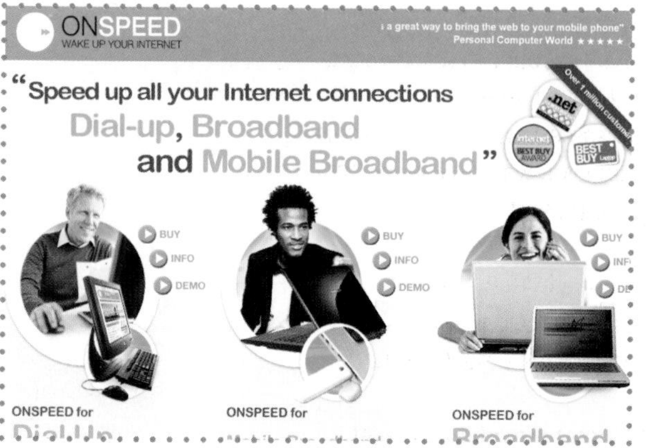

Watch your distance

If possible, try to connect your router or ADSL modem to the main telephone socket in your house. Also, if you connect the router or modem directly to a computer, use the shortest cables you can.

Use OnSpeed or add-ons

OnSpeed (www.onspeed.com) is a subscription-based service that increases the speed of your internet browsing. It claims to make both dial-up and broadband (of up to 2Mbps) up to five times faster and mobile broadband more than ten times faster. It works by reducing elements of a web page, such as image quality, so that less data is downloaded (this is called compression). It also holds ready-compressed versions of the most commonly visited websites so it can deliver them quicker. However, it won't make downloading a file, such as a music track or TV show any faster.

There are also add-ons you can download and install that will speed up your browsing in Firefox (see page 42).

Boost your Wi-Fi internet signal

If you use a wireless connection, you could try replacing the aerial. The longer the aerial, the better the signal and the further its reach.

SWITCH BROADBAND PROVIDER

Before deciding to switch, talk to your current provider. If you switch broadband provider before the end of any minimum contract term, you may have to pay a hefty broadband cancellation fee. As long as you're outside your minimum contract period, however, your broadband provider will be keen to keep your custom and may well offer you a much more attractive deal meaning that you might not need to switch.

The process you use to switch internet suppliers will vary depending on whether you're just switching broadband, or whether you're changing your home phone service at the same time.

Switch between ADSL broadband providers

If you're switching to and from ADSL broadband (broadband via a BT phone line), you'll need to use the MAC (migration authorisation code) process. A MAC is a unique code that identifies your broadband line.

1. Ask your existing broadband provider for your broadband MAC. Make sure you stress you're only asking for your MAC and not cancelling your broadband account; some broadband providers will see requesting your MAC as a sign you want to cancel the service, which is bad if you change your mind

2. Your broadband provider must provide a MAC on request and should send you the MAC within five working days. Your broadband MAC is valid for 30 days from the date it's issued

3. Give your MAC to the broadband internet provider you want to switch to. They should process your request and give you a transfer date

If you have problems switching between broadband providers because of difficulties obtaining a MAC from your existing broadband supplier, take a look at Ofcom's advice (www.ofcom.org.uk/complain/internet switching).

Switch to or from cable broadband

Cable broadband provider Virgin Media does not use the MAC broadband switching process. If you're switching your service to or from Virgin Media, you simply cancel your existing service and sign up to your new broadband service. You may need a new broadband line.

Switch your phone and broadband services simultaneously

If you're switching to or from a provider that offers phone and broadband services bundled together, you may not be able to use the MAC broadband switching process for technical reasons. However, under Ofcom's switching regulations, phone and broadband bundle providers are still required to make the switch as easy for you as possible. You can find detailed advice on the various broadband and phone switching processes on Ofcom's website (www.ofcom.org.uk).

Each of the three processes aims for the minimum possible disruption, though there's a chance you may experience some loss of service. In each case, ask your new supplier which broadband and phone switching process to use and how long the switch will take.

SURFING THE INTERNET

By reading and following all the steps in this chapter, you will get to grips with:

- **Navigating the web using a web browser**
- **Searching the internet for the results you want**
- **Getting the most from your web browser**

Surfing the internet

WEB BROWSERS

A browser is your window on the web. It is a software application that lets you view and navigate web pages, bookmark favourites sites, and download files such as music, video and pictures.

There are several main web browsers available. While they have the same job function, each has a unique appearance and different features. As web browsers are free to download and use, and easy to install and uninstall, you can try out a few and see which you like best.

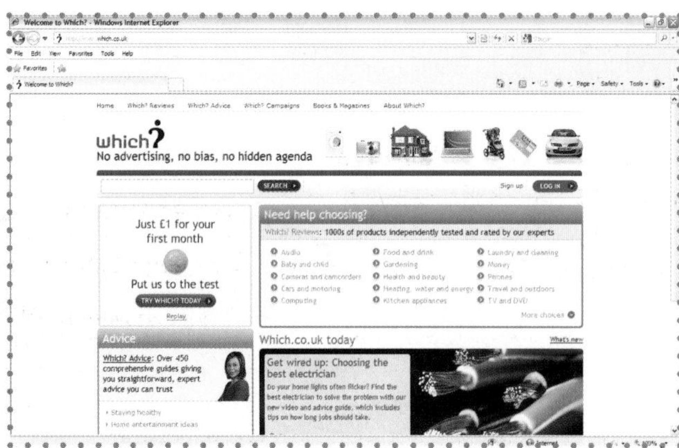

The most popular web browser is Internet Explorer, which comes pre-installed with Microsoft Vista and Windows XP. However, Microsoft's new operating system Windows 7 allows users to choose from several browsers including Microsoft's Internet Explorer (IE; pictured), Google Chrome, Mozilla Firefox and Apple Safari. Users can then select any one of these as their default browser.

How to install a web browser

1. Visit the website of the web browser you wish to use, such as www.firefox.com

2. Check the system requirements on the browser's download page to ensure it will work on your PC. You will need to check your PC system specifications to do this

3. Go to the **Start** menu and click **My Computer**

4. Click **View System Information** and then the **General** tab

5. If your PC specifications are OK, click the **Download** or **Download Now** button to begin the download process. Click **Save File** in the box

6. Choose **Next** to begin installation, and then click **Next** when prompted. Click **Finish** to complete

Launch a web browser

1. To launch the web browser on your Windows PC, click on **Start** in the bottom left of the screen

2. From the pop-up menu, click on **Internet**. The name of your browser will be listed underneath. Click it and the web browser window will appear in the centre of your screen

Change your default web browser in Vista

There are a number of ways in which you can do this:

- **Download and install the new browser** When installed, open the new web browser that you wish to be your default program. A message will be displayed asking you if you want to make this web browser the default web browser. Click **Yes**

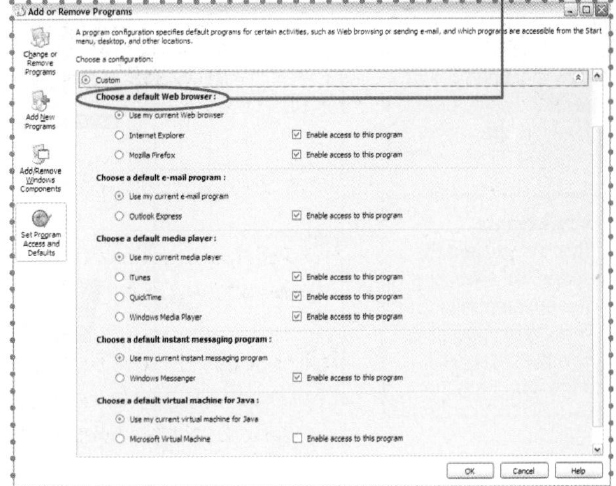

- **Through the start button** On the Windows desktop, click the **Start** button. Choose **Default Programs** on the list. You will be able to see a setting there for the default web browser that you want. Click next to it and exit the screen

- **In the browser itself** Open the web browser of your choice. Look for **Options** or **Settings** under the web browser **Preferences** to select it as the default. In Firefox, for example, click on **Preferences** under the Firefox menu. In the box that appears, click on **Advanced** and **General** and then make sure that the box that says **Always check to see that Firefox is the default browser on start up** is ticked

- To make Internet Explorer 8 the default browser, open Internet Explorer and click on the Tools menu and then **Internet Options**. On the panel, click **Programs**. Make Internet Explorer the default browser and tick the **Tell me if Internet Explorer is not the default browser box.** Click **OK**

Surfing the internet

YOUR WEB BROWSER

When you launch your web browser the first thing you will see is a web page. This is known as your home page and, each time you start your web surfing journey, you'll begin from here. The home page will have been already set by your choice of web browser but it is very easy to change to something you prefer (see page 27).

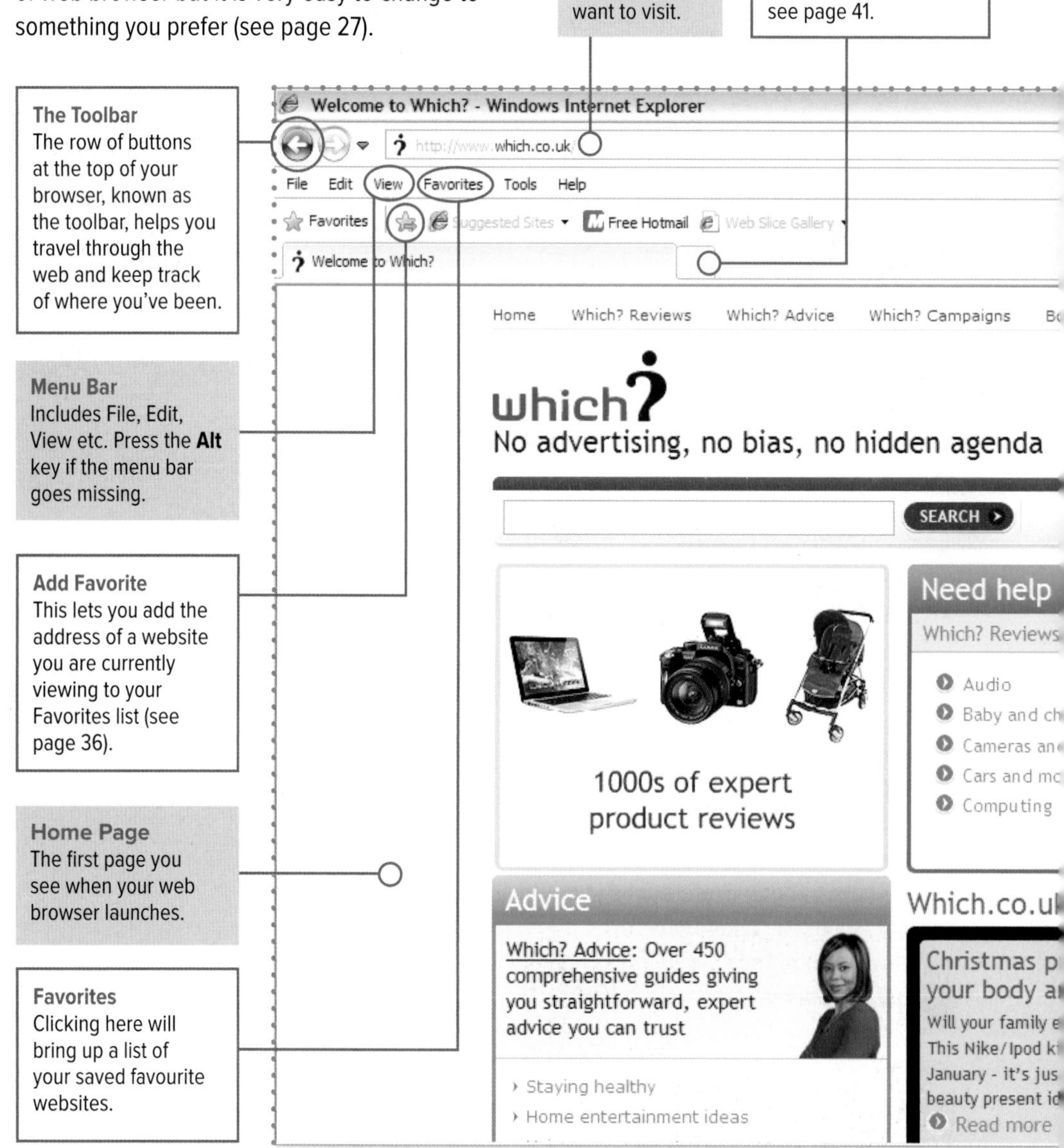

Compatibility View
Websites designed for earlier versions of Internet Explorer may not always display correctly in the latest version. If this is the case, click here to display the website as if you were using an earlier version of Internet Explorer.

Refresh
Clicking here shows any updates made to a web page during your visit. You can also use it if the page seems to have frozen before loading properly.

Stop
Clicking here will stop a page loading.

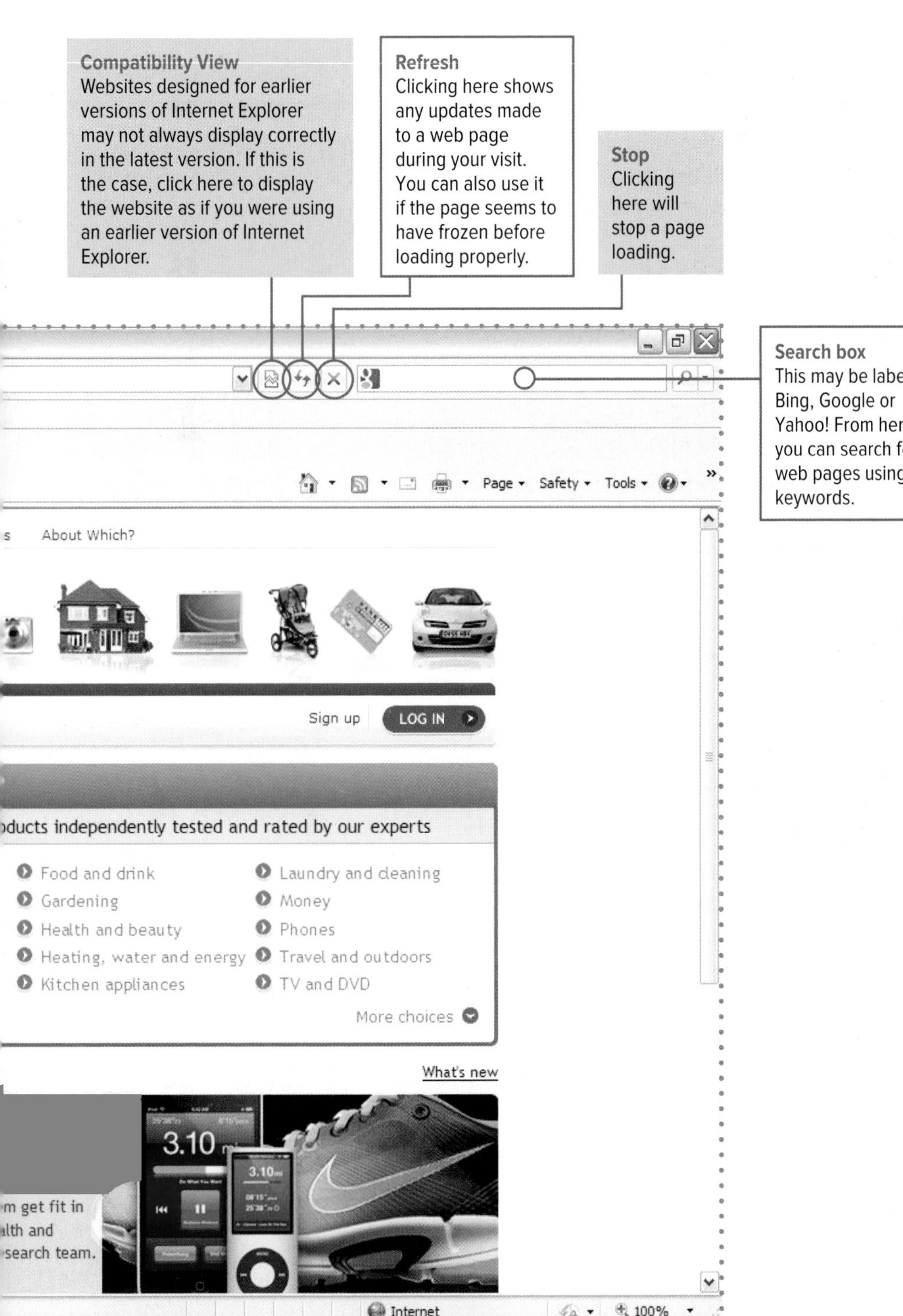

Search box
This may be labelled Bing, Google or Yahoo! From here you can search for web pages using keywords.

Surfing the internet

TRY THIS

You don't have to type http:// every time you visit a website. Just type everything after the last forward slash, and your browser will fill in the rest. For example, just type www.bbc.com rather than http://www.bbc.com

ENTER A WEB ADDRESS

Every web page has its own web address, often referred to as the URL (Uniform Resource Locator). For example, the Which? website is http://www.which.co.uk. If you already know the web address for a page, follow the steps below; if you don't and you need to search for one, see page 32.

1. Type the full address into the address bar
2. Press **Enter**

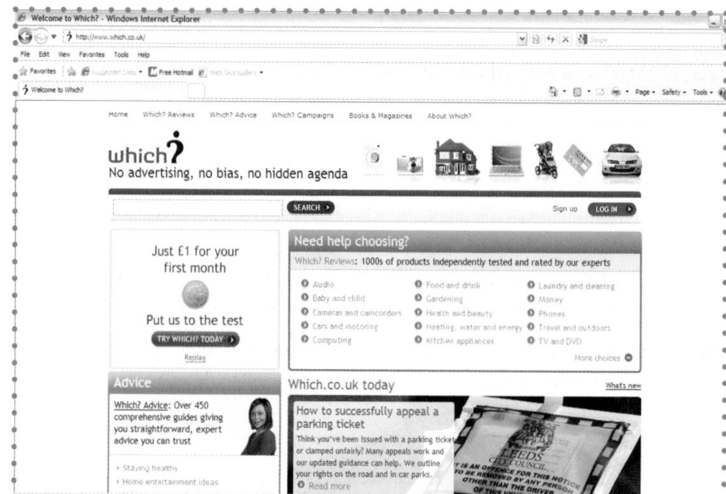

TRY THIS

If the web address you're typing ends in .com, you only need to type the words between the www. and .com and press **Ctrl** + **Enter.** For example, type BBC in the address bar and then press **Ctrl** + **Enter.**

NAVIGATE WEB PAGES

When you enter a website address in the address bar, that web page will appear to view. If you want to see another page of that site, or want to view an entirely different website, enter the new website address and a new page will load replacing the previous one.

Back and forward buttons

As you move between web pages, Internet Explorer keeps track of the pages you've viewed. So, if you want to return to the last page you looked at, click the **Back** button. Continuing to click it more than once will go back a number of pages equal to the number of times you click it. Once you've clicked the **Back** button, you can also use the **Forward** button to return in the same manner.

Recent pages

Rather than repeatedly clicking the Back and Forward buttons, you can use the **Recent Pages** menu to revisit a page you've looked at recently. Click the arrow next to the Forward button and select a website from the list.

Refresh

Clicking this button reloads the current web page, which is useful if it appears to freeze while loading.

Home Page

Clicking this icon will take you to your home page – the first page you see when your web browser launches.

Favorites

Most browsers allow you to mark websites that you visit regularly as 'favourites' or 'bookmarks' so you can access them quickly rather than typing in an address for them each time you visit. In Internet Explorer 8, these sites are called Favorites and you can choose to list them horizontally on the menu bar. Clicking on the name of a favourite website will launch that particular site. Altenatively, you can save them in a list, which is accessed by clicking the **Favorites** button.

History

Your browser stores a history of all the websites you have visited, which is handy if you want to revisit a site you looked at earlier or if you can't quite remember the web address. However, it's easy to delete this information either to save space or to protect your privacy. Here's how in Internet Explorer 8:

1. With your Internet Explorer window open, click **Tools**. Click **Internet Options**
2. Click **Delete Browsing History**
3. Tick the box next to **History**. Click **Delete**

TRY THIS

Flick backwards and forwards between web pages you've visited by pressing the **Shift key** and using the scroll wheel on the top of your mouse (up is forwards, down is backwards on the scroll wheel).

TRY THIS

Most web pages contain **links** to other pages. Links will often appear in a different colour, or as underlined text. Click on a link and the relevant web page will open up. You can check whether something is a link by hovering your cursor over it – if the mouse pointer turns into a pointing finger, it's a link and you can click on it.

TIP

To search a web page you're visiting, press **Ctrl + F** and enter the word or phrase you want.

SEARCH THE WEB

If you're not sure of a website's exact address or you want to find information on a specific topic, you can use a search engine.

The most popular search engine is Google (www.google.co.uk), but Yahoo (www.yahoo.com) and Microsoft's search engine (www.bing.com) are good alternatives. Simply type one of these addresses into the address bar to take you to its home page from where you can start your search.

Alternatively, the latest versions of web browsers Internet Explorer or Firefox have an instant search box located to the side of the address bar. You can type what you're looking for straight into this box and press **Enter**.

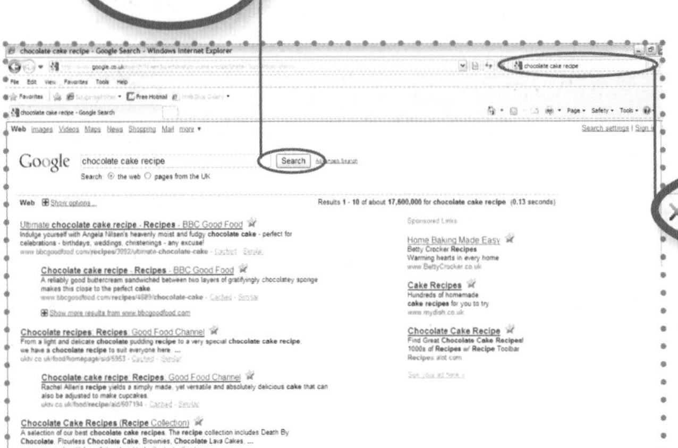

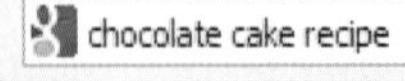

1. Click once in the **Search** box in the top right-hand corner of the toolbar
2. Type what you're looking for and press **Enter**
3. Results will be displayed on screen

If you can't see what you're looking for, click  at the bottom of the page to see more results.

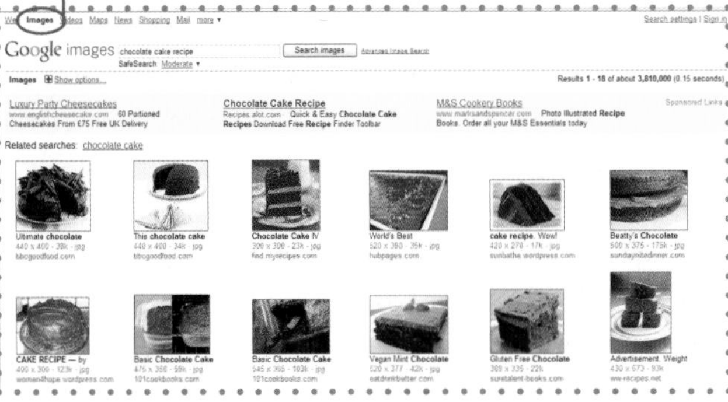

Search engines automatically search for text results first but you can also search for images and video. To search for an image, simply type what you're looking for into the search box and click on the relevant link or button (usually labelled **'Images'**) on your search engine's home page and press **Enter**.

In addition to **Web** and **Images**, Google also offers the search categories **News**, which search for news-related stories and **Shopping**, which looks for items for sale for whatever search term you've entered into the search box.

Add another search engine box

If you don't want to use the default search engine that appears on your web browser, you can switch to a different search engine, or add a specialist search engine box, for example, an eBay box, which will just search within the eBay site.

1. In Internet Explorer 8 click the arrow to the right of the magnifying glass icon and click **Find More Providers**
2. You'll see a list of options. Choose the one you want and click **Add to Internet Explorer**
3. Or click **Create your own Search Provider** if you can't see the one you want in the list of options
4. When you want to switch to a different search engine box, click the arrow next to the magnifying glass to show the list
5. Click on the search engine you want to use. Then in the box enter the word/s you want to search for and press **Enter**

INTERNET SEARCH TIPS

- Search engines don't worry about words such as the/a, so you don't need to include these in your search terms
- Be specific in your search. If broad search words such as 'car sales' yield too many results, try more specific words such as 'used car classifieds', 'used Honda car sales', or 'London used car classifieds'
- Using punctuation in your searches will make them more efficient. If you're looking for information on the TV show Antiques Roadshow, type "Antiques Roadshow" into the search window. Without the quotation marks, a search engine will look for websites containing either of the words separately
- If you aren't sure whether a word has a hyphen in it or not (email or e-mail, for example), keep the hyphen in; most search engines will check all variations
- Add a + symbol to keep certain words or phrases in the search results. For example, "city guides" + "San Francisco" will help you narrow the search for city guides for San Francisco only
- Similarly, place a minus sign (-) in front of a word that you do not want to appear in the search results. Typing in tiger -Woods, for example, will allow you to come up with results for tigers rather than the golfer
- Almost all search engines have an advanced search link that offers more detailed search criteria. Clicking on this brings up more search options such as the ability to look for websites with a specific domain such as .net, or find websites in a preferred language
- You can restrict searches to certain websites. For example, you can look up a computer error code on Microsoft's website by putting the code you're searching for in the search box and following it with site:microsoft.com. The search engine will search results from Microsoft's website only

- To avoid adult sites with explicit sexual content being included in your search results, activate **SafeSearch Filtering** on Google's home page. Click on Search Settings and choose a level of search filter. While not 100 per cent accurate, this filter will eliminate sites that contain explicit sexual content from the search results

Search for specific files

You can specify the type of document you want to search for. For example, you can narrow your search so that your results only include Word documents or PDF files. Follow the **Options** or **Advanced settings** links from your search engine's home page.

In Google, a quick way to search by file type is to include the word **filetype:** followed by the three-letter file extension of your desired file, followed by the keywords. Here are some examples of what to type:

filetype:pdf – Searches PDF files
filetype:doc – Searches Word documents
filetype:ppt – Searches PowerPoint files

Remember to include key words in the search query too (see below).

Jargon buster

File extension
The letters that appear after a file name. They show what type of document it is.

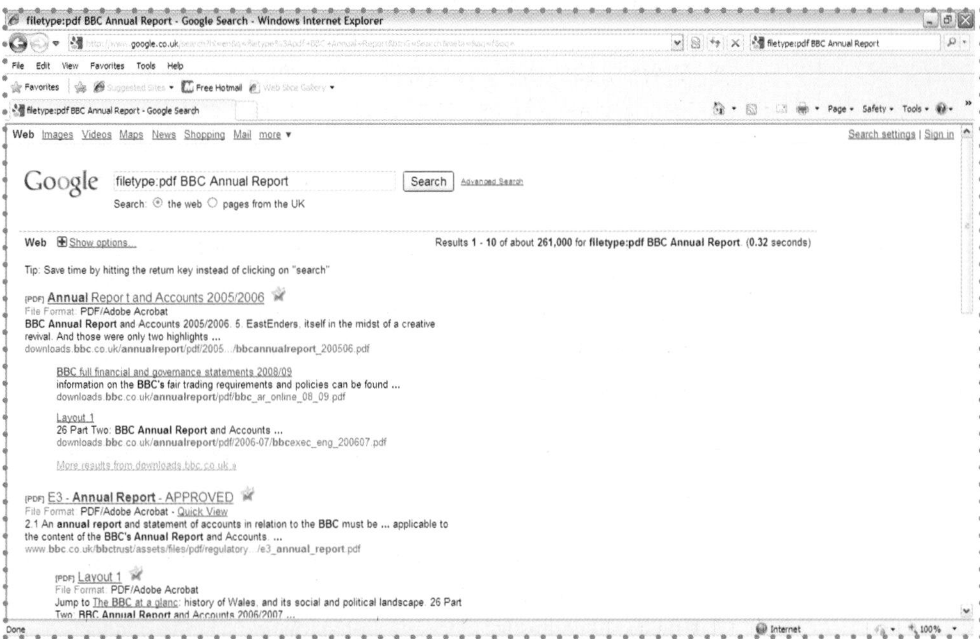

BOOKMARK SITES

Web browsers allow you to bookmark your favourite websites so that you don't have to type the address into the address bar each time. In Internet Explorer they are stored under Favorites and you will be able to simply click on the website's name to open the website quickly.

There are two ways to add a website to your Favorites list in Internet Explorer:

Add to the Favorites bar

This displays your favourite sites in a bar along the top of the web browser window.

1. Go to the website you want to add
2. Click the **Add to Favorites Bar** button 
3. A button with the website name will appear on the Favorites Bar. To go to the site simply click on the name

Add to your Favorites list

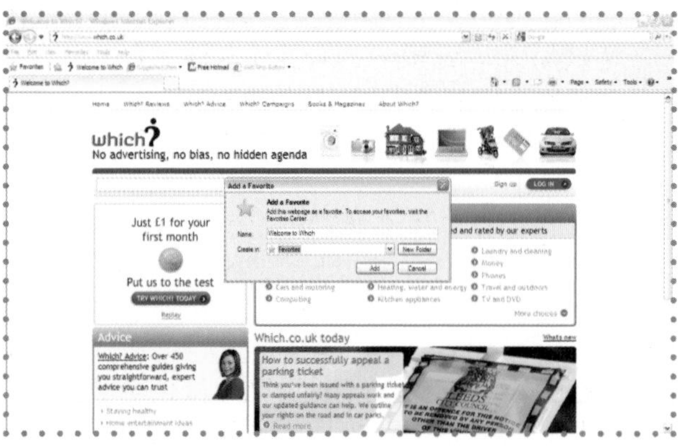

1. Go to the website you want to add. Click **Favorites**
2. Click **Add to Favorites** in the drop-down menu
3. In the box that appears, type a name for the website and click **Add**

Open a favourite web page in Internet Explorer

1. Click the **Favorites** button. Click the **Favorites** tab if it's not already selected
2. In the Favorites list, click the web page you want to open

MANAGE YOUR BOOKMARKED SITES

You can organise your favourite websites into separate folders, making them easier to find than if they are in one long list.

1. In Internet Explorer, click the **Favorites** button
2. Click **Organize favorites**
3. In the box that appears you'll see a list of your favourite links and folders
4. Click on a folder to expand it and see the links it contains
5. To create a new folder, click **New Folder**. When a folder icon appears, right click on it
6. Click **Rename** and type a name for it (for example, 'Holiday websites') and press **Enter**
7. When you've finished, click **Close**

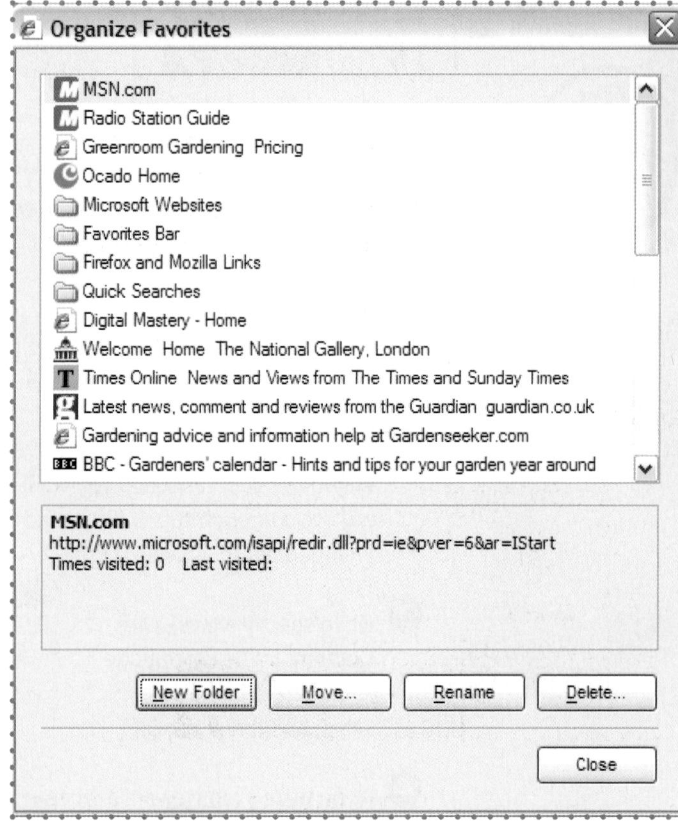

TIP

To rename an entry, right click on it, then click **Rename**. Type the new name and press **Enter**.

TRY THIS

To move a link or folder, click on it and drag it to the new position or folder. To delete a link or folder, right click on it, click **Delete**, then click **Yes**.

MAKE WEB PAGES MORE READABLE

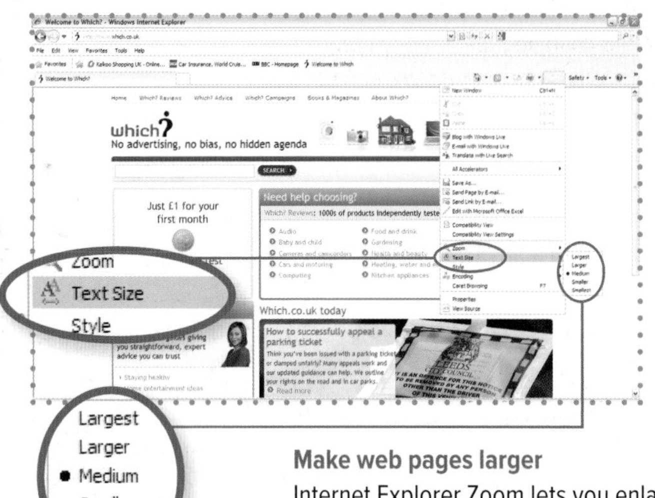

Internet Explorer 8 has several accessibility options that can help make web pages easier to read.

Change web page text size

1. In Internet Explorer, click the **Page** button, then click **Text Size**

2. Click the size you want

Make web pages larger

Internet Explorer Zoom lets you enlarge or reduce the view of a web page. Unlike changing font size, zoom enlarges or reduces everything on the page, including text and images. You can zoom from 10% to 1,000%.

1. On the bottom right of the Internet Explorer screen, click the arrow next to the **Change Zoom Level** button

2. To go to a pre-defined zoom level, click the percentage of enlargement or reduction you want. Holding down the button will cycle through 100%, 125%, and 150%, giving you a quick enlargement of the web page

3. Or, to specify a level, click **Custom**. In the Percentage zoom box, type a zoom value, and then click **OK**

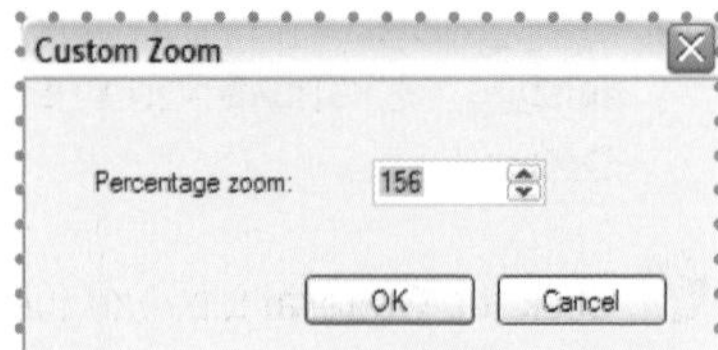

4. If you have a mouse with a wheel, hold down the **CTRL** key, and then scroll the wheel to zoom in or out (up for in and down for out)

5. From the keyboard you can increase or decrease the zoom value in 10% increments. To zoom in, press **CTRL + PLUS SIGN (+)**. To zoom out, press **CTRL + MINUS SIGN (-)**. To restore the zoom to 100%, press **CTRL + 0**

Change web page colours

You can change a website's foreground and background colours as well as the colour of the links (as well as changing the font type and size). These are all useful if you have poor vision, or need larger fonts or high-contrast colours for great legibility.

To specify fonts and colours

1. In Internet Explorer, click the **Tools** button, and then click **Internet Options**
2. To change the fonts, click the **General** tab, and then click **Fonts**
3. Specify the fonts you want to use, and then click **OK**

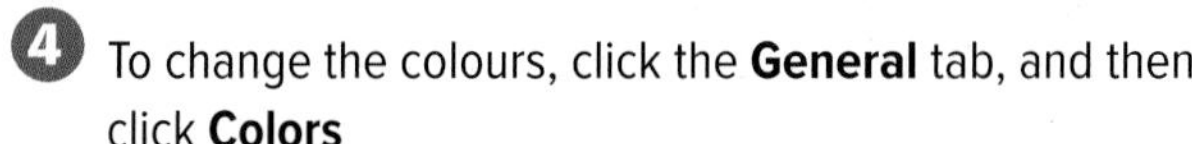

4. To change the colours, click the **General** tab, and then click **Colors**
5. Clear the **Use Windows Colors** check box, and then select the colours you want to use
6. When you've finished, click **OK** and then **OK** again

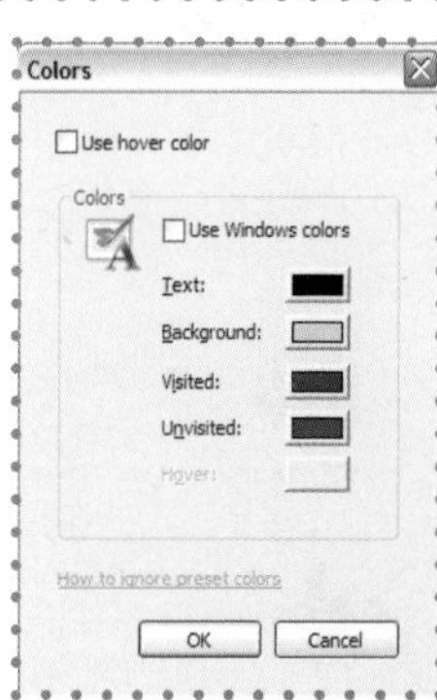

To make these your default fonts and colours

1. In Internet Explorer, click the **Tools** button, and then click **Internet Options**
2. Click the **General** tab, and then click **Accessibility**
3. Select the **Ignore colours specified on webpages**, the **Ignore font styles specified on webpages**, and the **Ignore font sizes specified on webpages** check boxes
4. Click **OK** and then **OK**

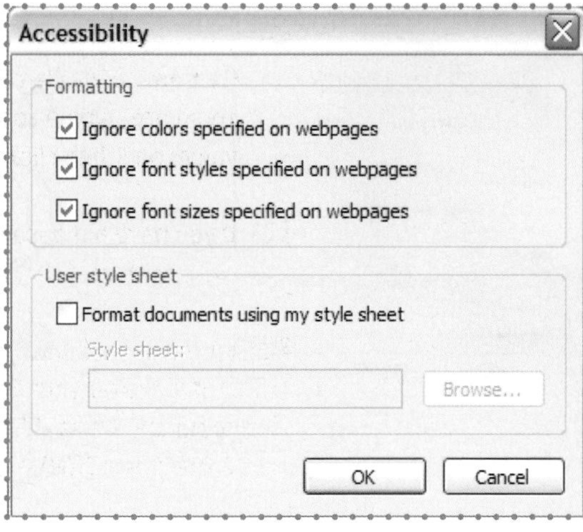

Surfing the internet

CHANGE YOUR HOME PAGE

Your home page is the first web page you see whenever you open the internet. This is usually set to a default page but you can change this to anything you want such as a particular news site, your webmail service (see page 60) or to keep up to date with a blog.

1. Go to the web page you'd like to use as your home page
2. Click the arrow to the right of the Home button, and then click **Add or Change Home Page**
3. Click **Yes** to save your changes
4. To go to the home page at any time, click the Home page icon 

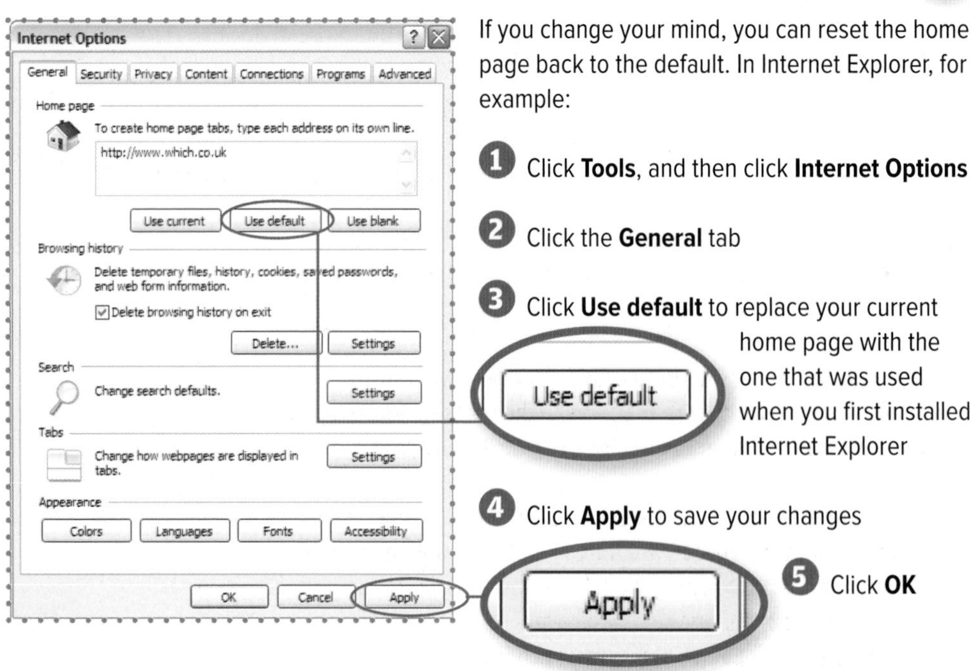

If you change your mind, you can reset the home page back to the default. In Internet Explorer, for example:

1. Click **Tools**, and then click **Internet Options**
2. Click the **General** tab
3. Click **Use default** to replace your current home page with the one that was used when you first installed Internet Explorer
4. Click **Apply** to save your changes
5. Click **OK**

TABBED BROWSING

Tabbed browsing allows you to open multiple web pages at the same time within the same browser window. This can aid navigation by letting you open a link in a fresh tab while keeping the old page open as a reference. To do this, right click the link and select **Open in New Tab** from the pop-up menu.

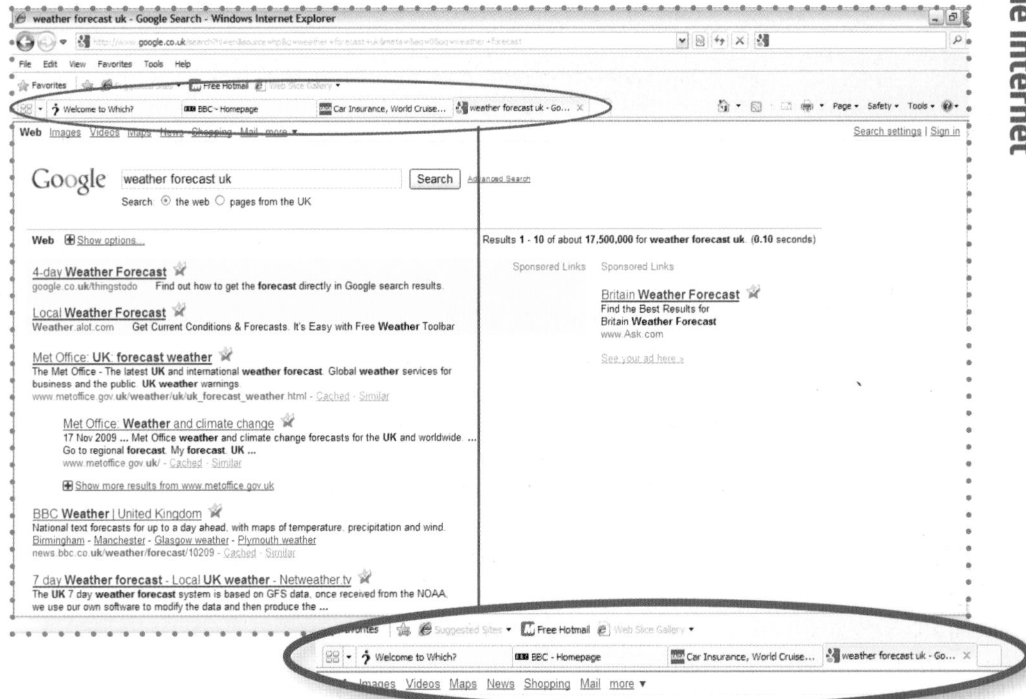

You can switch between tabs by clicking on the one you want along the top edge of the main window. To close a tab, click on it to highlight it and then click the grey **X**.

The alternative to tabbed browsing is to open a new window by clicking **File** and then **New Window.** Type in the website address you want into the new window's address bar to view that page.

If you want to view web pages side-by-side, simply resize the windows so you can see them on the computer screen at the same time (click and hold the bottom right corner of each window and drag to reduce or enlarge). Viewing two or more windows at the same time can be handy when you're comparing products or services.

EXTRAS FOR YOUR WEB BROWSER

All the popular web browsers provide support for add-ons, themes and plug-ins. These are small pieces of software that add a specific function to the web browser.

Plug-ins

Plug-ins make certain types of website content viewable or playable. Examples include: Adobe's Flash Player, Shockwave and Acrobat; Apple's QuickTime; Sun Java; RealPlayer and Windows Media Player.

Check what plug-ins you have installed

1. In Internet Explorer 8 click **Tools**, then **Internet Options**

2. From the **Program** tab, click **Manage add-ons**

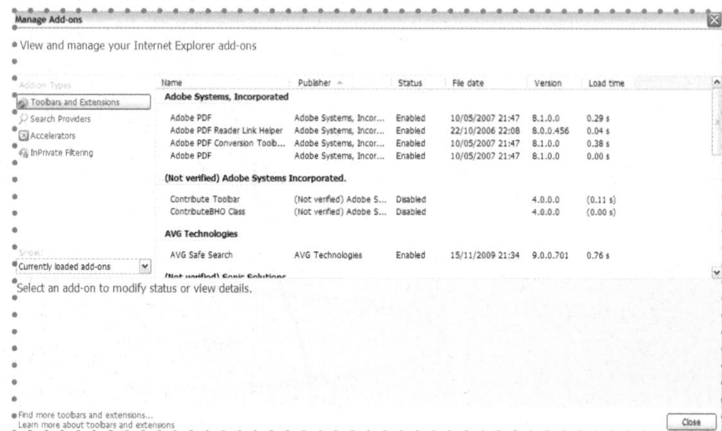

Or

3. In Firefox 3, click **Options** and then click **Applications**

4. Choose which plug-in is used to open different types of media content

Add-ons

Add-ons are free pieces of software added to your web browser to increase what it can do for you. They're sometimes referred to as 'extensions'. A huge variety of add-ons are available for each of the browsers. They are simple to download, install and customise to make your browser more flexible and your web surfing faster and easier.

STAY IN TOUCH

By reading and following all the steps in this chapter, you will get to grips with:

- **Sending and receiving email**
- **Avoiding spam**
- **Video chat using a webcam**

EMAIL EXPLAINED

Short for Electronic Mail, email refers to messages sent and received across the internet. To send and receive email you need an email account. This account will allow you to organise and store email that you wish to keep, as well as create an address book with important information such as phone numbers, postal and email addresses.

To grasp what email is all about, it helps to think in equivalent terms of traditional postal mail:

- **The email message** Rather than put pen to paper, you type an email message in an email program on your computer
- **Sending the email** When you've finished writing the email, you add the recipient's email address and press the Send button, which sees the email message head off across the internet
- **Mail server** Like postal sorting offices, mail servers transmit email messages from sender to recipient. Usually, emails are not delivered to the recipient directly, but are held at the nearest mail server to be picked up
- **You've got mail** If you've got new mail in your mailbox, you can click to open and read it. Your email program can also check for new email messages at your mail server and download them ready for you to read

To send and receive emails, you can either use an email client such as Outlook Express or Windows Mail, or a webmail account. Both share functions and features, although the difference lies in where email messages are stored.

Email client

An email client is an application that stores email messages on your computer. Using an email client means you can complete tasks such as reading email messages and writing messages when you're not online, but to send and receive emails you have to be connected to the internet. This was a useful feature when dial-up connections to the internet were common, but is less of an issue now as most people have 'always-on' broadband.

Webmail

Webmail accounts can only be accessed when you're connected to the internet, but the benefit is that you can access all of your emails from any computer or device that's connected to the internet, rather than just from your home computer.

SET UP A WINDOWS MAIL ACCOUNT

During setup you'll need to enter details about your email account, which will have been sent to you when you signed up with the ISP.

Enter your name

1. Click **Start** and click **All programs**
2. Click **Windows Mail**
3. The **Windows Mail setup wizard** should appear (if it doesn't, go to **Tools** and click **Accounts**)
4. Click the **Add** button and, in the window that appears, highlight the words **E-mail Account** and click **Next**
5. In the following screen, enter your name as you want it to appear in your emails (this can be in any form you like) and click **Next**

Enter your email address

1. Type your email address (as stipulated by your ISP). Click **Next**
2. Select the server type (as given by your ISP) from the drop-down list at the top of the next window
3. Underneath, you'll see two boxes for the incoming and outgoing server addresses. Enter the details provided by your ISP here
4. If required tick the box that says **Outgoing server requires authentication**. Click **Next**

Jargon buster

ISP
An Internet Service Provider is the company that enables and services your connection to the internet.

Security details

1. Enter your username and password into the boxes provided
2. If you don't want to have to enter your password every time you check your mail, put a tick in the box next to **Remember password** and click **Next**
3. Click **Finish** to exit the wizard. You can now use Windows Mail

Stay in touch

WINDOWS MAIL

There are lots of different email clients and most computers come with a default email application already installed. Windows Vista PCs, for example, come with an email client called Windows Mail (not to be confused with Windows Live Mail, which is a webmail account, see page 60). Windows Mail replaces Outlook Express, which came with previous versions of Windows. Microsoft's latest operating system Windows 7 doesn't come with an email client at all. You can download and use any email client you chose, or create a Windows Live Mail account.

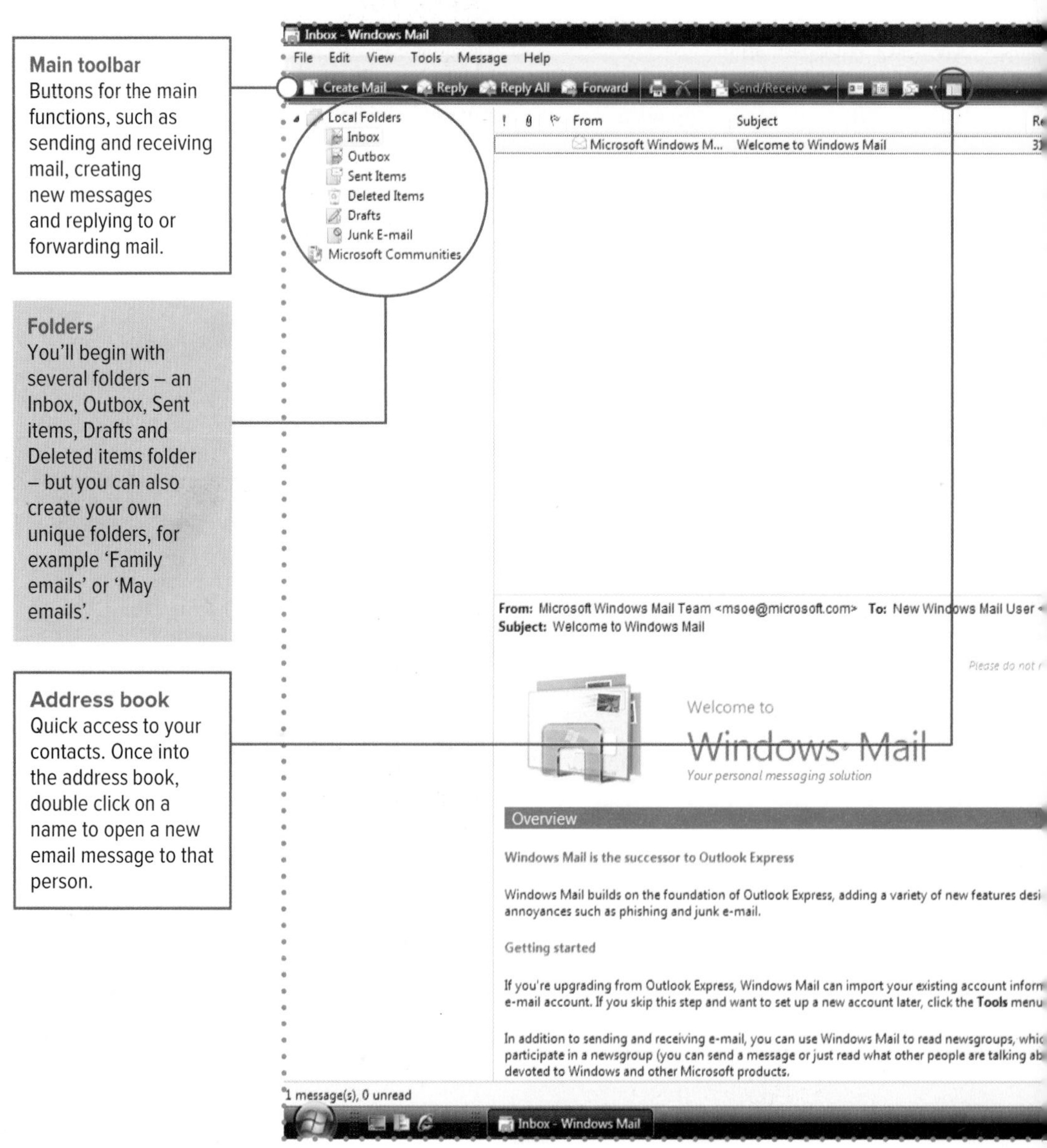

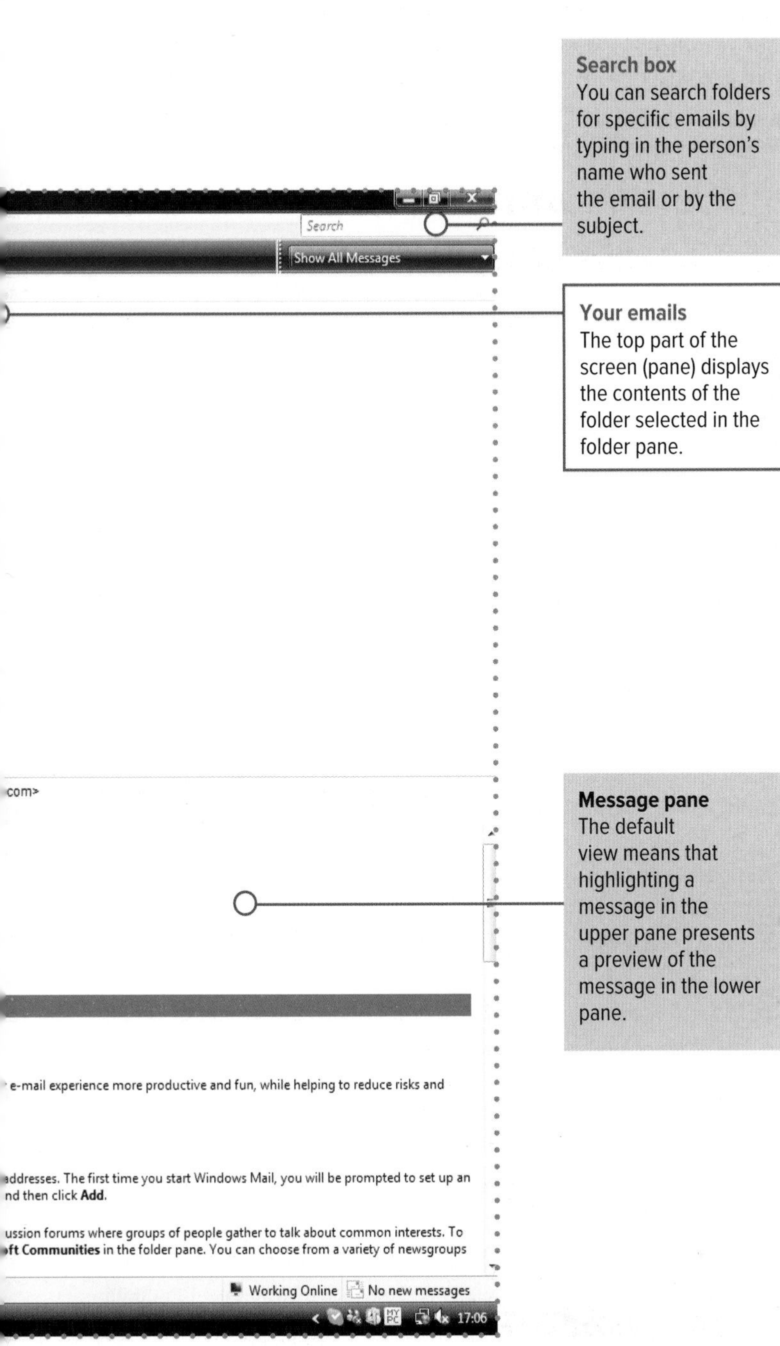

Search box
You can search folders for specific emails by typing in the person's name who sent the email or by the subject.

Your emails
The top part of the screen (pane) displays the contents of the folder selected in the folder pane.

Message pane
The default view means that highlighting a message in the upper pane presents a preview of the message in the lower pane.

Stay in touch

CHECK YOUR EMAIL

If you're connected to the internet when you open Windows Mail, it will check to see if you've got any messages and download these to your inbox. It will then check every half hour for any new messages. If you want to check in between, you can do this manually:

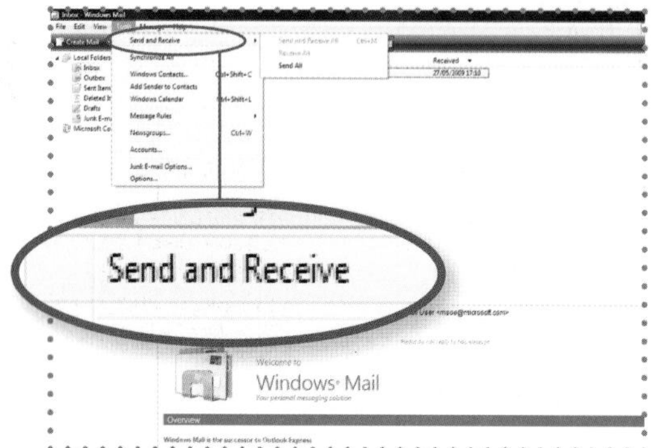

1. Make sure you're connected to the internet
2. Click **Tools**
3. Select **Send and Receive**
4. Click **Send and Receive All**
5. New messages will appear in your inbox

TIP
To send an email to more than one person, type a semi-colon between email addresses.

Open and read an email

1. Select **Inbox** from the folders list
2. Click once on the message you want to read and it will appear in the bottom half of the screen automatically
3. To open the message in a separate, bigger window, double click on the message in the inbox

Write and send an email

TIP
If you can't see the **CC** and **BCC** fields then click **View** and then **All Headers**.

1. Click **Create Mail**. A new window will appear
2. In the **To box**, type the email address of the person you're writing to. Or you can use your address book/contacts (see page 46 for more on this)
3. Most email programs also have CC (carbon copy) and BCC (blind carbon copy) fields that allow you to copy your email to others. When you use the CC field, all recipients are aware who has received a copy of the email. The BCC field can be used to hide email addresses so recipients are unaware of who else the email has been copied to

4. Type a title for your message in the **Subject box**

5. Type your message in the space below

6. When you're finished, click **Send**

Reply and forward an email

1. To reply to a message, open it and click **Reply** (top left of the screen). This will open a new window, with the recipient's email address already entered, where you can write your email

2. To forward a message, open it and click **Forward**. This opens a new window where you can write your email. You will need to enter the recipient's email address

TIP
With your message open, change the font size, style or colour in your email. Use the toolbar buttons.

Delete an email

1. In your inbox, click once on the message you want to delete

2. On the toolbar click **Edit**, then **Delete**

3. Alternatively, in the inbox, right click on the message and click **Delete**

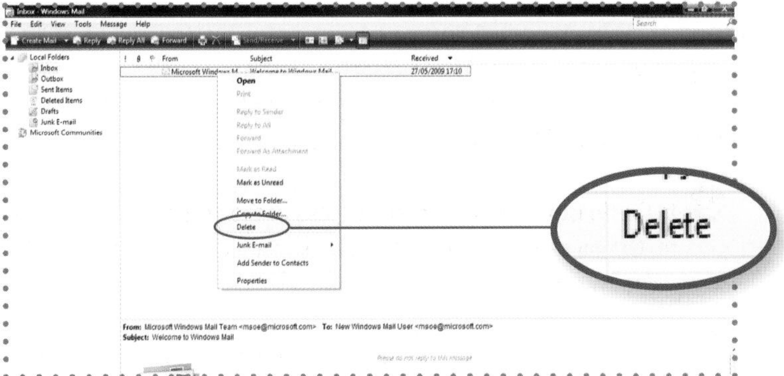

4. To select multiple messages, hold down the Ctrl key while you click each message you want to delete until they're all highlighted. Then follow step 2 or step 3

ORGANISE YOUR EMAILS

As your inbox begins to fill up with email messages, it's a good idea to use folders to sort and store messages. This makes it easier to find specific messages later. You might, for example, have a folder called 'Bills' to hold emails related to online payments, and another called 'Family' to store messages from family members.

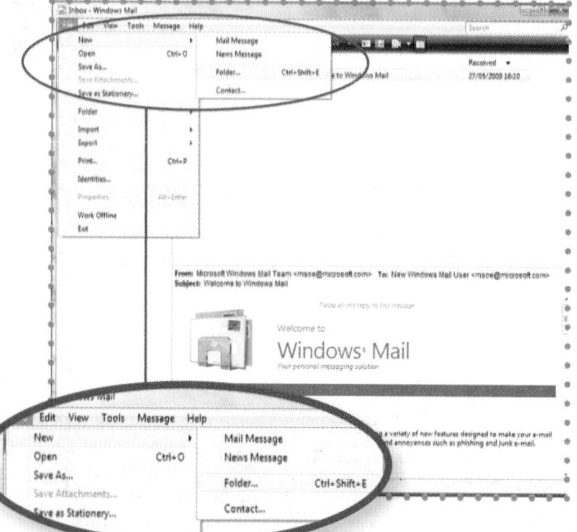

To create a folder

1. Open **Windows Mail**
2. Click the **File menu**, point to **New**, and then click **Folder**
3. Type the name of your folder in the **Folder name** box
4. In the **Select the folder in which to create the new folder** list, click the one you want

Moving messages to folders

You can drag email messages from the inbox into the folders manually by clicking on the email and holding down the mouse button as you drag it on top of your chosen folder on the left-hand side of the window. Alternatively, you can create rules that automatically move messages to certain folders as they arrive. You might, for example, create a rule to move mail from a specific person to a folder named for that person, or use rules to flag messages that you want to take action on later, or even delete unwanted messages automatically so that you never have to see them.

TRY THIS

You can click the **contains people** or **contains specific words** hyperlinks in the **Rule Description** box to specify the people or words you'd like Windows Mail to look for in messages. If you enter multiple people or multiple words per condition, you can use the **Options button** in the **Select People** or **Type Specific Words** boxes to further customise your rule.

To create a rule

1. In **Windows Mail**, click the **Tools** menu
2. Point to **Message Rules**, and then click **Mail**
3. In the **New Mail Rule** box, under **Select the Conditions for your rule**, select one or more check boxes to set up the criteria that will be applied to incoming messages

4 If you select multiple conditions, click the **and** hyperlink in the **Rule Description** section. In the **And/Or** box, click **Messages match all of the criteria** or **Messages match any of the criteria**, and then click **OK**

New Mail Rule

Select your Conditions and Actions first, then specify the values in the Description.

1. Select the Conditions for your rule:

- [x] Where the From line contains people
- [ ] Where the Subject line contains specific words
- [x] Where the message body contains specific words
- [ ] Where the To line contains people

2. Select the Actions for your rule:

- [ ] Forward it to people
- [ ] Highlight it with color
- [x] Flag it
- [ ] Mark it as read

3. Rule Description (click on an underlined value to edit it):

Apply this rule after the message arrives
Where the From line contains people
and Where the message body contains specific words
Flag it

OK Cancel

5 Under **Select the actions for your rule**, select one or more check boxes to determine how to handle messages that meet the conditions you selected

6 Click the underlined hyperlinks in the **Rule Description** section to specify the conditions or actions for your rule

7 In the **Name of the rule** box, click on the default name and then type a new name that describes your rule. Click **OK**

Creating a rule on a specific message

You can put all future messages from a sender in a named folder. To do this:

1 Click the message you want to use as a basis for your rule

2 Click the Message menu, and then click **Create Rule from Message**

3 Add the selected message's sender in the **Where the From line contains** condition

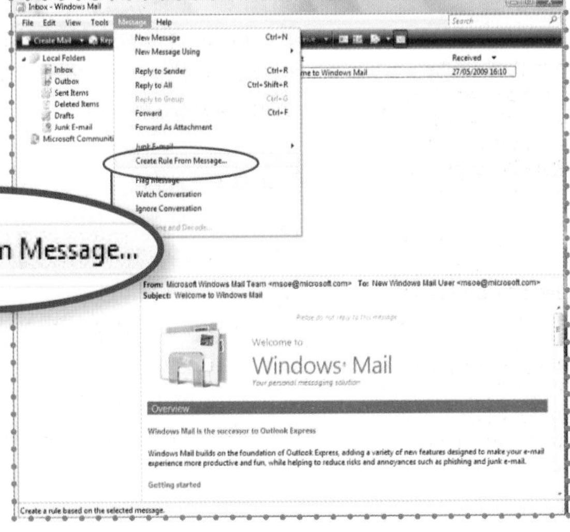

ADD AN ADDRESS TO WINDOWS CONTACTS

Once you're familiar with using email, you'll quickly build up a list of people you email regularly. Rather than typing out their email address each time you want to send them an email, you can make use of Windows Mail's Windows Contacts. Here's how:

1. Click **Start**
2. Click **All Programs**
3. Click **Windows Contacts**
4. Click **New Contact**
5. Type the information for your contact into the relevant boxes and click **OK**

Add a picture of your contact

1. Double click on the name of the contact
2. On the **Name and e-mail** tab, click on the dummy picture
3. Click **Change picture**
4. Choose the picture you want from your folders by clicking on it (see page 54) and then clicking **Set**
5. Click **OK**
6. To remove a picture, click **Remove picture** (in step 3) instead

ATTACHMENTS ON EMAIL

Sometimes you might want to send a picture or separate document with your email. Here's how:

Attach a file to an email

1. Once you've written your email, click the paper clip icon

2. Locate the file you want to send and click on it (photographs are likely to be in your **Pictures** folder)

3. Click **Open**

4. The file will appear in the **Attach** box

5. You can add more attachments in the same way. When you have attached them all, click **Send**

Open an attachment in an email you have been sent

1. Double-click on the email message that contains the attachment. Double click on the file attachment icon at the top of the message window

2. The attachment will open in a new window. You can save it from here

3. To save an attachment first before opening it, open the message as above and click **File** in the message window. Click **Save Attachments**

4. A folder list will appear. Select the folder into which to save the attachment

5. Select the attachment you want to save (if there's more than one). Click **Save**. Repeat for other attachments if there are any

BE CAREFUL

Attaching files and pictures to your emails can create unwieldy emails – if your email attachment is too big, you may see an error message that means it exceeds the email attachment limit for your account.

BE CAREFUL

Only open attachments if you know the sender. Those from unknown senders could contain viruses. See page 190 for more on computer security.

ATTACH A PHOTO TO YOUR EMAIL

Digital cameras can generate very large image files that may clog up another person's inbox if you attach them to an email. The size might even mean the image gets sent to the recipient's junk mail folder or is blocked altogether. Windows Vista, however, has a tool that lets you resize pictures for easy emailing. Consider what the recipient wants to do with it before choosing an image size (see point 4).

TRY THIS

In many email programs you can right click on an attachment and click Properties to see more information about it, including size and file type.

1. In Windows Vista, click 
2. Click **Control Panel**. Click **Windows Photo Gallery**
3. Click on the picture you want to email. Click **E-mail** at the top of the window

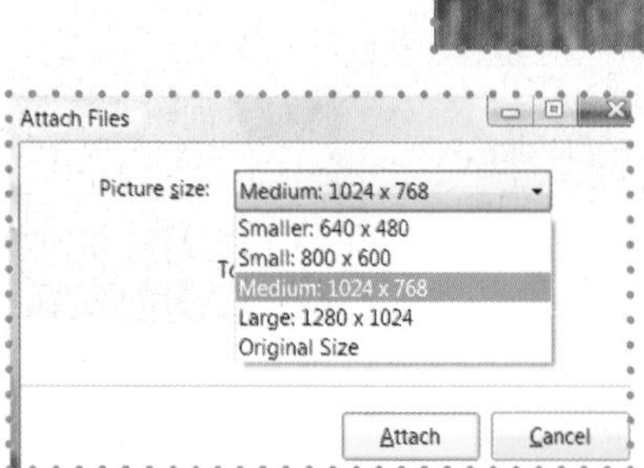

4. Choose a size from the drop-down menu. For viewing photos on screen the 'smaller' size is fine. This size will be suitable for printing photos at 4 x 6 inches. Both 'medium' and 'large' are suitable for printing photos sized 5 x 7 inches
5. You'll then see the estimated size of your attachment. Anything less than 1MB is fine to send via email. If it's OK, click **Attach**

SEND A SLIDESHOW VIA EMAIL

Rather than sending an email with a number of individual photographs, which can be cumbersome to open and view, consider sending friends and family a photo slideshow. The slideshow will play automatically when the email is opened and photos will be viewed in the order you want.

Create a slideshow

A good way to create a slideshow is to use an image editor such as Adobe Photoshop Elements. In this program, you can create a slideshow including a wide range of transitions (the moment when the slideshow moves from one photo to the next), then, when complete, compress the file to a smaller size as a PDF document so you can email it to your family and friends.

Choose images to include

1. Click on the **Start** button and click on **All Programs**. Click on **Adobe Photoshop Elements**
2. From the **Organiser Ctrl** + click the images you want to include in the slideshow
3. Click the **Create** tab from the **Palette Bin** on the right-hand side then click the **Slideshow** button at the bottom of the box
4. Alternatively, you can open the images from the **Editor**, click **Create** and then click **Slideshow**

Choose the transitions and duration

1. Click the **Slideshow** button. The **Slideshow Preferences** box will appear, complete with a thumbnail (a very small image) of the first slide you have chosen

2. A number of options will also appear. You can, for example, choose the length of time that each slide remains on show, along with the how one slide will transform into the next and the length of that transition

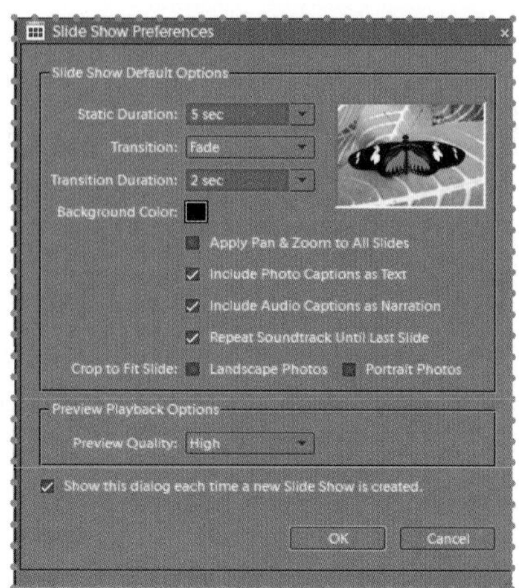

3. When you're happy with your selections, click the **OK** button. You'll then see the **Slideshow Editor** box

Change the slide order, add or delete slides

1. The **Slideshow Editor** box shows an overview of the slide show. You will see thumbnails of the images in order, any transitions you have selected and the static duration for each slide

2. To change the order of the slides, click on them, hold down the button and drag them to where you want them before letting go

3. To delete an image, right click the thumbnail and select **Delete Slide** from the menu that appears

4. You can add images easily too. Click the **Add Media** button close to the top of the box

5. Select **Photos and Videos from Folder** and then navigate to your folder of images. **Ctrl + click** the photos or video you want to add from your folder, and click **Open**. The photos or video will be added to the slideshow

Customise the look

1. To the right of the active image you will see an **Extras** list and a **Properties** list

2. You can customise the look of your active slide by adding text, choosing graphics from the selection on offer or adding your own narration. Click on the three icons located at the top-right of the **Slide Show Editor** box. The Picture icon will add graphics, the T icon allows you to add text, and the microphone icon can record sound if you have a PC equipped with a microphone

3. To add text, click the **T** icon, then click on and drag a text style onto the active image. Click the **Edit Text**... button under the **Properties** tab to change the words

4. You can also change the background colour of your slide and alter the static duration as well as enable a Pan and Zoom effect that zooms out from a part of an image until the full photo is displayed

5. To add a **Pan and Zoom** effect that zooms out from a part of an image until the full photo is displayed, right-click an image in the **Slide Show Editor** and select **Enable Pan and Zoom**. Resize the green box that appears on the active image by clicking and dragging the corners of the green box, and position it on the image where you want the Pan and Zoom effect to start

Set the transition type

1. Once you're happy with the order of your photos and have applied any affects such as text as above, you can change the transition of slides, which alters what happens when one photo replaces another on screen

2. The default setting is a two-second fade, which is usually fine for most slideshows. You can select from many different types of transitions, and there's even a random option

3. To change from the default transition, click on the small black arrow to the right of the transition's icon and select a new type from the pop-up menu, such as **Dissolve**

4. You can also apply the same transition to all the slides at once by selecting the same small black arrow and choosing **Apply To All** from the pop-up menu

Save the slideshow as a PDF

1. Once you're happy with your selections, click the **Output** button close to the top left of the box

2. The **Slideshow Output** box will appear. You can save your file as a PDF, as well as select the slide's image from the pop-up menu

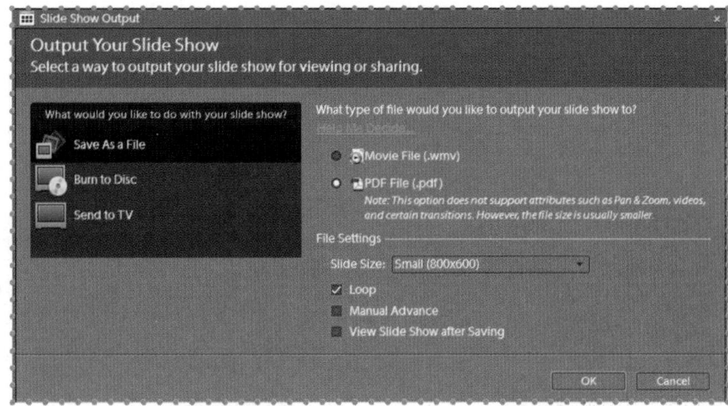

3. Select the **Small option** of 800 x 600 pixels so that the slideshow can be sent by email

4. Select **Loop** to replay the slideshow continuously or **Manual Advance** for the viewer to move from one slide to the next by clicking with their mouse

5. Select **View Slideshow** after **Saving** if you would like to see the show after creating it. Select **OK** and save the PDF file to where you would like to keep it on your computer

Send your PDF slideshow

1. Open your email program and attach the slideshow in the normal way of adding an attachment (see page 53)

2. Alternatively, right click the PDF and select **Send to** and then **Mail Recipient**

3. Now choose who you intend to receive your slide show. When your recipient opens the attachment, the PDF will automatically open Adobe Reader in full-screen mode and the slideshow will begin

Jargon buster

PDF
A PDF (Portable Document Format) is a popular file format that can be opened and viewed using Adobe Reader software. This is usually bundled with new PCs or it can be downloaded for free from the Adobe website.

USE A WEBMAIL ACCOUNT

There are a number of webmail accounts to choose from, including Google's Gmail (www.gmail.com), Yahoo! Mail (https://login.yahoo.com) and Windows Live Mail (home.live.com – this was previously Hotmail).

Create a Windows Live Mail Account

The first thing you'll need to do is set up a Windows Live ID, which will give you access to a personalised home page as well as a Windows Live Mail account.

1. Go to http://home.live.com. Click on the **Sign up** button

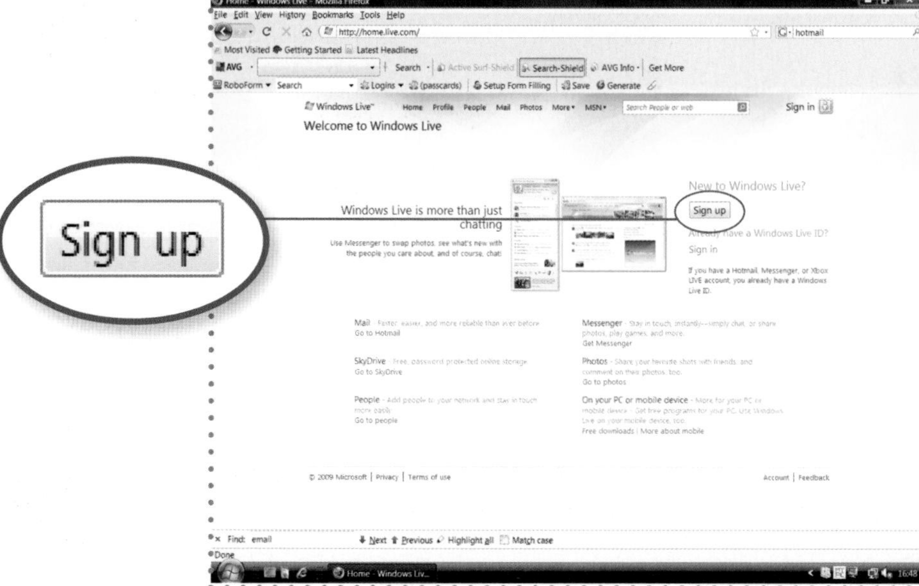

2. Enter a Windows Live ID (usually a version of your name) and click **Check availability**. If your preferred ID isn't available, Windows Live will suggest alternatives. For example, if JohnDoe isn't available, you may be offered JohnDoe323

3. Choose a password for your account. Enter an alternative email address (if you have one) so that Windows Live Mail can send you a reminder of your password if needed, or click **Or choose a security question for password reset**. Click the drop-down arrow and choose a reminder question

4 Enter your personal details and copy the series of characters – the captcha – at the bottom of the screen. Click **I accept**

5 To make changes to your profile click **Profile**

6 Click **Edit profile details**

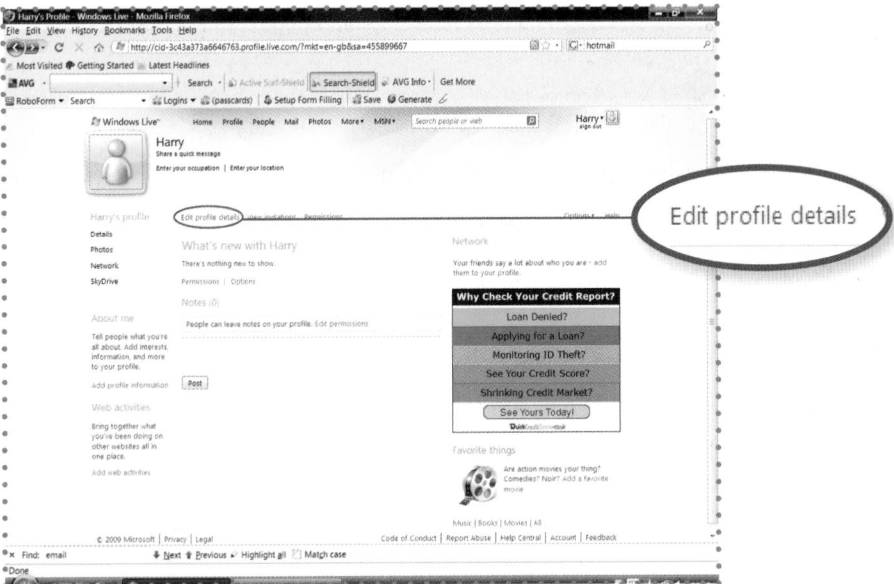

7 Click the relevant buttons to add a picture, enter your age, contact information and so on. Avoid adding any sensitive information

8 Windows Live Mail's default setting is to share your profile publicly. To change this, click on the link that currently reads **Everyone (public)** under Contact info. Untick the box that says **Everyone (public)**

9 Tick the box that reads **My network**, which means your information is only accessible to those in your contact list, not to others. Click **Save**

Jargon buster

Captcha
A common feature used in filling out forms or sending messages online. Consisting of an image of a distorted word or collection of numbers that you need to copy, they're designed to check that the user is a human and not an automated program sending spam messages.

Send an email

1. Go to home.live.com. Log into your Windows Live Mail account with your Windows Live ID and password

2. On the home page click **Mail** to access your Windows Live Mail (alternatively you can bookmark http://mail.live.com to go straight to your email account – see page 36 for more on bookmarking)

3. To send an email, click **New**

4. Type the email address of the recipient in the **To** box or click on **To**: to reveal any friends' addresses you have added to your Contacts

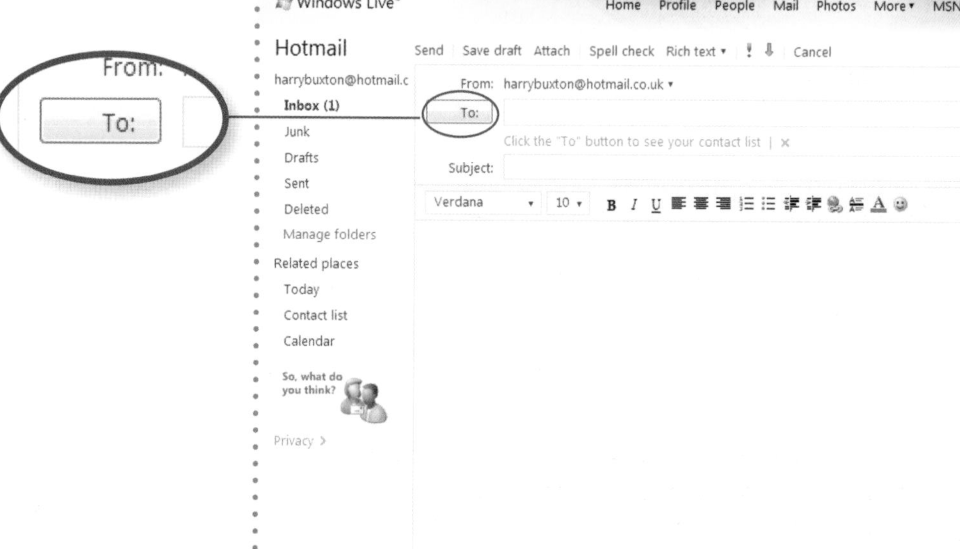

5. Enter a subject line for your email and type your text

6. Click **Send**

Filter emails

To filter emails so that they automatically go into one folder, you'll need to set up a new folder.

1. Click **Manage Folders** on the left-hand side of the screen

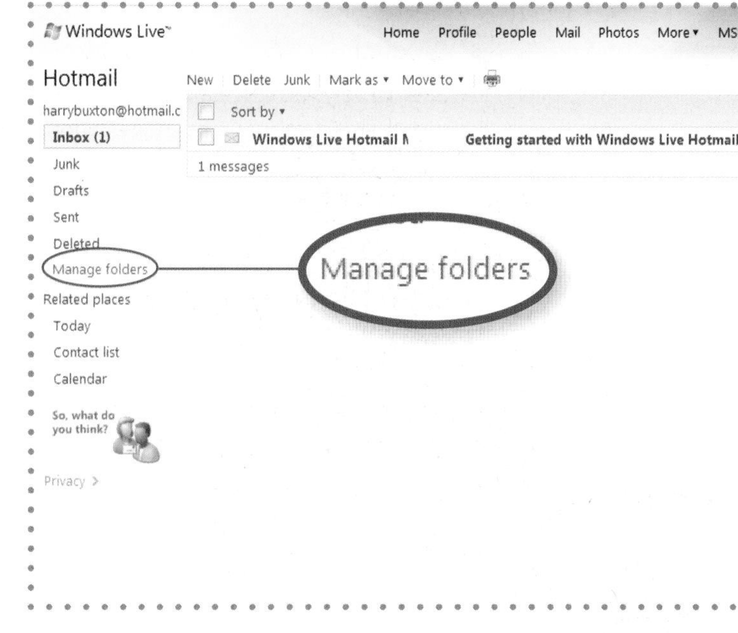

2. Click **New** and give your folder a name (this can be anything – for example, 'Work friends')
3. Press **Enter**
4. Click **Options** (on the right-hand side of the screen), then **More Options**
5. Under **Customize your email**, click **Automatically sort e-mail into folders**
6. Click **New Filter**
7. Select **From address** and **Contains** from the drop-down menus (if they aren't already selected) and enter the email address of a work friend (you can only enter one address at a time)
8. Put a dot next to the new 'Work friends' folder you created in step 2
9. Click **Save**. The emails from that person will now automatically go to that folder

BE CAREFUL

If you've set up a filter, remember to check that new folder you've created for emails from those people.

Stay in touch

SET UP A GMAIL ACCOUNT

Gmail (also known as Google Mail) is another popular webmail service.

1. Type mail.google.com in the address bar of your browser

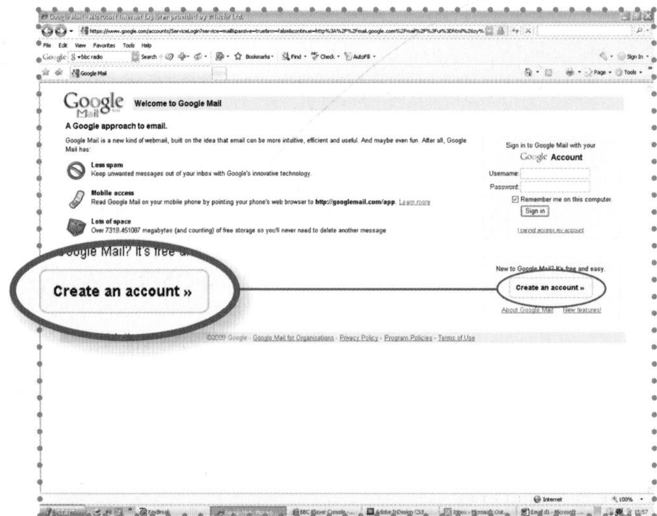

2. On the Google Mail home page, click **Create an account**

3. This will open a registration page asking you to fill in your details (for example, creating a login name and password). If your chosen name isn't available, you'll have to enter an alternative

4. Once you've done this, click **I Accept/Create my Account**

Send an email on Google Mail

1. Go to the web page mail.google.com to log into your account. Enter your username and password that you created when you set up the account. Click **Sign in**

2. You can now start emailing. Click on **Compose Mail** (top left of the screen) to write an email

Send instant messages to friends on Google Mail

1. Click **Add contact** in the Chat menu on the left-hand side

2. Enter your friends' email addresses. Click **Send invites** to invite them to chat

3. To chat with a friend, make sure they are online (when they are also logged into Google Mail, they will have a green dot next to their name) and click on their name to open a window where you can type your messages

DEAL WITH SPAM

The electronic equivalent of junk mail, spam can clog up your inbox. Spam emails may also contain offensive material and can be carriers of viruses and phishing scams (see page 190).

Your ISP will use spam filters on their email server in an attempt to prevent spam from reaching your inbox and webmail accounts usually feature spam filters too. You can also change your email program's junk email settings to filter out certain types of message automatically.

Filter junk mail in Windows Live Mail (Hotmail)

1. With your Windows Live Mail account open, click **Options** at the top right of your screen. Click **More options**

2. Under **Junk Mail**, click **Filters and Reporting**

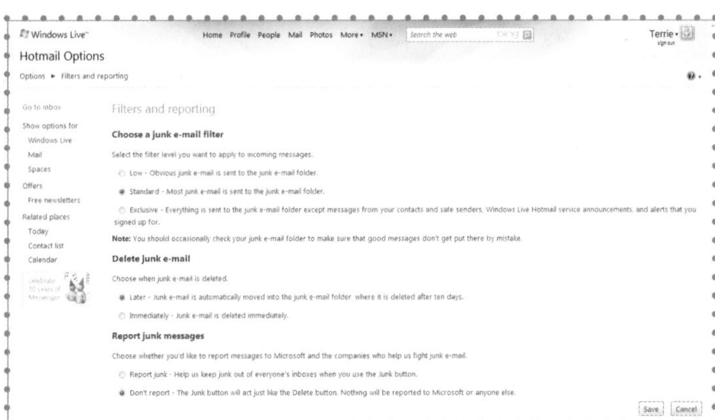

3. From the list that appears, you can select how your account deals with junk mail. Click **Save** at the bottom of the page when you've chosen

Filter junk mail in Windows Mail

1. With your Windows Mail account open, click **Tools** on the toolbar

2. Click **Junk E-mail Options.** A window will appear. Here you can choose the level of protection you want

3. Make your choices and click **Apply**. Click **OK**

BE CAREFUL

Never reply to spam emails or click on an 'unsubscribe' link within them as this confirms that your email address is genuine. Simply delete them without opening the message.

Stay in touch

SET UP A WEBCAM

A webcam is a video camera attached to a computer that transmits images across the internet. It's a great way to stay in touch with friends and loved ones, particularly those who are abroad. Both you and the person you're talking to will need a webcam and a broadband connection. New PCs/laptops often have an integrated webcam in the screen. If not, you'll need to buy a separate webcam, which you then attach to your monitor.

1. Run the set-up CD included with the webcam. This will install the software that the webcam needs to work with your computer

2. Check your webcam manual for instructions on how to attach the webcam to your computer

3. Place your webcam at around eye level, and an arm's length from your face to ensure that people aren't squinting to see you or staring up your nose

4. When prompted, plug the webcam into a USB port on your computer. Windows Vista should recognise it and the software will set up the webcam's camera and the built-in microphone

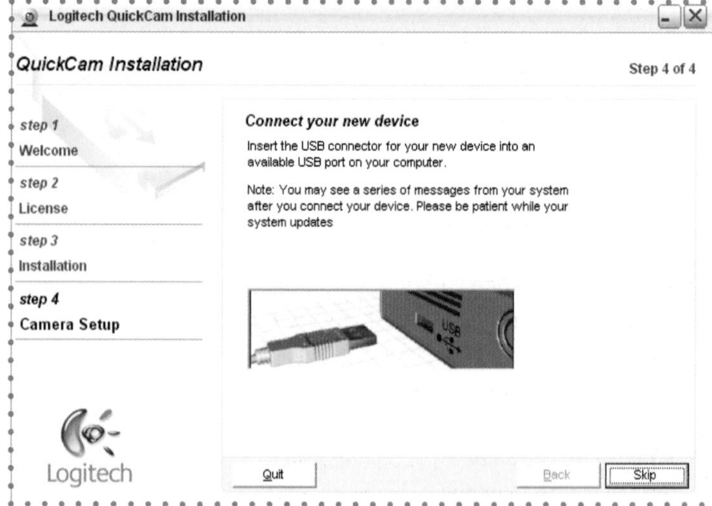

5. Most webcam software provides shortcuts to the popular instant messaging services Windows Live Messenger and Skype (see page 70), and often links to Yahoo! Messenger and AOL's AIM too

HOW TO VIDEO CHAT WITH WINDOWS LIVE MESSENGER

To use a webcam to talk to distant friends you need to install video-chat software. There's a wide choice of free video-chat software available that lets you exchange text, sound and video messages with other users. However, as you need to use the same software as your friends and family, check which software they use first.

Download Windows Live Messenger

1. Download the Windows Live Messenger program from get.live.com/messenger/overview
2. Click **Get it free** and follow the steps
3. Click **Run** to start Windows Live Installer (it will take a few minutes)
4. Once it's installed, a Windows Live Messenger window will pop up on your desktop. This is the window you'll see each time you log in

Set up your Windows Live account

1. In the Windows Live Messenger window, click on **Sign up for a Windows Live ID**
2. A web page will open. Choose a username and password. You may have to try more than one username if someone else has already taken your first choice
3. When your username has been accepted, enter it into the Windows Live Messenger window along with your password, to log in

Stay in touch

TIP
Open Messenger at any time by double-clicking on the **Messenger** icon in the taskbar.

Configure Windows Live Messenger

1. Windows Live Messenger will run automatically every time you start Windows. If you don't want it to, click **Tools** on the menu bar at the top of the Messenger window
2. Click **Options**
3. Click Sign In on the left-hand side and untick **Automatically run Windows Live Messenger when I log on to Windows**
4. Click **OK**

Set up your webcam with Windows Live Messenger
Make sure the sound output (PC speakers or headphones), sound input (microphone in the webcam) and the video input (the webcam) are all working. Onscreen instructions will help if you're having problems.

1. Click **Tools**, as in step 1 above
2. Click **Audio and video setup**

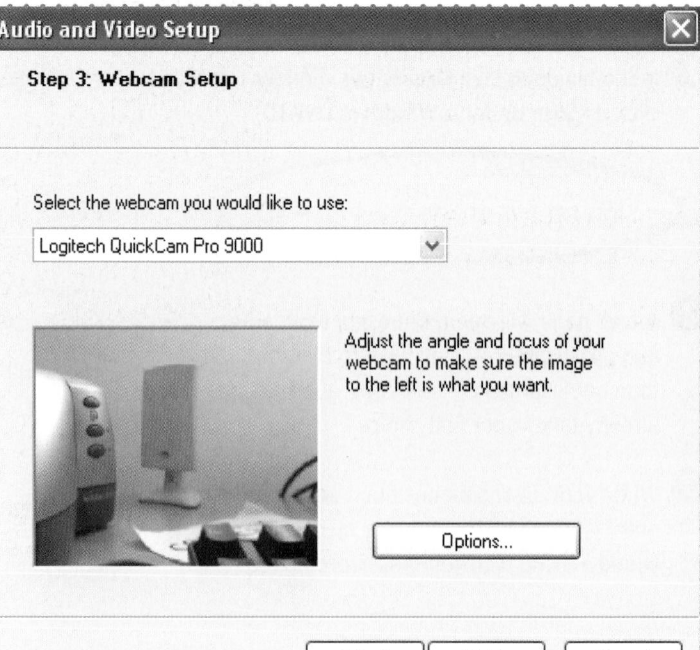

TRY THIS
You can also send written messages. Double-click on your friend's name and type your message in the window that appears. Every time you press **Enter** your words will appear immediately on their screen.

3. Follow the instructions onscreen. You'll then be prompted to speak to make sure the microphone is picking up your voice

4. You'll see the image that your webcam is seeing. This should be you! Adjust the position of the webcam until you're centred. When you're happy, click **Finish**

Find your friends

1. To find someone else using the same program, click the icon in the Windows Live Messenger menu bar. Enter your friend's instant messaging address (the same as their email address)

2. Click **Add contact**

3. A request will be sent to them. When they accept, they'll appear in your list. If they're online at the time, it may take only seconds

Make a call

1. Agree with your friend when you'll be online. In the Windows Live Messenger window, right click on your friend's name

2. Click **Video** and then **Start a video call** to let them know you want to chat

3. When they click **Accept**, you should see each other

MAKE PHONE CALLS ONLINE

Making phone calls over the internet is often referred to as VoIP (Voice over Internet Protocol). VoIP calls are usually cheaper than standard landline or mobile phone calls, and in some cases are completely free. All you need to make and receive VoIP services like Skype is a basic microphone headset, though you can buy a dedicated Skype handset.

Download and install Skype

1. Open your web browser and type www.skype.com/intl/en-gb into the address bar. Press **Enter**

2. Click **Download Skype**

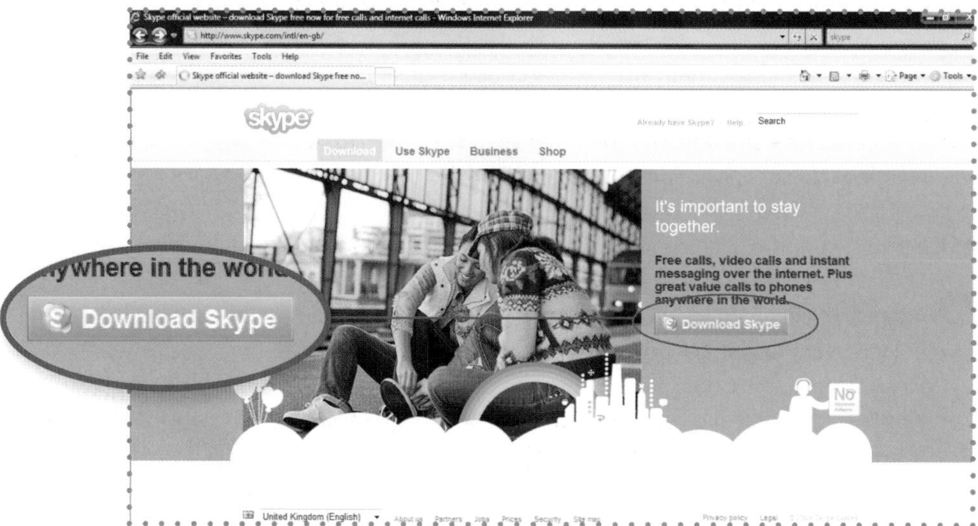

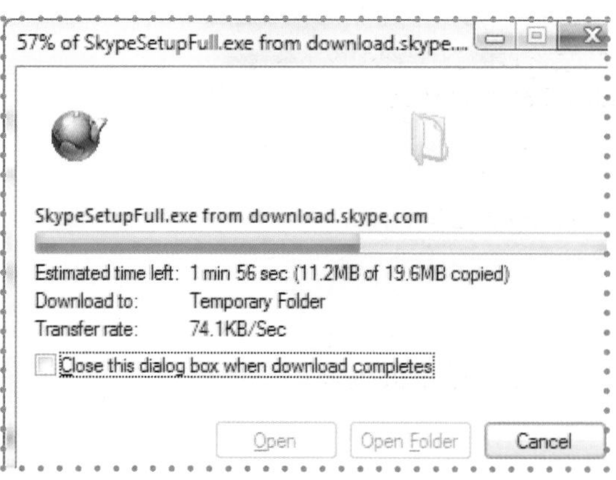

3. When the File Download box appears, click **Run**

4. Click **I agree – install**. A window (left) will appear showing the progress of the download

5. Once the file has downloaded, click **Finish**

Create an account

1. Once you've finished installing the software, there will be a **Thank You** screen. Click **Start Skype**
2. In the **Create Account** window that opens, enter your name and choose a Skype name and password
3. Check the tick box and click **Next**
4. Fill out your email address on the next screen and enter your Country/Region and your nearest city
5. Finally, check or uncheck the boxes as required and click **Sign In**

Set up

1. When you first sign in to Skype, the **Getting Started** wizard will launch. Connect your headset or handset if you're using one
2. If you're using a standard microphone headset, you should find it has two plugs attached to it. Insert the pink or red one into your computer's microphone socket (this should also be pink/red or marked with the icon of a microphone)
3. Plug the green one into the headphone output (also green or marked with a stereo sound waves icon)

Make a test call

1. You'll find a Skype Test Call contact listed in your Skype contacts. To make your test call, click the green **Call** button next to this contact
2. Instructions should prompt you to record a message after the beep
3. You should then be able to hear the message you recorded. If you can't, onscreen instructions will tell you what to do (you may need a headset if you don't have one already)

Stay in touch

Add contacts

1. Ask your friends to send you their Skype names. You can then add them to your Skype contacts by clicking the **New** button

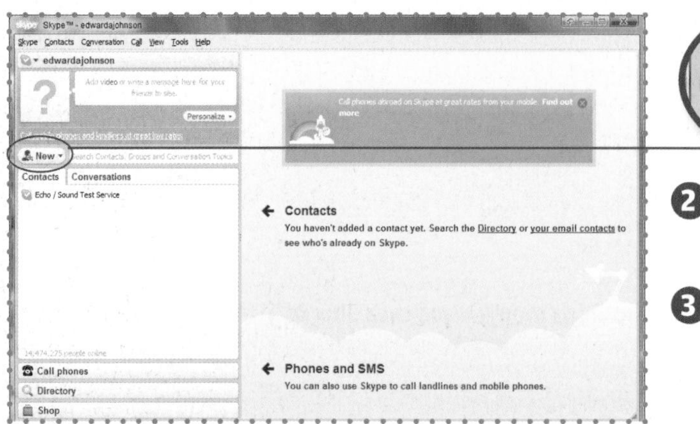

2. Click **New Contact** and enter their Skype name

3. Alternatively, you can search for people using their email address or full name. Enter the name and click **Find**

4. Select people from the list that appears and click **Add Contact**

5. Click **Close** when you're done

Make a Skype call

1. Double click on the icon that appears on your desktop or in the system tray. Select the **Contacts** tab in the main Skype window and find the name of the person you want to call

2. Click on their Skype name and then click the green **Call** button

3. If they aren't listed, type their Skype name (you'll need to get this from the person you want to contact) into the box towards the top of the Skype window and click **Search Directory**

4. When you receive a call, a window will pop up asking whether you want to accept or reject it. You must be logged in to Skype to receive a call

NEXT STEP

You can call a landline or mobile using your Skype account, but you'll need to buy Skype credits. Go to **Account** and click **Buy Skype Credit**. A wizard will launch that will take you through the process. Then, to make a call, click on the **Call Phones** tab in the main Skype window.

FIND INFORMATION

By reading and following all the steps in this chapter, you will get to grips with:

- **Finding accurate information online**
- **Watching TV and listening to radio online**
- **Downloading music, video and podcasts**

TRUSTWORTHY WEBSITES

From email messages, opinions, comments and recommendations, to photos, video, and music, the internet lets us share information and content with others around the world. You can find information on just about every topic imaginable – but how can you be sure that what you're reading is accurate and genuine?

Anyone can publish anything on the web, and it can be hard to determine either a web page's author or their knowledge and qualifications on a given subject. It's also difficult to decide whether a web page is a mask for advertising, product sponsorship or is simply biased in some way. To help decide if information on a website can be trusted, consider the following:

Accuracy

Does the website have an **About** or **Contact** button with details for those responsible for the site? Click these to find out about the site's author or the company/institution behind it.

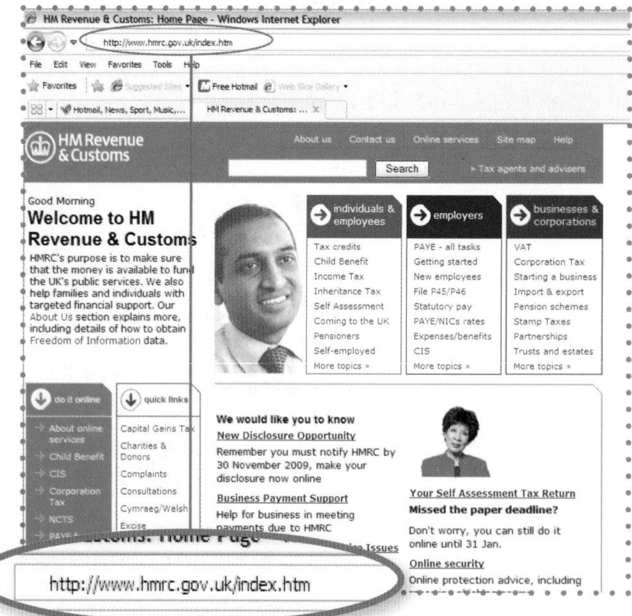

Authority

Does the website provide information or is it a sales site? Look at the site's web address – those ending in .edu and .gov are for educational and government sites only; those ending .org, are mainly used for non-profit organisations, such as charities.

Sites ending in .com, .net as well as country specific sites such as .co.uk are usually commercial sites that make money through advertising or selling products.

Objectivity

Does the website clearly state its objectives? Consider whether it promotes just one point of view, product or service? Is its advertising support, if it has any, obvious? If it is not clear, the information it presents may be biased.

Currency
Some website information can be very out of date. Check that links to other sites (if it has any) work, as out-of-date links are often a sign that a web page is rarely updated. Scroll to the very bottom of the page. Websites often state the last date that they were updated.

Coverage
Can you view the information you need fully or are you limited by payment requests, browser technology, or software requirements?

If you can answer yes to all or most of the above, you will able to decide that a website is trustworthy in the information it provides.

Sponsored search engine results

When using a search engine to look for information online, be aware that some of the results displayed are 'sponsored' links. While search engines such as Google never sell their search results, they are funded by displaying relevant links from companies interested in advertising their products or services.

Remember, paid-for links appear at the top and right-hand side of the search engine's results page and are labelled as 'Sponsored Links'. On Google, for example, those in the yellow box are sponsored; those below it are simple search results.

Find Information

TRY THIS

If you like a particular news source, such as a newspaper, type its name into Google (www.google.co.uk) to go to that website. You can then bookmark the newspaper's home page (see page 36) to be able to return to the site easily in the future.

HOW TO FIND NEWS ONLINE

There are lots of websites that deliver news, but it's important to be able to trust the source of the news and information you're reading or watching. Traditional news organisations, such as the BBC and Sky, as well as newspapers are all trustworthy sources of news. Specialist destinations, such as Which?, also deliver reliable sources of news on their areas of knowledge, such as consumer issues.

Some sites such as Google and Yahoo! deliver news taken from lots of news sources, and are a good way to get an overview of different news topics quickly. You can also search news within them.

Type http://news.google.co.uk into the address bar of your web browser. This will show a page of news stories, including UK, world, entertainment and business. The source of the story, such as CNN International, will be listed, along with how recent the story is.

Create a personalised news channel on Google

1. If you have a Google account (see page 78) and are signed in, click **Add a section** in the upper right of the screen

2. Click the **Add a custom section** button. Type in a **Section Title**, such as 'My Local News' then enter two or three keywords for your local area, such as 'Brighton and Hove'. A new section will appear containing just those news stories that contain those words – presenting you with a handy digest of local news

3. You can create as many personalised channels as you wish, and Google will remember your preferences next time you visit the site

4. To remove channels, click the x-shaped buttons on news sections – you can add them back in by clicking the **Edit this page** section again

5 To read a story, click on the headline. This will take you to the news story on its original site. To go back to Google News, click on the **Back** button on your web browser

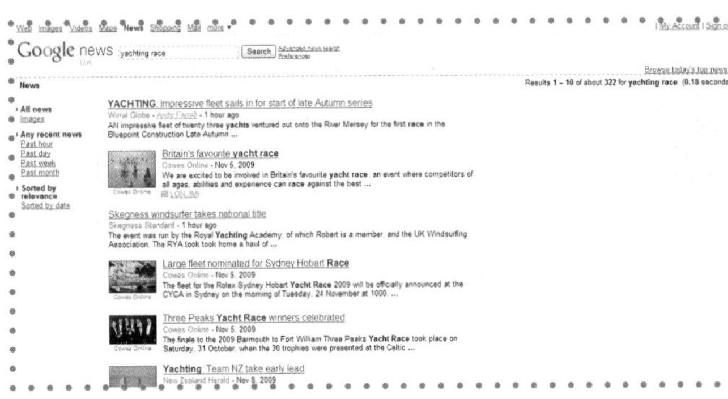

6 Type in a search phrase, such as 'yachting race' into the search box at the top of the page, and click **Search News**. This will return a list of news stories containing that search term

Sharing and getting news

Many websites allow you to share stories you find interesting with others via social networking sites (see page 154). Some websites will also let you sign up to a newsletter so that you can have a digest of their news stories delivered to your email inbox.

1 Type the address into the address bar of your web browser, for example www.which.co.uk/news. This will show the latest news stories on the Which? website. Click on a headline to read a story

2 At the bottom of the story, click on the envelope icon beneath the phrase **Share**, **Bookmark** or **Subscribe**. Enter the details that are requested to email a friend with a message and link to the news story

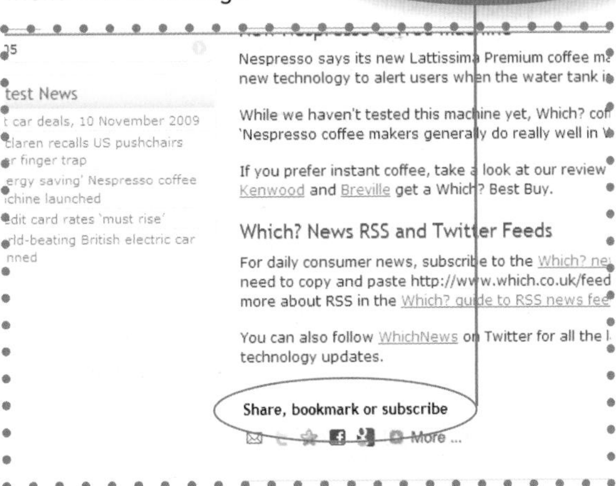

3 To sign-up to an email newsletter, which are usually free, look for a link inviting you to sign up. In this case, click on the **Sign Up** to the Which? technology email. Enter your email details to get a weekly email digest of the news emailed to you

HOW TO USE NEWS FEEDS

Keeping tabs on your favourite websites can be time-consuming. And sometimes you'll find there's nothing new to read. But there's an easy way to keep track of the latest news without even visiting the website concerned. If the website supports RSS (Really Simple Syndication), you can access its latest articles, normally in the form of headlines and news summaries, delivered to your computer screen via a news reader.

Most regularly updated websites should have a feed available – this is a file that tells the news reader about the site's articles and where to find them. You can tell if a site has a feed by looking for a distinctive RSS (see orange button in image on left) or XML logo or link.

By building up a list of favourite feeds, you'll see headlines of the latest stories from multiple websites. To read the whole article, click the headline and the website it comes from will open in your browser.

Using a News Reader

To get started, you'll either need to sign up to a web-based news reader (which can be accessed from your normal web browser, such as Internet Explorer), or download suitable software. The good news is that many of these readers are free. Here's how to use Google Reader.

1. First, register for a Google Account. On the **Google Mail** home page, click **Create an account**. Choose a user name and a password

2. Once signed in, click on the word **More** at the top left of the screen. From the drop-down menu, select **Reader**

3. A quick way to get started is to choose pre-packaged bundles of feeds. You can always add or remove individual feeds later. There are hundreds of packages to choose from either by category or recommendation by experts. To view bundles click on **Browse for stuff** on the left-hand side of the screen

4. Several bundles will be spotlighted. You can click **View all** next to each one

5. To choose a bundle, click the **Subscribe** button next to it

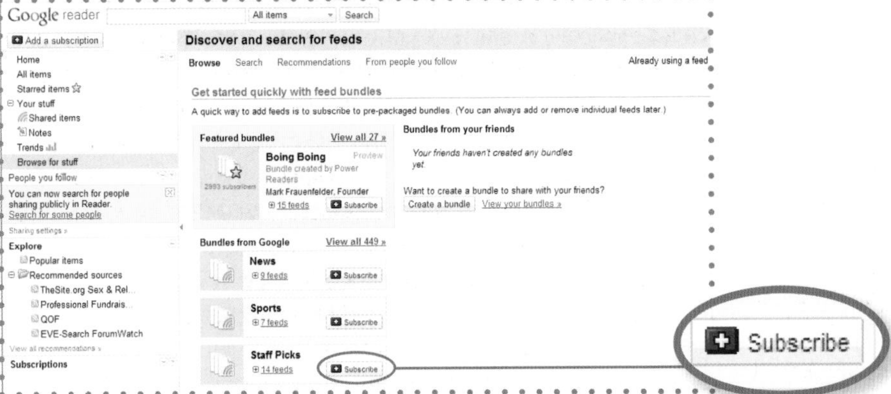

6. The individual news feeds will appear under **Subscriptions** on the left-hand column of the Reader page. Click on any one to bring up headlines and stories from that source

7. As you read headlines in each feed, they are marked as 'read'

8. If you're visiting a favourite website and wish to add their news feed, click the RSS button and select Google (or whatever news reader you're using) from the list of web-based readers

9. On the following screen click on **Add to Google Reader**. The news feed will appear in the left-hand column

Google Reader lets you do a lot more with your news feeds. You can rate news items, share them with others online or email them to friends and family.

FIND A WEATHER FORECAST

There are lots of websites that offer the weather forecast, but they differ in ease of use and levels of commercial advertising. Typical websites to try include http://news.bbc.co.uk/weather/, www.metoffice.gov.uk and http://uk.weather.com/. These have a similar range of features, but this example uses http://news.bbc.co.uk/weather/.

1. Type http://news.bbc.co.uk/weather/ into the address bar of your web browser. You will see a screen with a large map of the UK showing the current weather. On the right-hand side is a column for finding out the local weather, adding other locations and switching values such as Celsius and Fahrenheit

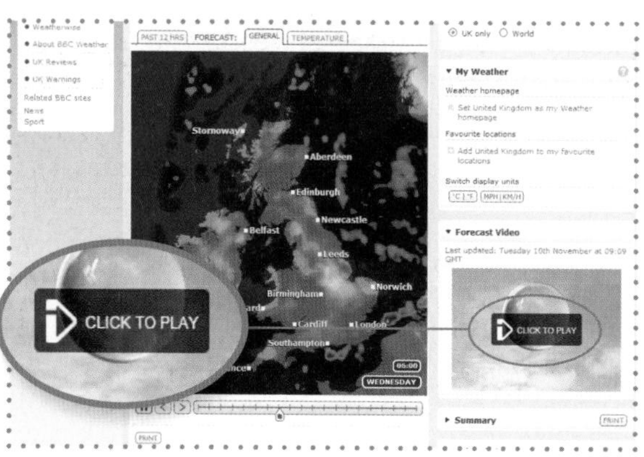

2. To see a national forecast, click the **Play** icon at the bottom of the large UK map. This will show how the weather will change in three-hour periods over the following four days

3. Click the **Temperature tab** immediately above the main map to see the temperature changes over the same period

4. Click the **Key** button in the upper-right above the map to see a guide to map information such as temperature colours and rainfall levels

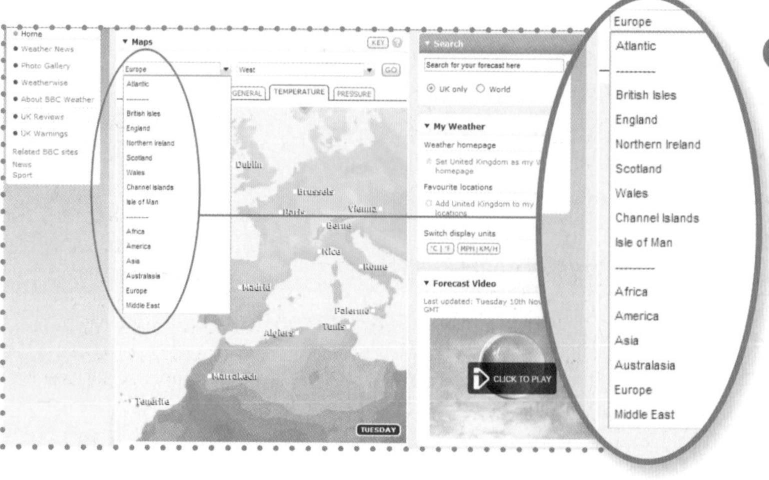

5. To see the weather in different global regions, click the upper-left menu above the map that reads British Isles. From this pop-up list, select a region, such as Europe, and then click **Go**

Get the local weather forecast

National weather is fine for the bigger picture, but a local forecast can help you plan home or holiday activities.

1. To find a local forecast for your area, type your postcode or town into the **Search** box at the top of the right-hand column. Click the **UK only** option, then click the **Search** button

2. You'll see a page that shows weather for the local area, with a 24-hour forecast and a four-day forecast. At the bottom of the page click the **UV, Pollution and Pollen** bar to see current levels, and the forecast for the following four days

3. If you want to print the forecast, click the **Print** button in the top-right of each forecast section

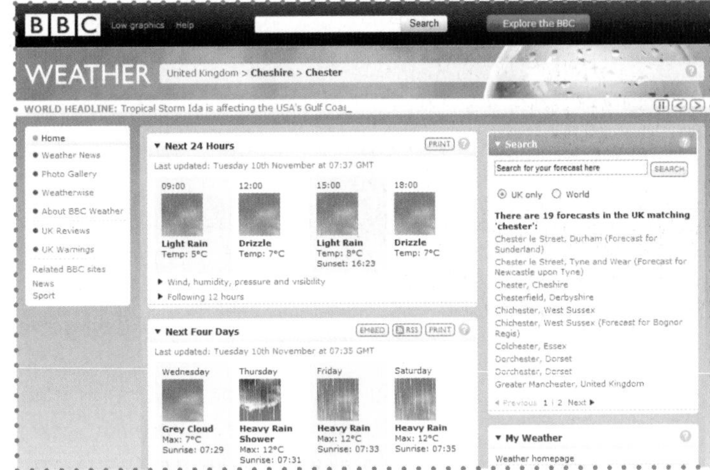

4. In the **My Weather** section in the right-hand column, you can click **Set [your postcode]** as my **Weather homepage**. This will then show the local weather each time you visit the site without you having to search

5. If you'd rather watch the weather forecast, click the **Click To Play** button in the right-hand column to watch both regional and national weather forecasts from the BBC. Make sure your computer's volume is turned up

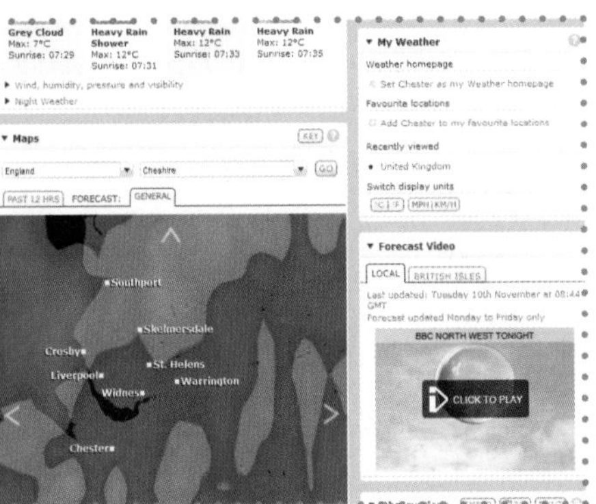

There are lots of other related weather links in the **My Weather** section of the BBC website, including tide tables, sports forecasts, shipping forecasts and climate change.

FIND HEALTH ADVICE AND GP SERVICES

Increasing numbers of people are turning to the web for basic information concerning illnesses, symptoms and treatments rather than visiting a GP. The danger is that lots of online advice can be incorrect, potentially harming your health or giving you a false sense of security. However, some health advice, such as that offered by NHS Direct, can be useful in certain circumstances.

Using NHS Direct symptom checker

If you're feeling unwell, then it is best to contact your GP or call the NHS Direct helpline on 0845 4647. If you simply want to check your symptoms, however, NHS Direct has an interactive guide to help give you an idea of what is wrong.

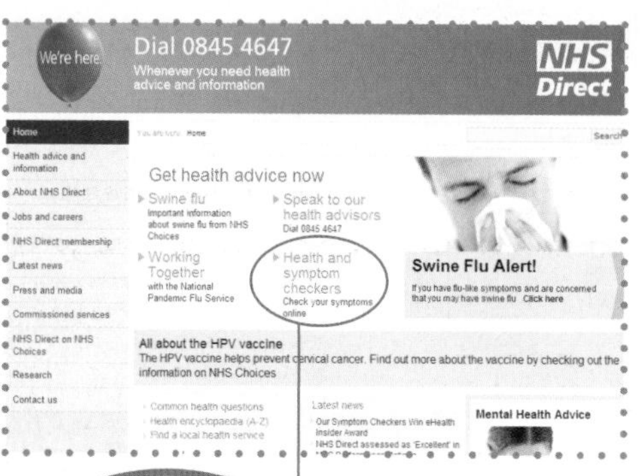

Health and symptom checkers
Check your symptoms online

1. Type www.nhsdirect.nhs.uk into the address bar of your web browser. On the main page that opens, click on **Health and symptom checkers**

2. Various different health checkers will appear, such as cold and flu and mental health advice. Click on the lowest box titled **Self-help guide**

3. You can either browse symptoms from an A–Z list – simply click on **Search by A–Z** and then the letter that you think will lead you to your symptom. For example, if you click on **W**, you will find information on Wheezing, Wounds and Whiplash, among others. Then click on the relevant links below these headings

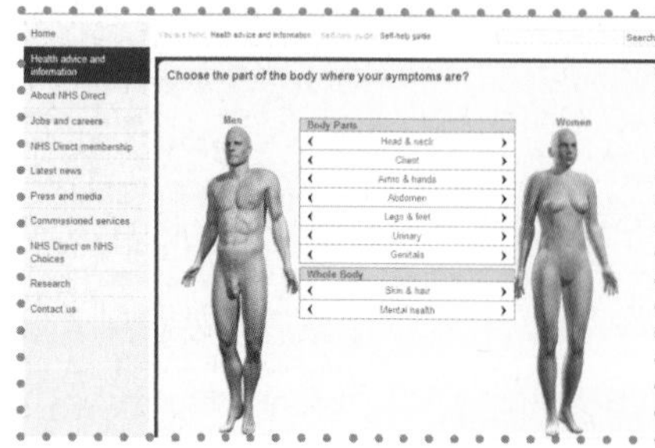

4. Alternatively, you can use the interactive body map. Click **Search by body** map. Choose the body part affected for either male or female, such as skin and hair. From the sub menu that appears, choose the symptom that is the best match

5. In either case, a series of **Yes/No** questions will follow. Answer them accurately to get a recommended course of action, such as self-care at home to making an appointment with a GP

Find a local GP's surgery

Changing your GP, for example if you have moved to a new area, can be a challenge. Sites such as NHS Direct offer interactive tools to help find a local surgery.

1. Type www.nhsdirect.nhs.uk into the address bar of your web browser. Near the bottom of the main page that opens, click on **Find a local health service**

2. The next page allows you to find local GPs, dentists, chemists, hospitals, emergency and urgent care services and opticians

3. Click on **GPs**, then type your postcode into the **Search** box in the centre of the screen. If you're new to the area, then tick the box labelled **Only show practices accepting new patients**. Click **Search**

4. You can arrange the results in alphabetical order or according to distance by clicking the arrow next to **With closest to you shown first**

5. You can also compare services by clicking on the **Detailed Comparison** button. This will show them side by side, and you can compare specific information, such as **Parking** or **How Patients rate the practices** by clicking on the arrow to the left of each subject

Victoria Cross Surgery	The Hermitage Surgery	Whalebridge Practice	Carfax NHS Medical Centre	Park Lane Practice
Add to shortlist	Add to shortlist	Add to shortlist	Add to shortlist	Add to shortlist

▸ GPs at this practice
▸ Extended opening & availability of appointments
▸ Clinics and other services offered at this practice
▸ How patients rate this practice overall
▸ What patients say about staff at this practice
▾ What patients say about the practice itself

Victoria Cross Surgery	The Hermitage Surgery	Whalebridge Practice	Carfax NHS Medical Centre	Park Lane Practice
96% of patients surveyed said the practice was very clean	100% of patients surveyed said the practice was very clean	96% of patients surveyed said the practice was very clean	93% of patients surveyed said the practice was very clean	97% of patients surveyed said the practice was very clean

▾ About Cleanliness of GP practice

96% of patients surveyed said it was very easy or easy to get into the building	99% of patients surveyed said it was very easy or easy to get into the building	97% of patients surveyed said it was very easy or easy to get into the building	98% of patients surveyed said it was very easy or easy to get into the building	97% of patients surveyed said it was very easy or easy to get into the building

6. Click on the **Map** button to get an overview of where the GP practices are located

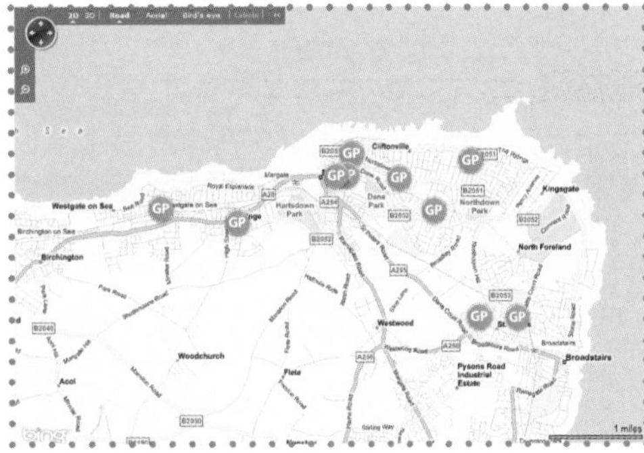

7. As you look through, you can select several GP surgeries by clicking **Add to shortlist**. At any time you can click **View your shortlist** to look at your list of options

8. Once you have chosen a surgery, click **Find out how to register** for details on registering with them

find information

HOW TO FIND RESTAURANT INFORMATION ONLINE

Whether you're planning a family get together, a romantic dinner for two or just grabbing a quick bite, the internet can make finding and booking the perfect restaurant a piece of cake.

There are loads of websites that list restaurants with full contact details. Many allow you to search for restaurants by city, area or postcode, by cuisine type or by price bands. You can search via restaurant ratings and read customer reviews. Some websites even allow you to book a table at your selected restaurant online.

Find a restaurant

Toptable is one of the UK's biggest restaurant search and reservation sites.

1. Type www.toptable.com into the address bar of your web browser. It will usually open on the UK site and you can specify your location in the **Location** box of the **Venue Finder**. If it doesn't, click **Change location** in the left-hand menu and you can then specify the area you would like to search. In this example, we've chosen Bristol

2. Select the number of people dining, and the date and time. If you wish, from the drop-down menus, you can choose a cuisine type such as Italian and a price band to refine your search. Then click **Go**

3. A list of restaurants will be displayed. If this is long, you can sort by restaurant name, any price offers, how other diners have rated them, and their popularity on the site by clicking on the relevant link – **name**, **offers**, **rating** or **popularity** – at the top of the page

4. Click on a restaurant's name and you will be shown more details including a review by toptable, a sample menu and customer reviews

5. A list of available time slots for booking a table will be listed. Check the number of diners and date is correct, then simply click on the time you want

6. You'll be taken to **Your Details** page. To book a table through the site, you'll need to register and create an account. Either click **New User** if this is the first time, or enter your login details if you've used the site before

FIND AND BOOK THEATRE TICKETS

Buying theatre tickets online is quick and easy and can save you both time and money.

Precautions to take when buying online tickets

- Look at the event's official website to check the list of official ticket sellers
- Check prices (including all the fees) from a few ticket sellers before you book – this could save you money
- Make sure that you have the ticket seller's name and contact details from the site so you can get in touch if there's a problem
- Read the ticket seller's terms and conditions of sale carefully
- Don't assume, because the website address ends in .uk, that it is a UK company
- Pay by credit card if you can, as this makes your credit card company jointly liable if the ticket seller breaches their contract with you. If you can't get a refund directly from the ticket seller, you should be able to claim from your credit card company
- Check the description of the ticket on offer – the date and time of the event, the venue and location, the seating arrangements and the face value of the ticket. You have a right to this information with the Consumer Protection from Unfair Trading Regulations 2008

Use the STAR website

Ensure that whoever you're buying tickets from is a member of the Society of Ticket Agencies and Retailers (STAR). Type www.star.org.uk into the address bar of your web browser. On the site, you will find advice on buying tickets and a list of approved members, such as Lastminute.com and Ticketmaster, who are legitimate sellers of concert and theatre tickets.

Booking a ticket with Lastminute.com

1. Type www.lastminute.com into the address bar of your web browser. Once the page has loaded, you will see the different types of ticket you can buy on the site across the top of the screen. Click on the **Theatre** button

2. In the **Search** box on the right-hand side, type the name of the play under event name. You can also add other information for your search if you have specific dates or number of tickets in mind. Click on the **Search** button

3. Select a ticket type by price or what's involved in the package, then click **Continue**

4. You will see show information and ticket prices. Click on the second tab for venue information

5. Click **Check availability** to see possible show times

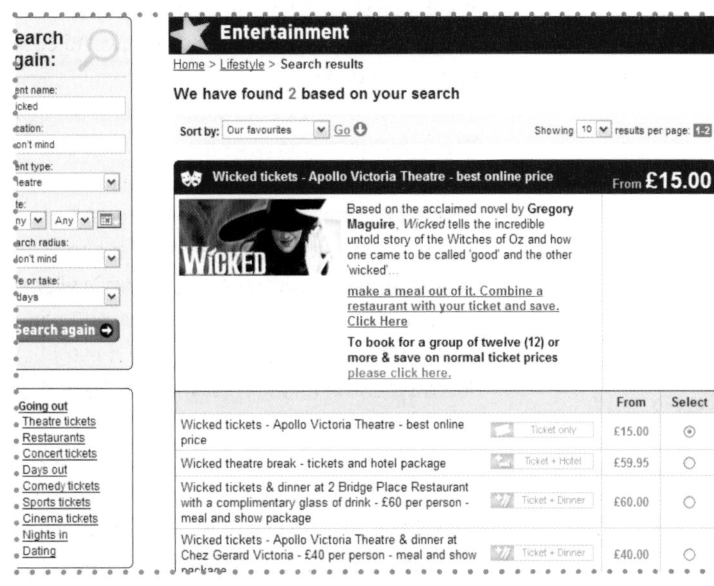

6. Choose a date on the calendar that appears on screen, then click **Choose tickets**. Using the pop-up menus, choose the number of each ticket type you want. Click **Choose tickets**

7. Enter the name of the person making the booking. Click **Add to basket**

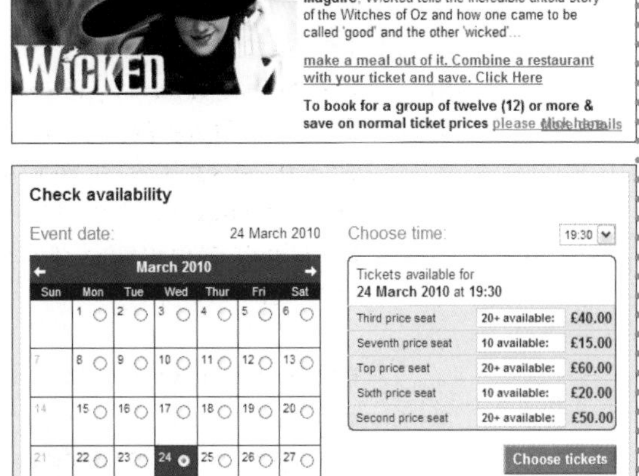

8. If you're happy with the pricing, click **Proceed to checkout** to pay for your tickets using a credit card and provide the delivery address. If this is your first time on the site, you will need to register and provide an email address so that Lastminute.com can send you a confirmation email of your purchase

FIND AND BOOK CINEMA TICKETS

Using the internet, it's possible to watch trailers of new and forthcoming films, find cinemas and film showing times near you, reserve specific cinema seats, and book and pay for tickets online for collection at the cinema.

Choose a film

There are lots of ways to find local cinemas, including using search sites such as Google and Yahoo! You can also go direct to individual cinema chain websites such as Vue, UCI and Odeon. For example:

1. Type www.odeon.co.uk into the address bar of your web browser. You'll see a page that has information about new films, and options to book tickets and find cinema locations

2. Scroll down the page using the web browser's right-hand scrollbar to view a list of some of the films currently showing

3. To see a trailer of the film, click the **View Trailer** button underneath the image of the film. This will take you to a page that plays a short clip of the film. On this page you can also find out information about the cast, director, plot and advice from the British Board of Film Classification (BBFC) about the film's suitability. Make sure the volume on your computer is turned up

4. Scroll down the page to read customer reviews of the film, as well as to see similar films that are also showing

5. Once you've chosen a film, you will see a large map of the UK. Click the + and – buttons to zoom in, and click the arrow buttons to move around to locate a cinema near you where the film is showing

Book tickets

Once you've found the film you want to watch and the cinema showing it, you can book the tickets online and pick your seats before leaving home.

1. To book a film, either use the **Back** button to go to the main home page or type in www.odeon.co.uk

2. In the **Book Now** box, choose the cinema and film from the pop-up menus. Next, choose the day and time you'd like. Click **Go**

3. You'll be asked either to log in (which stores your details so you don't have to add them again in the future), or continue without registering. To continue without registering, in the **Continue With My Booking panel**, click **Next Step**

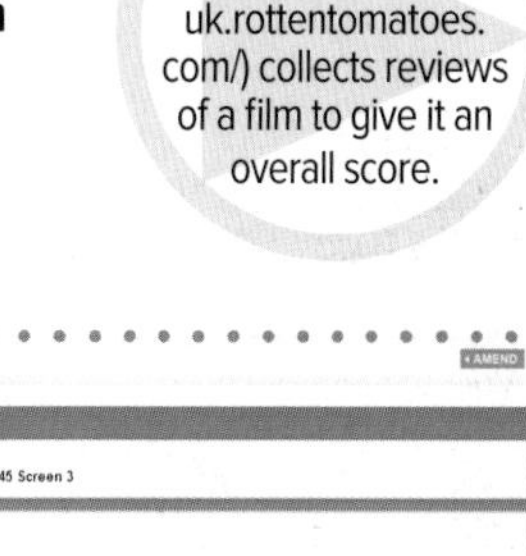

TIP

Rotten Tomatoes (http://uk.rottentomatoes.com/) collects reviews of a film to give it an overall score.

4. In the left-hand panel, click the + and – buttons to increase or decrease the right number of tickets

5. Click the mouse cursor on the **Your seats** section of the panel, hold down the mouse and drag it onto the seats you like in the seating plan. Let go

6. You'll be asked to enter your details including an email address – this is important, as a confirmation reference will be emailed to you. Once done, you'll head to a payment screen to enter your payment details using a credit card

7. Once payment has been confirmed, you should print either the payment confirmation screen or the confirmation email when it is sent to you and take it with you to the cinema

8. To pick up your tickets, you will need the credit card that you used to book the tickets with whether you pick them up from a machine or the box office

BOOK TRAVEL ONLINE

The internet is a fast, safe and convenient way to book travel. You can compare prices, look at hotels and create your perfect holiday, but it can be daunting to know where to start and how to book. A good travel website should:

- Tell you exactly what's included in the price
- Offer named accommodation
- Offer a secure booking page
- Make it clear early on how much it costs to pay with a credit card
- Have understandable terms and conditions
- Be cheaper than phoning or booking in person
- Have a good FAQ section to help you solve any problems

Book a flight online

Online travel agents, such as ebookers or lastminute.com, don't receive commission for selling flights with some no-frills airlines, so they may charge a transaction fee if you book with them. To avoid this, book directly on the airline's website. In this example we've used popular low-cost airline easyJet.

TRY THIS

Good travel websites show you the prices either side of the date you want to travel so, if it works with your plans, tick the option for flexible date as you may save money.

1. Type www.easyjet.com into the address bar of your browser and press **Enter**

2. On the right-hand side of the screen is a panel with three tabs across the top. The **Flights** tab should be highlighted by default. If it isn't, click on the word **Flights**

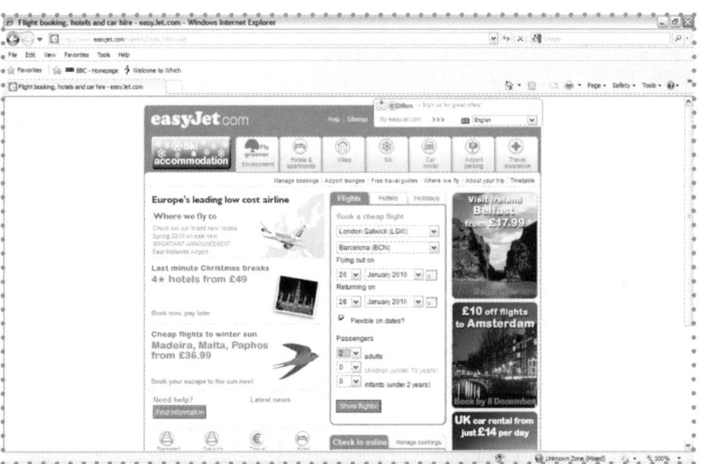

3. In the panel that appears, select the airports you wish to travel to and from, the dates you wish to fly and the number of passengers travelling. If you can travel on alternative dates, tick the box **Flexible on dates?** Then click the **Show flights!** button

4 You'll be shown the flights available for those days of travel, plus a day before and a day after. You can view flight details and prices for the three weeks around the dates you have specified or look at cheapest fares available per month

5 Select a date and flight time for both the **Outbound** and **Return** journey by clicking on the box showing the date and time you wish to travel. Then click **Continue**. A panel on the right-hand side of the screen will now show your shopping basket with the flights you've chosen, standard luggage options and travel insurance. Click on each item to add or change details, such as adding additional suitcases to your luggage. When you've finished adjusting these options, click **Continue**

6 You'll be offered the chance to book a hotel room by viewing prices, ratings and reviews of various hotels at your destination as recommended by easyJet. If you just want to purchase flights, click the **Continue** button under the Basket panel on the right-hand side of the screen

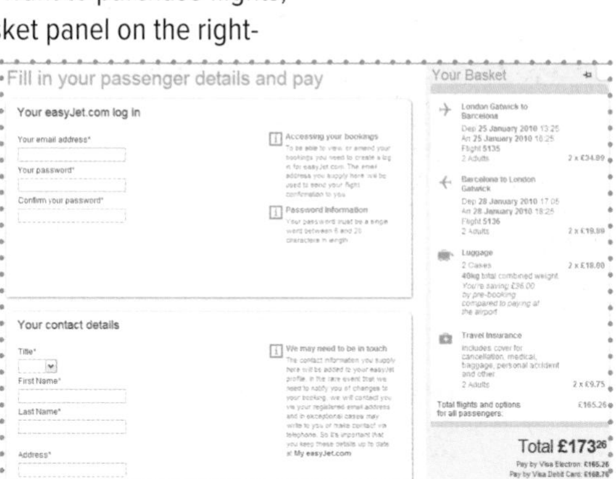

7 If you've booked through the website before, you'll need to enter your username and password, then click **Continue**. If not, click **I'm new to easyJet.com** and then click **Continue**

8 As a new customer, fill in your email address, choose and confirm a password, fill in your contact details, passenger details and payment details. Tick the box to confirm you have read easyJet's terms and conditions (click the **Terms and conditions** link to read them first) and then click **Book Now** to purchase your flight tickets

9 The ticket information will usually be emailed to you. Ensure that you print out any relevant ticket information and take it with you when you travel

BOOK A HOLIDAY ONLINE

1. Type the website address of your chosen travel agent into the address bar of your web browser and press **Enter**. In this example, we've used Thomas Cook at www.thomascook.com

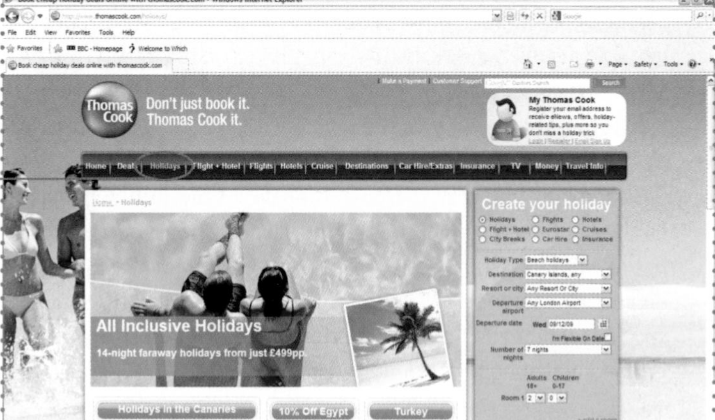

TRY THIS

Travel websites update their prices continuously throughout the day according to demand. Mondays and Tuesdays tend to be busier than other days of the week for flight websites, while Sundays are busiest for holiday sites. Web 'traffic' also seems to fall off towards the end of the month when people are waiting to be paid.

2. Click on **Holidays** on the top menu bar to see details of special offers. Begin your search in the **Create Your Holiday** panel on the right-hand side of the screen. Enter details of your desired destination, departure airport, dates of travel and number of people travelling. Then click **Search**

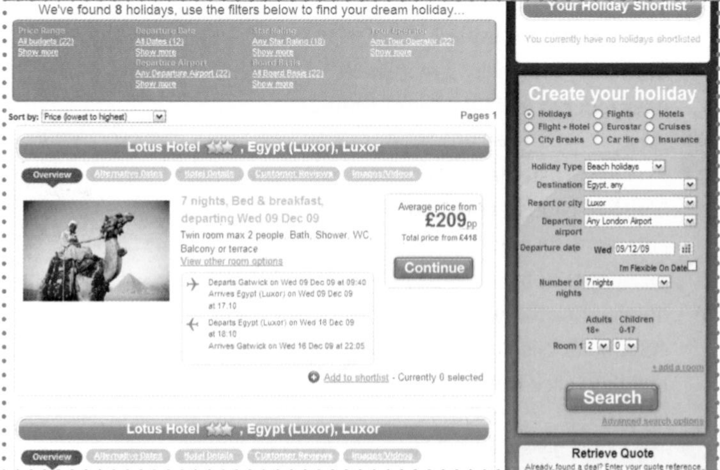

3 The next screen will show a selection of holidays. Click on one that interests you to see more details about the accommodation, flights and optional extras such as insurance. Click **Continue**

4 You will see a reference number on this screen which relates to your choice of holiday. Take a note of this number. Should you not proceed with booking the holiday at this time, use this number in the 'Retrieve Quote' box on the home page when visiting the site again to go directly to this holiday without having to search again

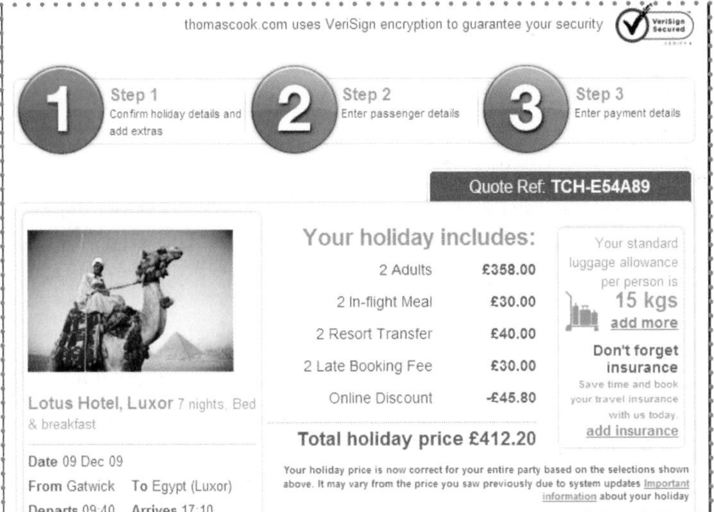

TRY THIS

If you don't want to spend ages browsing the internet, price comparison sites such as www.traveljungle.com and www.travelsupermarket.com will scour hundreds of travel sites to find the best prices on rooms and flights.

5 On the following screen fill in passenger details. Then click **Continue**

6 On the next screen enter your payment details and click **Pay Now** to complete the purchase of your holiday

7 Your holiday details will usually be posted to you, but print out any confirmation information or email to keep as a reference for your holiday booking

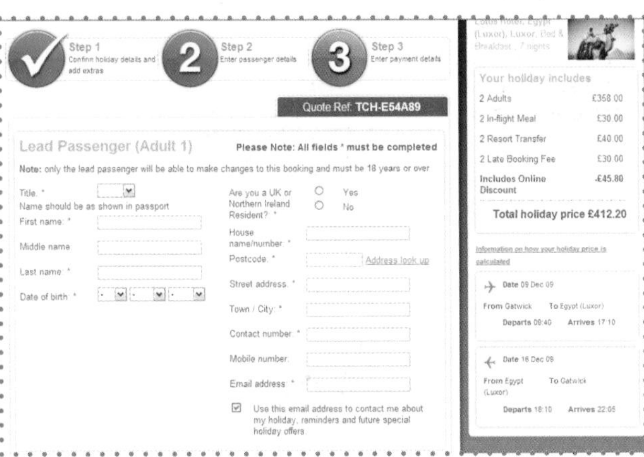

PLAN A ROUTE WITH GOOGLE MAPS

Google's free map service can provide comprehensive route planning tools so you can plan your journey, avoid traffic congestion and even print out turn-by-turn directions to take with you.

Plan a route

1. Type http://maps.google.co.uk into your address bar. Google Maps will appear showing a map of the UK with major cities

2. Click on **Get Directions** on the left-hand side. Two search boxes labelled **A** and **B** will appear, along with a small menu to select how you are making the journey, for example by car or by foot

3. Type the start destination into box A (here, NW1 4DF). Type the end destination into box B (here, SG14 1LH). You can type in postcodes, street numbers and names, and even business names. You can also add further directions for multi-destination journeys

4. Click **Show options**. You can set a few basic options here – showing the route in miles or kilometres, or avoiding motorways (labelled Highways on Google Maps) or tolls

5. Click **Get Directions**. The main picture will show the route and a turn-by-turn description of the route, including distance and time, will appear down the left-hand side

Changing route options

You can fine tune the directions, share your map and get live traffic information to help plan your journey.

1. Across the top of the main map image are buttons labelled **Traffic**, **More**, **Map**, **Satellite** and **Terrain**. Click **Map** to show a clear, illustrated map of the route and area. Click **Satellite** to show a

photographic bird's-eye view of the route, and **Terrain** to show contours of the area

2. Click **More** to show public transport and webcams, among other options

3. To find out the traffic situation on your route, click **Traffic** to get a live traffic update. Green areas show good-moving traffic, while red and black areas show traffic trouble spots. Click **Change** to switch from live traffic to view traffic movement at a particular time of day

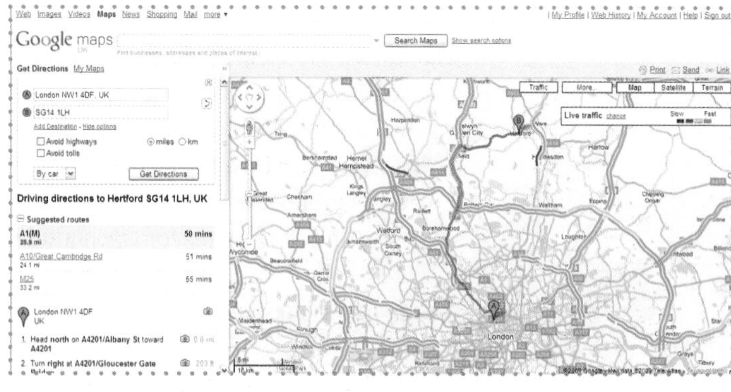

4. You can see your route in more detail by clicking each journey stage in the left-hand pane. This will zoom in on the main map and highlight that stage. If available, a street-level photo of that stage will also appear, with the route shown in 3D over the photo

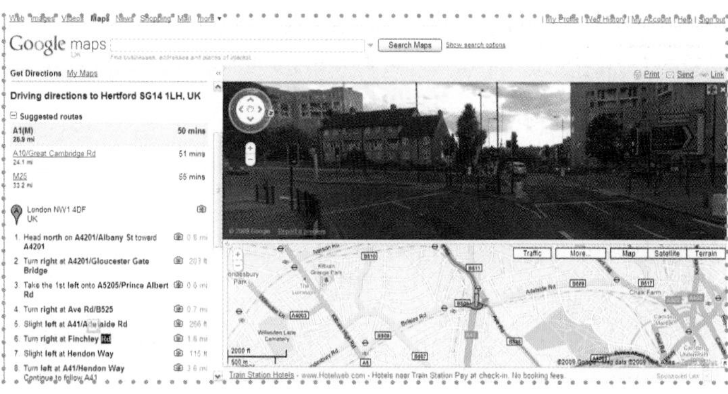

5. Click **Print** in the upper-right-hand of the screen to print the turn-by-turn instructions. You can click on **Text only**, **Maps** and **Street View** to get different amounts of detail printed. Click the **Include Large Map** checkbox to print a larger map of the entire journey. When you've set all your options, click **Print**

6. Alternatively, click **Send** to email a link to the map and route. You can also send the route to specific makes of car or directly to supported brands of satellite navigation devices

CREATE A MAP WITH GOOGLE MAPS

Google Maps is a map service that you can view in your web browser. It can show basic or custom maps and local business information, including business locations and contact details.

But Google Maps also has other handy features, such as My Maps. This allows you to create custom maps to which you can add descriptive text, photos and videos. You can also share your map with others. This is great for businesses who want customers to find them easily via their company website, but also for anyone looking to create a one-off map for use in an email or on a personal website, for example, to let people know how to get to a party.

You can even view your map in Google Earth, a website that offers maps and satellite images for pinpointed regional searches.

Create and customise your map

1. You will first need to create a **Google Account**. On the Google Mail home page, click **Create an account**. Choose a user name and a password

2. Type http://maps.google.co.uk into the address bar of your web browser. Click **My Maps** at the top left of the screen, then **Get Started**

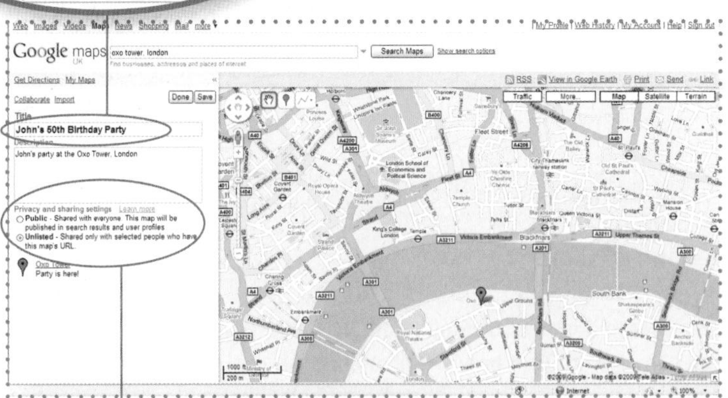

3. Give your map a title, such as 'John's 50th Birthday Party'

4. In **Description** you can add a more detailed description of your map, such as location, time and parking details

5. Under the **Description** box, you will see **Privacy and sharing settings** with two options: **Public** and **Unlisted**

6. Choose **Public** if you want your map published in search results and user profiles – ideal if your map is for promoting a business

7. If you're creating a one-off map for other purposes, select **Unlisted** to share it only with the people to whom you send the map's web address

8. Click **Save**

9. Create your map. Follow the instructions on the website to add location markers (for the party venue, for example) and other details. When you're happy with the settings, click **Done**

Share Your Map with Others

1. Under **Created By Me**, you will see a list of any maps you've created. Click on the link of the one you wish to share

2. You will see a menu bar offering various options for sharing your Map: **RSS**, **View in Google Earth**, **Print**, **Send** and **Link**

3. To compose an email from within **My Maps** containing a link to the map, click **Send**. This is a good option for one-off maps

4. To share a link to your map and post it on a website, or email it from your own email, click **Link**. A window will appear with two text fields. One contains the web address of your map, which you can copy and paste into an email

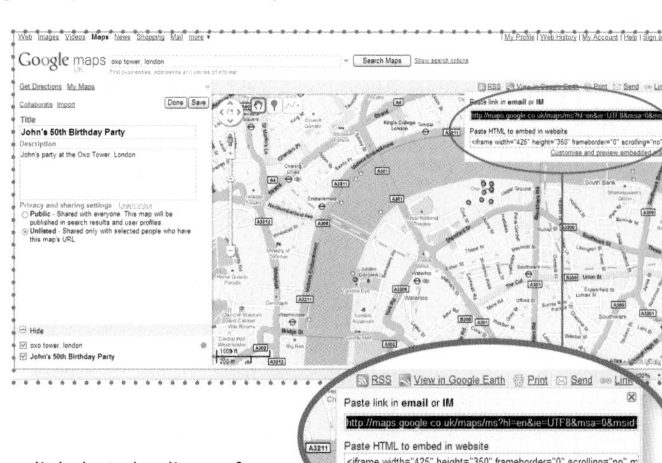

5. The other contains the same link, but also lines of HTML code (the language code used by all websites). You can copy and paste this into your website or blog to embed the map into that site. To preview or resize the map before doing this, click **Customize and preview embedded map**

Find Information

USE A POSTCODE FINDER

Realising you're missing the postcode on a friend or family member's address is annoying, particularly at Christmas time when you're sending lots of cards through the post. Luckily, there's a free, quick and easy way to find postcodes online at Royal Mail's Postcode finder.

The Royal Mail's Postcode finder is intended for personal use only and is limited to 15 searches a day. If you need more than this you can ring the Royal Mail helpline listed on the web page.

TRY THIS

The Royal Mail's website offers a wide range of useful information including delivery and postage costs and advice on wrapping goods, as well as items you can buy (see also page 120).

1. Type www.royalmail.com into the address bar of your web browser and then click on the **Personal Customers** button on the right-hand side of the screen

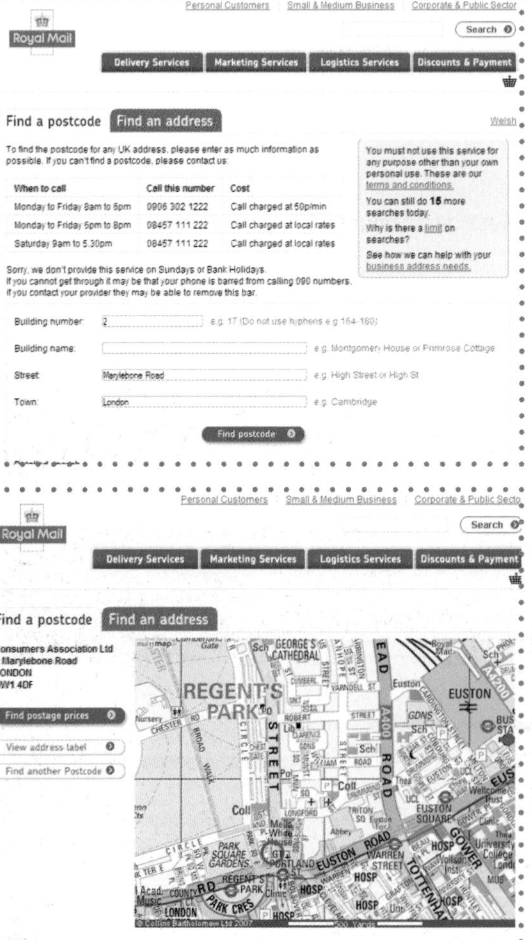

2. On the Personal Customers screen, click on the **Postcode Finder** button on the far right
3. Type in the house or building number in the first box
4. Type in the building name or house name in the next box. For example, Hanover House or Woodland Cottage
5. Then fill in the street name and the town name in the appropriate boxes
6. Press **Find postcode**
7. You will then see a screen, which asks you to read a short sequence of letters and number. Type them into the box. This stops the Postcode Address Finder being exploited by automated systems. Press **Continue**
8. You will then be presented with the full address and postcode as well as a map that shows the location of the address

WATCH TELEVISION ONLINE

With a fast broadband connection (at least 2Mbps) you can watch TV programmes on your PC over the internet. The most popular service is iPlayer from the BBC, which lets you catch up on virtually all BBC TV shows that have been broadcast in the past seven days.

You can either watch these shows in a lower-quality 'streaming' mode directly on the iPlayer website or you can download crisper, full-length shows to your computer. If you use the download method, you'll have 30 days to start watching them – and you won't have to be connected to the internet to do so.

First, however, check with your ISP about your monthly internet usage allowances, which are calculated by the amount of data you download from the internet. If you exceed your allowance you may be charged extra or your broadband speed may be temporarily reduced. Downloading an hour-long programme will use up around 600MB of your monthly allowance.

Browse for a programme

1. Type www.bbc.co.uk/iplayer into the address bar of your web browser. The week's TV highlights are listed in a scrolling panel at the top of the home page

2. Click on **TV Channels** to browse by channel. Or click on **Categories** to search through categories that include **Drama**, **Music**, **News**, and **Children's**

3. Alternatively, you can type in the programme name in the **Search** box at the top of the page. Titles that fit the search will come up. Choose the programme and episode you want, and click on the link to visit the show's page

TV Channels

Categories

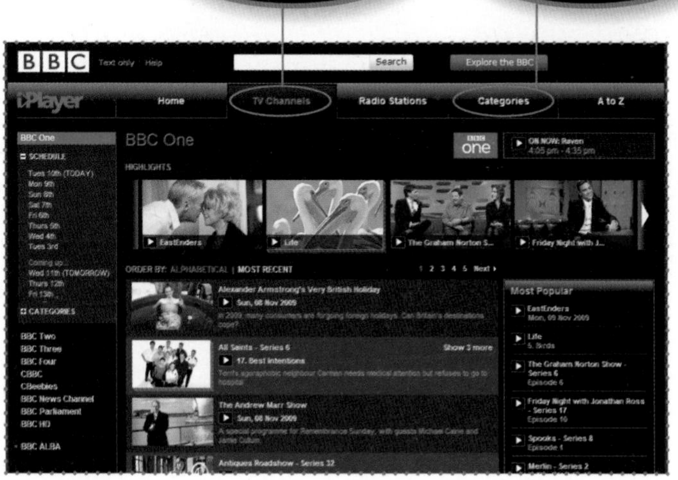

View a programme directly from the website

1. When you choose a programme, a large **Play** icon will show in the middle of the screen. When you click this, it will automatically start streaming to your computer

2. To view in full-screen mode, click the square icon at the bottom right of the viewing screen. To exit full-screen mode, press the **ESC** key

3. To increase or decrease the volume, click on the volume icon and move the pop-up slider up or down to suit

BE CAREFUL

BBC iPlayer uses peer-to-peer technology. This means your PC is helping others to download shows faster by uploading files to others' computers. If you have upload limits or if this is causing your computer to slow down, click **Settings** and untick the box under **Peer-to-peer Network Participation**.

Monitor your progress

If you encounter problems with interruptions or pauses during viewing, check the progress indicator underneath the viewing screen. The white bar shows how much of the show has been made ready (or 'buffered') for viewing. The pink bar shows how much of the show you've watched. The white bar always has to be ahead of the pink one in order for you to watch the show smoothly, so you may need to pause the show until the white bar progresses far enough. If it doesn't, your broadband connection may be busy and you'll need to try again later.

Downloading shows for viewing

1. Choose your programme as on page 99. Instead of clicking the **Play** icon, click **Download** underneath the viewing screen

2. The first time you do this, you'll be prompted to install the iPlayer Download Manager software. Click **Save** to acquire it and double click on the file to install the software. Follow the setup steps as prompted

3. Once installed, you'll return to the iPlayer website. When you click the **Download** link this time, your show will start downloading via the software. Progress is indicated on the iPlayer Download Manager screen

TRY THIS

Other TV channels including ITV, Channel 4, Five and Sky offer their own online TV viewing options. Search for and visit the website of each TV channel for viewing information.

View the downloaded show

Once your show is downloaded, it will be stored on your computer for 30 days. However, after you click to view it the first time, you will have just 7 days to watch it before it is deleted.

1. Launch the BBC iPlayer Desktop from the **Start** menu

2. Once the BBC iPlayer Desktop appears, click the **Downloads** tab. Click on a programme listed and then click **Watch Now**

3. As with streaming, you can view shows in full screen mode by clicking the icon (see page 100). Press the **ESC** button to exit this mode

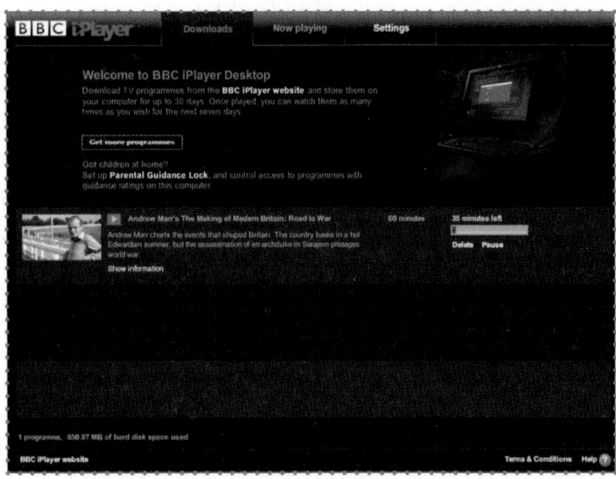

LISTEN TO RADIO ONLINE

Radio stations worldwide have been broadcasting, or streaming, live music and radio programmes on the internet for years. While some radio stations are now making more use of podcasts (see page 110), many broadcast their live shows – allowing you to listen to lots of different radio stations from around the world.

Get started

Broadcasters usually stream media in either Windows or Real format, so you'll need Windows Media Player or the free version of RealPlayer to be able to listen. Windows Media Player is included with most PCs, but some broadcasters' websites need RealPlayer so you'll need to download it if requested – simply follow the onscreen instructions.

When installing RealPlayer, print and read the licence agreement carefully. It includes instructions on how to turn off the 'service' messages that pop up on screen periodically. You can also decline marketing emails by unticking the appropriate boxes during the installation process.

Find a radio station

Finding an online radio station is much like finding any other website on the internet. However, there are some specialist radio directories that can help you get started.

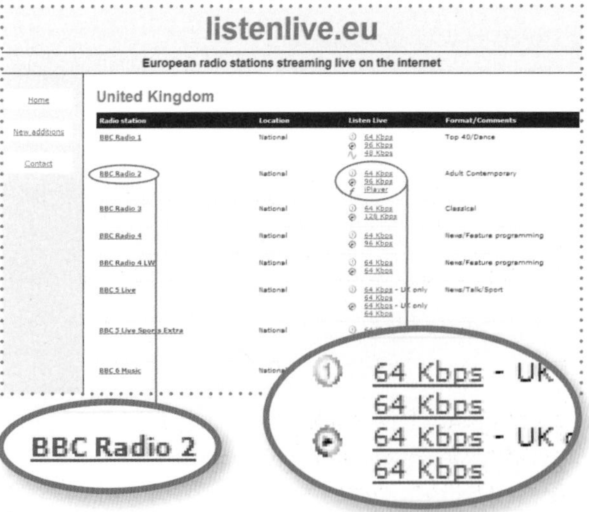

1. In the address bar of your web browser, type www.listenlive.eu. This site contains a list of over 4,000 European radio stations online. From the first page, click on **United Kingdom**

2. The next page shows UK radio stations, along with several options of how to listen to each station. A guide to the icons is located at the bottom of the web page

3. If you want BBC Radio 2, for example, click the **96kbps Windows Media** link for that station

4 A box will appear on the screen asking whether you want to download or run a special file. Click **OK to download**; Windows Media Player software will launch and the radio station will start playing. You can browse the internet while the radio plays

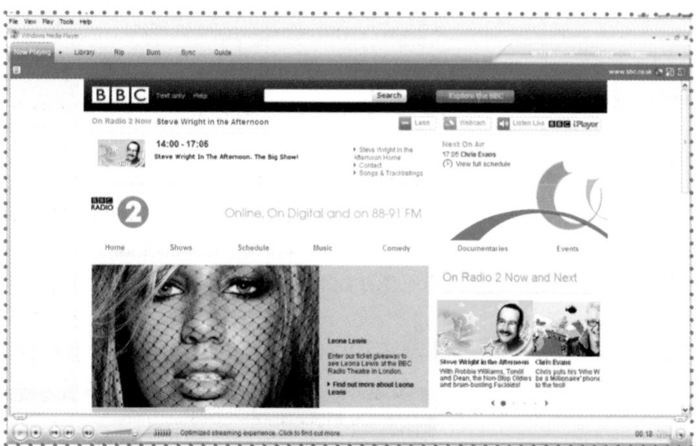

Finding a local radio station

Local radio stations can also be found by using the radio location service on web sites such as the BBC.

1 Type www.bbc.co.uk/local into the address bar of your web browser. A map and text links will appear. Click on the region you want

2 On the next page click **Listen Live** on the right-hand column to listen to the live broadcast of the radio station. A new window will appear that will play the radio station. You can minimise this window but, as long as you keep it open, you can browse the internet with the main browser window and the radio station will keep playing

Listen again services

If you missed your favourite radio show, don't worry. With listen again services you can listen to radio programmes up to seven days after they have been broadcast.

1. Type www.bbc.co.uk/radio into the address bar of your web browser. On the screen that appears, choose a radio station from the options running across the top of the screen

2. Click **Listen again** in the right-hand column

3. Scroll through the list of shows, times and DJs to choose the show you missed, then click on the name of the programme you want. A new window will launch and you can listen to the radio show through your computer's speakers

LISTEN TO STREAMED MUSIC

Instead of downloading music from the internet to your PC (see page 107), you can listen online using a free streaming service such as Spotify or Last.fm. This is legal (the artists are paid royalties for the music you choose to listen to) and there is a wide choice of music.

Last.fm is a popular website that makes suggestions about the kind of music you might like based on the music that you already listen to. Once you download the software, it works by watching what you listen to on your own MP3 music player or music software on your home PC.

Join Last.fm

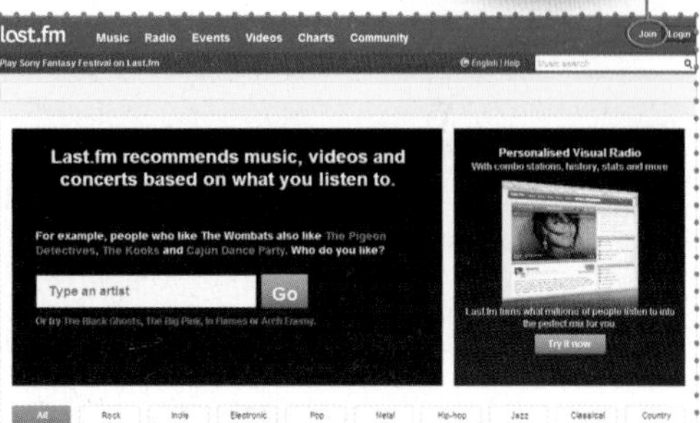

1. Type www.last.fm into the address bar of your web browser. Click on the **Join** link in the top right-hand corner of the home page to go the registration page

2. Create a username and click **Check availability** to check that it's not already taken. Enter your email and a password

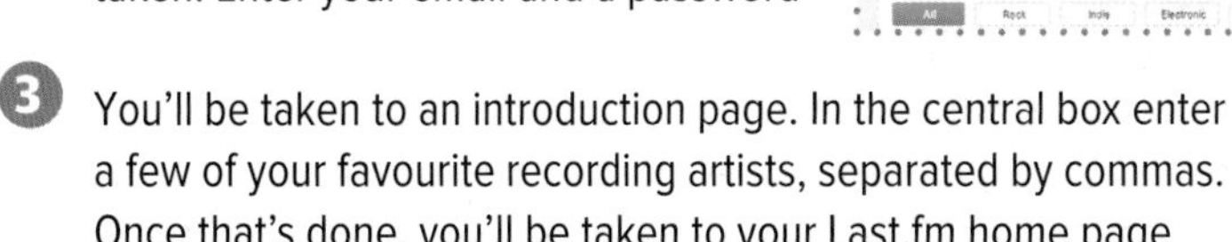

3. You'll be taken to an introduction page. In the central box enter a few of your favourite recording artists, separated by commas. Once that's done, you'll be taken to your Last.fm home page

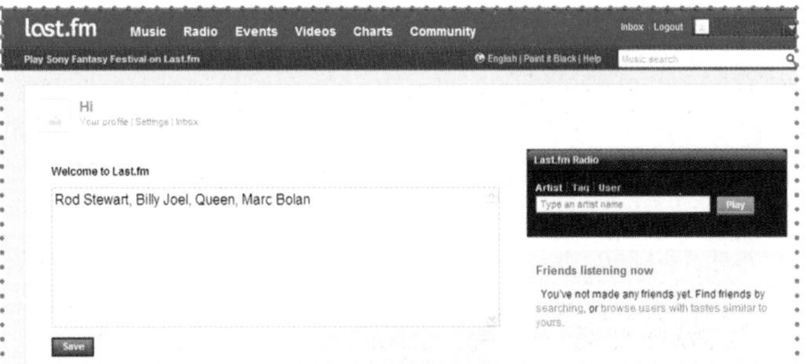

TRY THIS

When using www.lastfm.com, if you click the **My profile** icon, you can see a list of tracks that have been recently played, including ones you have recently loved or banned.

Download and set up the software

In the centre of your home page is a set of links to the software, with a version for your PC's music software (such as iTunes), a version for iPods, one for Windows Media Players and one for iPhones.

1. Click on the software logo that matches the one for your PC's music software. For software players and the iPod, after you download

TRY THIS

While importing listening history is important to Last.fm, you don't have to do it. You can choose instead to start Last.fm from scratch and let it learn about the music tracks you listen to after you install the Last.fm software.

the software, you'll be asked to select the language the software will use, where you'd like the program to be installed on your hard drive, where you want it to appear in your start menu, and whether you want an icon to appear on your computer desktop

2. Then click **Remember my password** – this saves you having to enter it each time

3. The setup wizard is where Last.fm learns what you listen to with your portable music player. Click **Browse** for it to find your music application such as iTunes on your computer hard drive. The options available on PC include iTunes and Windows Media Player. You can choose one, or both

4. If the correct option is shown, check the box and click **Next** to download the plug-ins for your music program

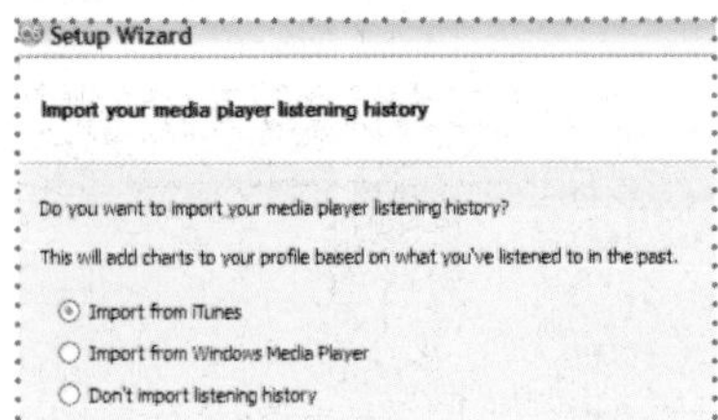

5. You'll be asked if you want to import your listening history – the information about what music you've listened to in the past. To import your listening history, select the player you use to listen to music and click **Next**. It may ask if it can start your music player. Click **Yes**

Search for and listen to music

1. Start the Last.fm application on your computer by double-clicking on the icon. A screen will ask you to enter the name of an artist or a 'tag' to start your own Last.fm radio station

2. You can request the music of a specific artist, which can be any band or solo artist. Or enter a tag – a keyword for a style of music, such as 'rock', 'country' or 'disco'

3. Last.fm will continue to play songs for as long as you leave it running. You can either listen through the track, at which point Last.fm finds and starts another track, skip a track to jump to the next track, or you can stop and return to the original radio station menu. You can also 'ban' or 'love' each song as it plays which will help Last.fm choose songs in the future

HOW TO DOWNLOAD MUSIC

As well as playing CDs and listening to music online, you can download music from the internet. You can buy individual music tracks or even whole albums from sites such as iTunes, HMV and Tesco. For example, with HMV:

1. Type www.hmv.co.uk into the address bar of your web browser and press **Enter**
2. Click **Downloads** on the page that loads
3. Search for the song or album you want to buy by inputting keywords into the **Search** box. Click on your choice
4. Click **Add to basket**
5. When you've finished shopping, click **Checkout**
6. HMV uses a Download Manager to download your music. This appears as a window showing the progress of your downloads

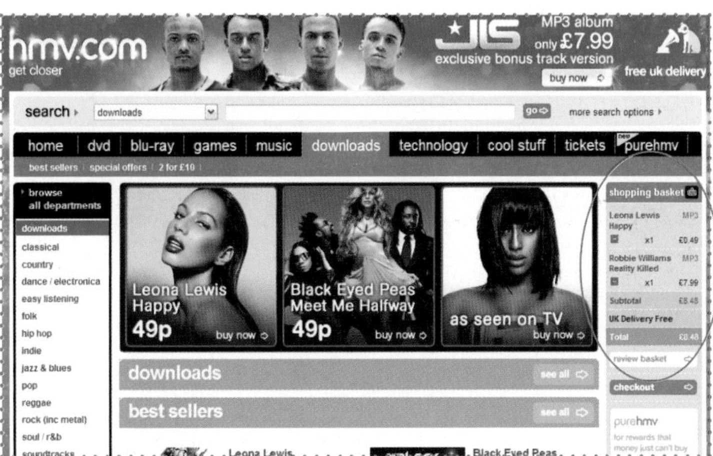

7. When it's finished, your music will appear in your Music folder. From here you can transfer it to an MP3 player or listen to it on your computer using software like Windows Media Player

Choosing the right audio format

There are lots of different digital audio formats and not all are compatible with the same media player software or portable music players. Most downloaded audio, however, is either in MP3, AAC and WMA formats.

WMA stands for Windows Media Audio and is Microsoft's format of choice, while AAC stands for Advanced Audio Coding and is used by Apple. On a PC, you can download a free software player that supports a particular format but, before you download any music or podcasts, check that your music player is compatible with that specific format.

HOW TO SET UP AN ITUNES ACCOUNT

If you own an Apple iPod or listen to music on your PC or Mac, the chances are you've downloaded and installed the latest version of iTunes. The iTunes Store on the iTunes website is Apple's online digital media store that sells songs, albums, TV shows, films and film rentals, and audiobooks. It offers free podcasts and other educational content.

Download from the iTunes store

To download an item from the iTunes Store, you need an iTunes Store account.

1. Type www.apple.com/uk/iTunes into the address bar of your web browser

2. Choose **Store** and then **Create Account**

3. Choose either **Create New Account** or, if you already have an account, enter your Apple or .Mac ID or AOL screen name

4. If you're creating a new account, you'll be asked to agree to the iTunes Store's terms and conditions. Read these, check the box, then click **Continue**

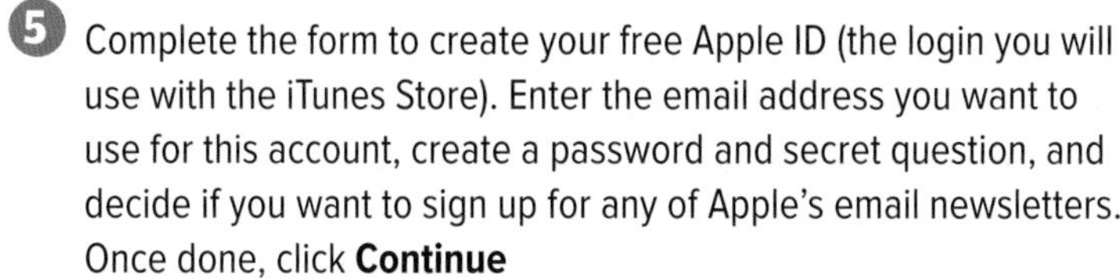

5 Complete the form to create your free Apple ID (the login you will use with the iTunes Store). Enter the email address you want to use for this account, create a password and secret question, and decide if you want to sign up for any of Apple's email newsletters. Once done, click **Continue**

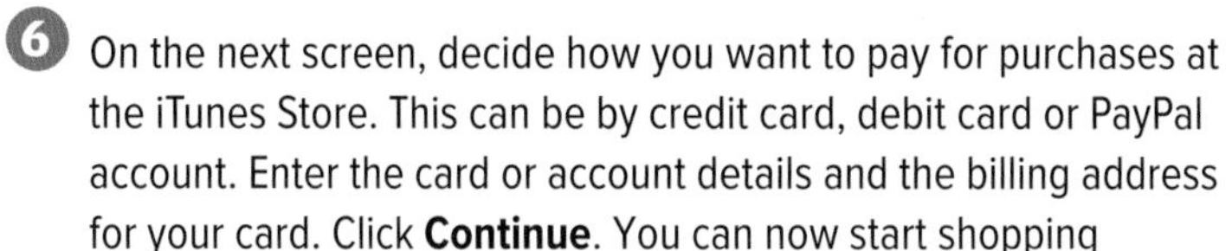

6 On the next screen, decide how you want to pay for purchases at the iTunes Store. This can be by credit card, debit card or PayPal account. Enter the card or account details and the billing address for your card. Click **Continue**. You can now start shopping

Decide how to buy items

The iTunes Store offers two options when it comes to buying items – One-Click shopping or a shopping cart. One-Click shopping means that you just click a **Buy** button, the download will start and you will automatically be charged for that item. With the shopping cart option, when you click the **Buy** button, your purchase is added to a shopping cart that you can review and edit before you pay. While One-Click is more convenient, there's no chance to change your mind, so, if you like to think about purchases, you may want to choose the shopping cart.

To switch between these buying options, you need to change an iTunes setting.

1 Select the **Edit** menu and choose **Preferences**

2 Click the **Store** tab

3 Tick either **One-Click** or **Shopping cart**

4 Once you've made your selection click **OK**

DOWNLOAD A PODCAST

A 'podcast' is a simple idea. It's like tuning into a radio show but, instead of listening to a live broadcast, you download a programme – known as a podcast – over the internet so that you can listen to it whenever and wherever you want. Like radio shows, podcasts are often published at regular intervals so you can set your PC to download an updated show automatically as soon as it's published on the internet. Then you can either listen to it on your PC or transfer the podcast to your digital music player.

Podcasts are usually free to download and consist of audio files and, occasionally, video files. There are podcasts on almost every topic you can think of from political debates to comedy sketches, and informative podcasts on anything from money tips to the latest gadgets.

Find a podcast

1. Type either www.podcast.com or www.podcastingnews.com into your address bar. These podcast directories contain links to different types of podcasts; simply click the different topic headings to find one on a subject you're interested in

2. You can subscribe to podcasts by using the free media player program, iTunes (perfect for people with iPods) or via software, such as Juice, which works with Windows Media Player

Download a podcast using iTunes

1. If you use a Mac, you will already have iTunes installed on your computer. PC users will need to check

2. Click **Start** then **All Programs** and look for an iTunes entry in the list

3. If it's there, launch the program and click **Help** then **About iTunes** to check that you have version 7 or later. To install iTunes from scratch or update an old version, go to www.apple.com/uk, click **Download iTunes** and follow the onscreen instructions

4. Open iTunes and click the **iTunes Store** icon in the left-hand panel

5. Click the **Podcasts** link in the box in the top left. A range of podcasts, including new releases and the most popular ones,

will appear onscreen. More are available by clicking on the various tabs, such as **What's Hot**, or scrolling down to browse through various topics

6 When you see a podcast you like the look of, click it. On the next screen, click **Subscribe** and then **Subscribe** again

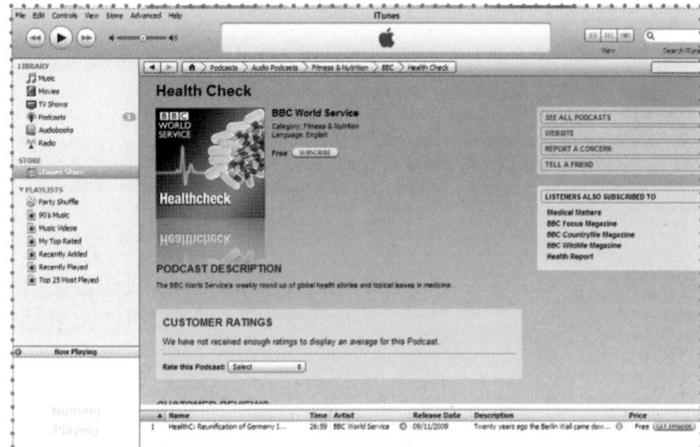

7 Every time a new episode of your podcast is available, iTunes will automatically download it from the internet. To listen, click **Podcasts** in the left-hand panel of iTunes and double click the podcast's name. Podcasts you haven't listened to will have a little blue dot next to them

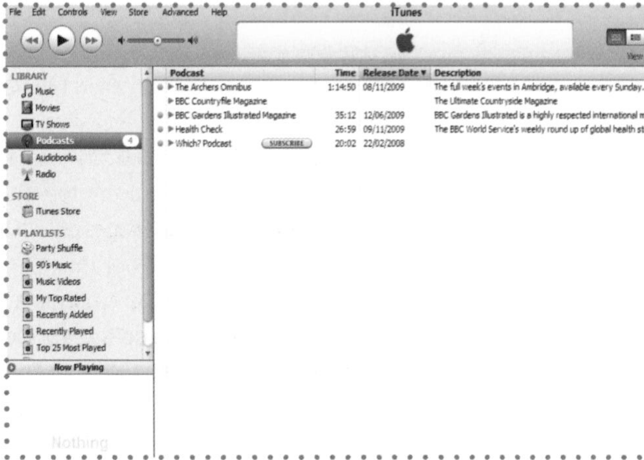

8 To delete a podcast, right click on it and select **Delete**

9 You can subscribe to podcasts manually – click **Advanced** on iTunes' top menu bar and, from the drop-down menu, click **Subscribe to podcast.** In the box onscreen, type in the website address of the podcast you wish to subscribe to

Get Podcasts without iTunes

If you use Windows Media Player and don't want to use iTunes to subscribe to podcasts, you could use other software such as Juice.

1. Type http://juicereceiver.sourceforge.net/ into the address bar and follow the onscreen instructions to install it on your PC

2. Click the **Add new feed** button and type in the web address of the podcast you want. Alternatively, click the **Podcast directory** tab and browse for a podcast you like. Double click on it. Click **Save**

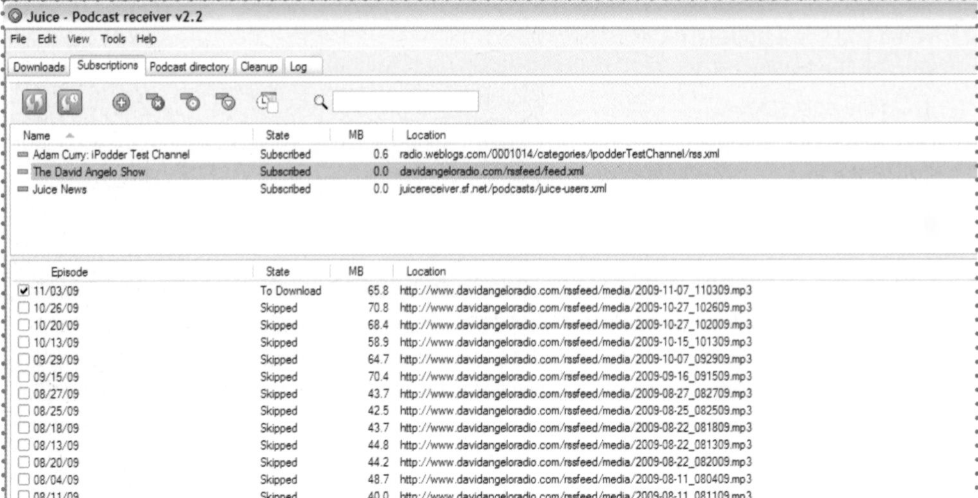

3. Juice creates a folder called **My Received Podcasts** in your Documents folder

4. If you have an MP3 player other than an iPod, it's likely that you'll use Windows Media Player (WMP) to transfer files to your device. Click **Start** then **All Programs**. Click **Windows Media Player**

5. Click the **Library** tab on the top toolbar and then **Add to Library**. In the box that appears, click **Add** and, from the pop-up menu, click **Add Folder**

6. Navigate to your Document folder, click on the My Received Podcasts folder and click **OK**. Once your podcast has been imported into Windows Media Player, you can then sync it with your portable music player

ONLINE ACTIVITIES

By reading and following all the steps in this chapter, you will get to grips with:

- **Online banking and bill payments**
- **Finding love and friendship through online dating**
- **Tracing your ancestors and family tree**

SET UP AN ONLINE BANK ACCOUNT

Nearly half the UK adult population bank online, and it's not hard to see why. Online banking means no more queuing at counters, no more worrying about closing time and no more waiting for a statement to arrive in the post. You can check your balance, pay bills, review direct debits, cancel standing orders and transfer funds between accounts, all without leaving home.

You can set up an online account using your existing bank account, or open a new internet-only account.

With your own bank

1. Type the address of your bank's website into the address bar. You'll find this on your bank statement or other correspondence

2. On the bank's home page, click on **Register** underneath the heading for internet banking

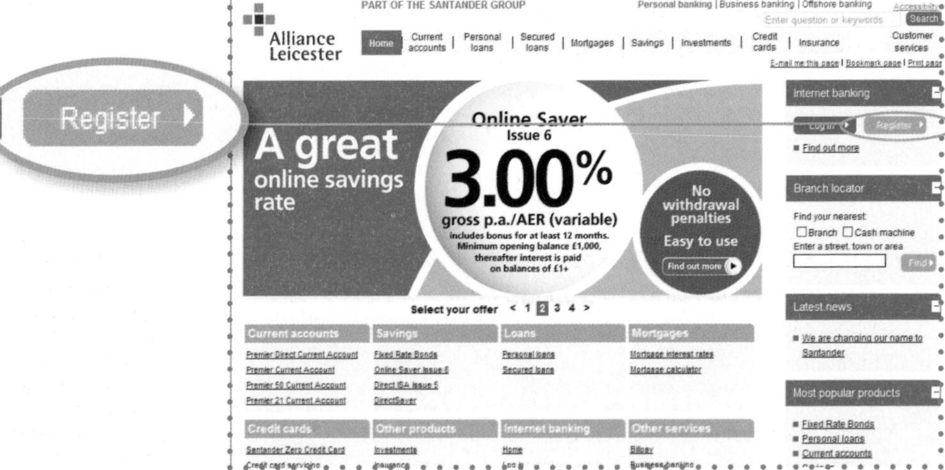

3. You'll need your bank sort code and account number at hand. Type them in when prompted, along with your personal details (this is likely to include your name, address and date of birth). You may also need a User ID or specific login details – contact your bank to check these

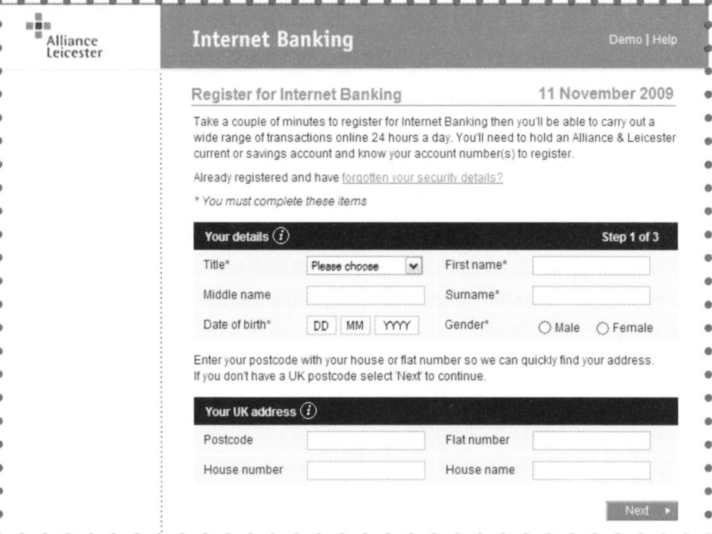

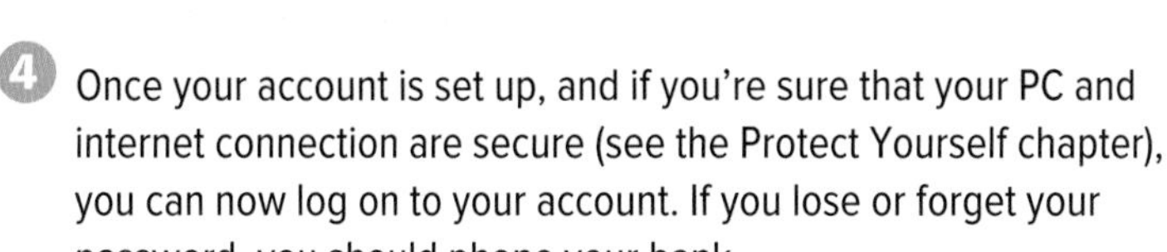

4. Once your account is set up, and if you're sure that your PC and internet connection are secure (see the Protect Yourself chapter), you can now log on to your account. If you lose or forget your password, you should phone your bank

5. Always remember to log out of your account when you're finished

With another bank

1. If you want to set up a new account online, enter that bank's website address in the address bar, go to the current account section, click on your desired account and fill in the form that appears

2. You'll usually get a decision on whether your application has been successful within a couple of minutes

3. As above, ensure that your PC and internet connection are secure before logging on to your account

TRY THIS

Many banks offer free security software or a subscription for a certain period when you sign up. Always check the terms and conditions before you subscribe to anything. For more on securing your computer, see page 190.

BE CAREFUL

Only access your account by using the website address provided by the bank. This means you can be certain that you are on the correct website when you enter your details. Never follow a link from an email claiming to be from your bank.

PAY BILLS ONLINE

The traditional ways of paying bills are fast becoming obsolete. From utility bills and TV licences to council tax, we are being encouraged to pay for services online as companies rush towards a future of paperless billing.

Some banks and building societies now charge a fee for processing paper bill payments and service providers such as utility companies offer discounts to those customers choosing to pay online.

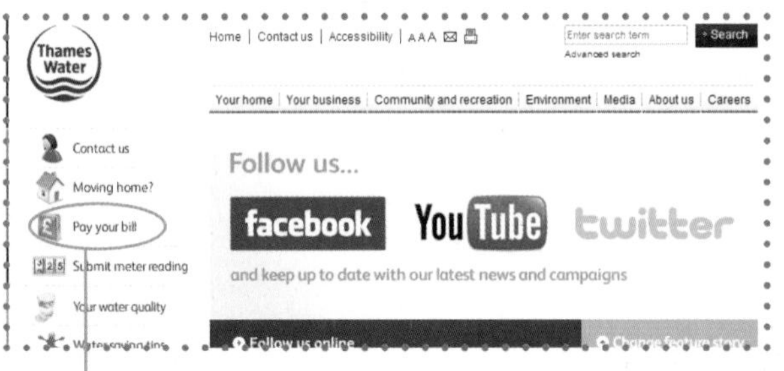

Pay online at the provider's website

1. Most energy and utility companies will have a button or a link on their home page saying **Pay Your Bill** or **Pay Your Bill Online**. Click on this
2. You will be asked to fill in your account number (this can be usually found at the top of your paper bills or statement). You need to give your full name, contact telephone number and the address of the property concerned. Finally, you'll need to provide your credit or debit card details
3. Enter the amount you wish to pay
4. Check through the details and click **Confirm**

Pay online from your Bank or Building Society account

Many banks and building societies allow you to pay bills online, as long as you're set up for internet banking. If you are, here's how to do it.

1. From your account page select the **Pay a bill** option
2. Enter the account number and the sort code of the company you wish to pay. This can be found on the company's website, on your paper bill under payment options, or by telephoning the company. Your bank may allow you to search for these account details by typing in the company's name but, as some companies have more than one account, it is best to double check

3. Enter the amount you wish to pay

4. Enter a reference number that will tie this payment to your account with the company whose bill you're paying. This is usually your account number or a reference supplied by the bill provider

5. Check the amount and click **Confirm**

Pay online with BillPay

Alliance & Leicester's BillPay lets customers (of any UK bank or building society) who hold a debit card, and in some cases a credit card, make regular or one-off payments online. A large number of local councils, water companies and utility companies accept payments using BillPay.

1. Type www.billpayment.co.uk into your address bar and click **New Users Register Here**

2. Read through and accept the Terms and Conditions, and complete the online registration form

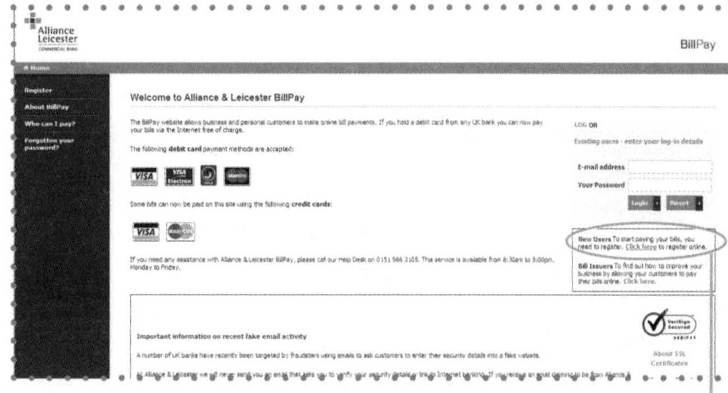

3. Choose a password and select the companies you wish to pay from the list of available companies in the drop-down boxes

4. Have the bills you wish to pay to hand, as you will need to enter your customer reference number

5. For security reasons, you'll also be asked to enter a brief security question and answer should you forget your password

6. Once registered, click the **Pay a Bill** button

7. On the **Payment Form,** select a company to pay, enter the total amount of your bill, the type of card you wish to use, the card number, expiry date and issue number (where applicable)

8. Click **Submit Payment Request**. Confirmation of your payment will then be displayed on screen

BUY CAR TAX ONLINE

When it comes to buying and renewing your car tax, you can stand in line at the Post Office with your MOT certificate and insurance documents, or you can take the easy route and buy your car tax online.

The DVLA has set up a special car tax website that lets you either apply for a new tax disc or declare your car off the road with a Statutory Off Road Notification (SORN). To get started, you'll need your number plate and the 16-digit reference number shown on your car tax renewal reminder (which you should have received in the post) or the 11-digit reference number on your car's V5c registration document/ logbook.

Pay your car tax

 Type www.taxdisc.direct.gov.uk into the address bar. Click the blue road sign that reads **Apply for a tax disc NOW!**

Directgov
www.direct.gov.uk Straight through to public services

Return to Directgov Motoring | Welsh/Cymraeg | Page Text Too Small?

Home
Apply for a tax disc NOW!
Declare SORN
Vehicle Enquiry
Common Questions
Have Your Say
Page Text Too Small?
Contact Us

Welcome

to the DVLA's vehicle online services

FREE PRIZE DRAW • WIN ONE OF THREE SEAT CARS

You can apply for a new tax disc or, if you intend to take the vehicle off the road, declare Statutory Off Road Notification, known as SORN, directly over the internet.

You can also use the Vehicle Enquiry service to check what information DVLA holds on its database about a vehicle.

If you tax or SORN on-line or by phone this month you will be entered into a FREE prize draw for one of three brand-new SEAT Ibiza ECOMOTIVE cars.
For more information on the Prize Draw, (including full terms and conditions) please visit www.dvlaprizedraw.org

How does it work?

- You tell us the vehicle. You will need either the 16 digit reference number shown on your renewal reminder, or the 11 digit reference number from your Registration Document/Certificate (also known as the Logbook) and your vehicle registration mark (numberplate).
- For a new tax disc we check the vehicle is insured and, if applicable has an electronic MOT Test Certificate/GVT Certificate or entitlement to disability exemption.

2 This page asks a series of car tax-related questions. You'll need to answer **Yes** to all five of these. (If you can't answer Yes, you will be unable to buy or renew your car tax online and you'll need to contact the DVLA for advice) When you've done so, click **Next**

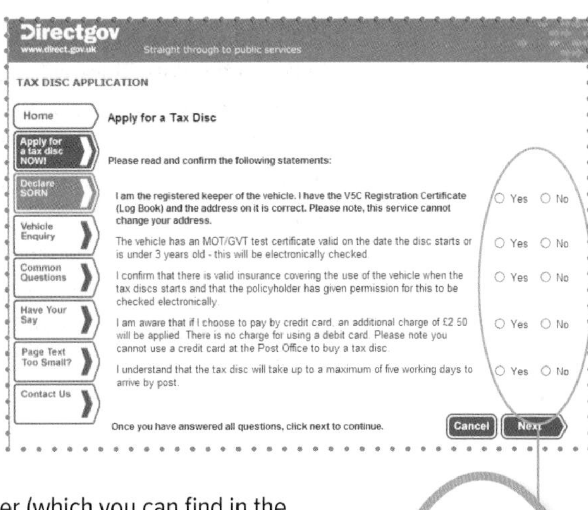

3 Type the reference number from the reminder into the box near the top of the screen. If you don't have a reminder, type your car's number plate and document reference number (which you can find in the car's logbook) into the boxes below. Click **Next** to continue

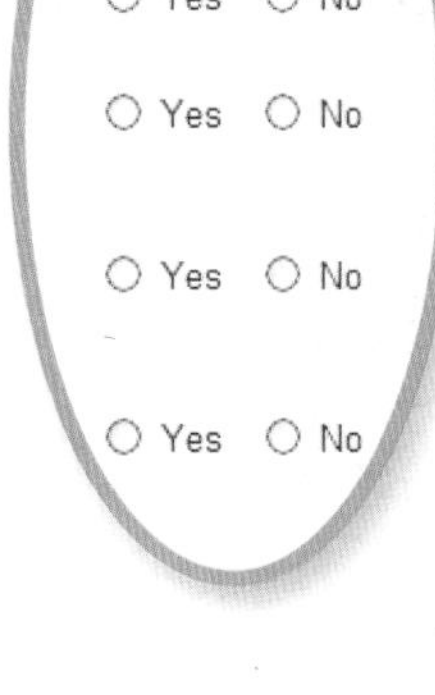

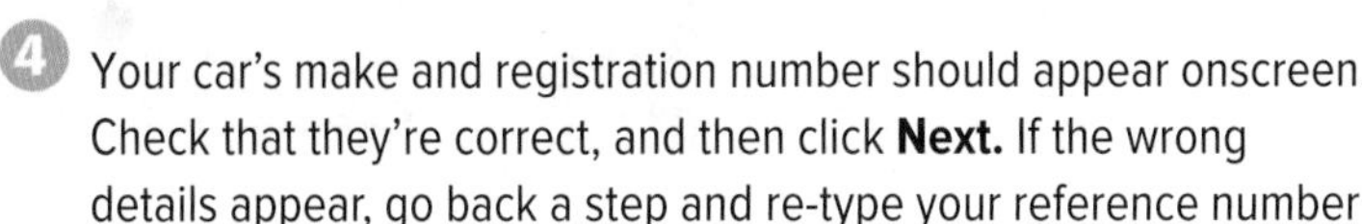

4 Your car's make and registration number should appear onscreen. Check that they're correct, and then click **Next.** If the wrong details appear, go back a step and re-type your reference number

5 Should you wish to do so, you can enter you vehicle's mileage on the next screen to help prevent mileage fraud. Click **Next** to continue

6 The website will check the DVLA's database to confirm that your vehicle's insurance and (if applicable) MOT details are up to date. It will then confirm this

7 Click the button beside the type of tax disc you would like to buy (six or 12 months). Click **Next** to proceed to the payment page

8 Enter your credit or debit card details and your email address, and then click **Next**. Note that credit card payments are subject to an additional charge

9 Check the details of your transaction and click **Pay now**. You can now print a copy of this confirmation – or just note down the reference number – for your records. Once you've completed the step-by-step process above, you should receive your new car tax disc within five working days. Letters confirming receipt of SORN declarations can take up to four weeks to arrive

BUY PERSONALISED STAMPS

You can capture and share your treasured family celebrations, from birthdays and weddings to new arrivals, with a set of personalised stamps from Royal Mail.

Ordering personalised stamps – known as Smilers – from the Royal Mail website is easy.

1. Type www.royalmail.com into your address bar and click on the red button marked **Personal Customers**

2. Under the heading **Mail help and advice**, click on the link **Create your own personalised stamps**

3. Click **Start here** and choose either a rectangular or a circular frame for your stamp

4. Click **Browse** and navigate to the picture you want to use on your computer and double click on it. Click **Preview your photo**. You may need to wait a few seconds for the picture to appear onscreen

5 The next screen displays a number of buttons to help you edit the picture that will appear on your personalised stamp. Click on these to zoom in on your photograph, change its position, rotate it, or even create a mirror image so you're seeing double. When you're happy, click **Choose a stamp design**

6 You can order first class stamps to accompany your Smilers. Use the left and right arrows to scroll through the 16 pre-set designs. When you find one that you like, click on it and then click **See your Smilers**

7 Choose whether to order 10 or 20 Smilers. Click **Buy Now** and enter your payment and address details

Online Activities

FIND LOVE ONLINE

Looking for love? You're most certainly not alone. Around six million people in Britain admit to using the internet to find a partner and there's over a thousand online dating sites out there hoping to help you narrow the search.

How online dating works

Unlike traditional introductions agencies, online dating agencies do not make background checks or have personal contact with site members. Instead, singles register with an online dating website and create an online dating profile page by writing about themselves, answering survey questions and uploading photographs.

Users can then browse the profiles of other site members to find someone they like, or search for suitable dates using keywords, location or criteria such as age range. Many online dating sites also nominate and recommend potential matches through a computerised system of selection. Once you've found someone you'd like to get to know better, you can get in touch using the site's built-in communication tools.

Signing up to an online dating site

1. **Choose a site** Look at a few sites before settling on one to subscribe to. Many dating sites cater exclusively for certain groups or people with a common lifestyle or interest. For example, specialist online dating agencies for more mature singles

include Dating for Seniors (www.datingforseniors.com), Senior Friend Finder (http://seniorfriendfinder.com/) and 40 Plus Dating (www.40plusdatinggroup.co.uk).

2 **Costs** Most online dating agencies allow new members to register and set up an online dating profile free of charge, but charge a subscription fee for certain important features such as tools for communicating with other members. Prices vary considerably depending on how many months membership you sign up for in advance. As a guide, a month's online dating membership typically costs between £10 and £25, though many offer daily, weekly, six-monthly or annual package deals which offer bigger discounts the longer your subscription

3 **No costs** There's a growing number of free online dating services, such as www.plentyoffish.com and www.flirtbox.co.uk. They generally work like social networking sites (see page 154) and make money through advertising

BE CAREFUL

Stay safe. When a profile can be read by so many people, it's best not to volunteer any personal information such as your employer's name, favourite local shop or your contact details.

PlentyOfFish
Free Online Dating

REGISTER | MAIL/PROFILE | HELP | ONLINE (53487) | SEARCH | RATING | FORUMS | CHEMISTRY | UPGRADE

Searches: Basic Advanced Marriage Username | My City | No Emails | Not Viewed

The Plentyoffish Relationship Chemistry Predictor (POFCP) measures five broad dimensions of personality that are each essential for building a romantic relationship.

We measure...

Factor 1: **Self-Confidence** This dimension was created to measure the extent to which an individual feel comfortable with him or herself. The items in this dimension reflect elements of self-confidence in both private and public contexts.

Factor 2: **Family Orientation** This dimension was developed to assess the degree to which a person possess a family orientation.

Factor 3: **Self-Control** This dimension measures the extent to which a person exerts control over sundry aspects of their lives and the lives of others.

Factor 4: **Social Dependency/Openness** This dimension measures the extent to which a person is open to and dependent upon other people.

Factor 5: **Easygoingness** This dimension taps into characteristics associated with being relaxed and psychologically flexible.

Currently 9,716,202 Plentyoffish users have taken the test. Login to see your matches or signup to take the test.

Username

Password

TRY THIS

Many online dating sites allow users to record and upload video and audio clips to their online dating profiles. You might want to try these out.

Making contact

Once registered, if you want to get in touch with another single on an online dating site, use the site's communication tools. These vary from site to site, but the most common options to look out for are outlined below.

- **Online dating webmail** When signing up to an online dating site, you'll be allocated an online email inbox allowing you to send and receive emails when on the site
- **Online dating instant messaging** This lets you exchange short messages with other online dating site users in real time. If another member is online at the same time as you, their profile will show an instant messaging prompt that will open a new window. You then just type in a message and wait for a response
- **Online dating chat** Similar to instant messaging, online chat enables you to exchange messages with other site users in real time. The difference is that online chat takes place in an established area of the online dating website and you join existing conversations with multiple or single online daters
- **Online dating video messaging** If you have a webcam and your dating site offers video messaging, you can send or accept invitations to have live chats with other members

Online dating abbreviation buster

Getting your words right when dating online is not always easy, particularly with all the abbreviations that are used online. Here are some of the most common:

ASL age/sex/location
AFK away from keyboard
BFN bye for now
BRB be right back
BTW by the way
FS Financially secure
GSOH good sense of humour
IMHO in my humble opinion
IRL in real life

TRACE YOUR FAMILY TREE

The internet has made it easier for people to trace their family background now that many historical records, such as the 1901 census, are available online in searchable formats. Dozens of websites have also popped up with information to help people find their ancestors.

Where to start

1. Gather as much information as you can about your closest relatives. Look for birth, death and marriage certificates and quiz older relatives to ensure your information is as accurate as possible. Arm yourself with a full name (preferably including a middle name), year and place of birth

2. For England and Wales, the 1911 census and each previous one back to 1851 are available to be viewed online on websites partnered with The National Archives. To find out more about a particular census visit The National Archives (type www.nationalarchives.gov.uk/records/census-records.htm into the address bar)

3. Here you'll see a list of census years with details of The National Archives' partner sites that hosts those records

4. Choose the census you wish to search and click one of the links provided. For example, in the case of the 1891 census, you can choose to search records for either **England, Wales, Channel Islands** or **Isle of Man** – clicking on one of these links will take you to those specific records on the partner site

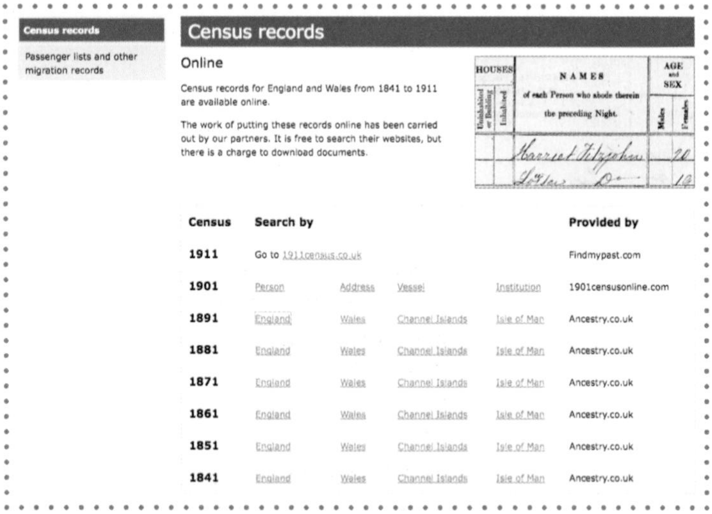

Census records

Passenger lists and other migration records

Census records

Online

Census records for England and Wales from 1841 to 1911 are available online.

The work of putting these records online has been carried out by our partners. It is free to search their websites, but there is a charge to download documents.

Census	Search by				Provided by
1911	Go to 1911census.co.uk				Findmypast.com
1901	Person	Address	Vessel	Institution	1901censusonline.com
1891	England	Wales	Channel Islands	Isle of Man	Ancestry.co.uk
1881	England	Wales	Channel Islands	Isle of Man	Ancestry.co.uk
1871	England	Wales	Channel Islands	Isle of Man	Ancestry.co.uk
1861	England	Wales	Channel Islands	Isle of Man	Ancestry.co.uk
1851	England	Wales	Channel Islands	Isle of Man	Ancestry.co.uk
1841	England	Wales	Channel Islands	Isle of Man	Ancestry.co.uk

5. Whichever census and category you choose, you will be presented with search form. Enter as many details as you can about your ancestor and click **Search**

6. You will be presented with a list of possible relatives listed by name, date and place of birth, parish and county they lived in and possibly their occupation too. To find out more information, click on the name of a potential ancestor

What does it cost?

You have to pay to see the census detail. Several different websites host the same census and the amount of information provided for free varies, so it's worth searching the internet for other sites that offer census details to get the best deal (see page 127 for tips on searching).

To view original documents via the National Archives 1901 census data you have to pay a minimum charge of £5. This gives you access to the online records for a week, during which you can download your chosen census images at a cost of 75p each.

Ancestry.co.uk, which hosts censuses from 1851 to 1901, offers a subscription service (£200 to view records worldwide or £70 for a UK-only subscription). There's a free 14-day trial, but remember to cancel the trial within the fortnight if you don't want to take it up or you'll be charged. An annual subscription might sound expensive, but you may be surprised at how many ancestors you uncover during that time.

If you don't want to pay at all, you can view the documents at The National Archives in Kew, London, for free.

Scotland and Northern Ireland

To search for ancestors living in Scotland go to Scotland's People (www.scotlandspeople.gov.uk) or for Ireland try the Irish National Archives (www.nationalarchives.ie). Ireland's census records are not online and the 1901 records were destroyed by fire.

Top online tracing tips

- **Watch out for spelling mistakes** Names can be, and often were, spelled in different ways. Some websites let you use an 'alternative spelling' option when searching, which could prove fruitful

- **Allow for transcription errors** It pays to think laterally when searching for ancestors. If you can't find a relative, try searching for a sibling in the same household or try another census. Also, different websites use different transcriptions of the same census so, if you can't find an ancestor on one website, try another

- **Scour war records** The Commonwealth War Graves Commission (www.cwgc.org) contains records of the British and Commonwealth personnel who died in the First and Second World Wars, often with details of the battle or location they died in, the regiment and the cemetery where they are buried

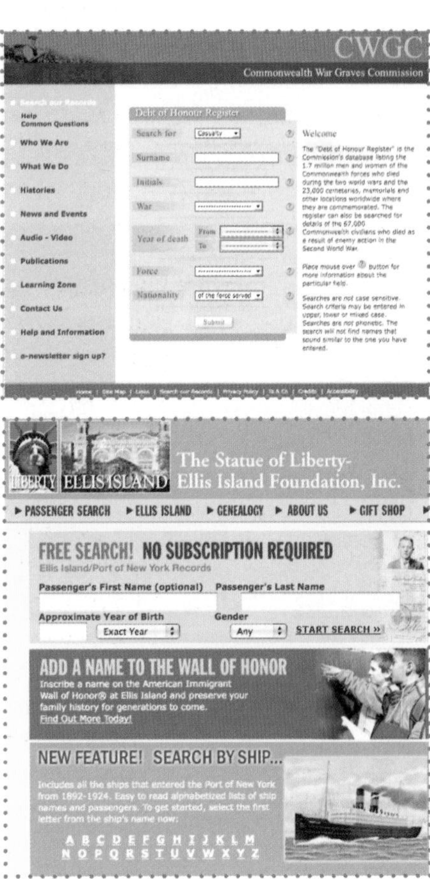

- **Finding relatives abroad** The Migration Histories section of the National Archives website provides fascinating information on tracing ancestors from Caribbean, Irish, Jewish and South Asian communities. In addition, lots of people emigrated to the US and Canada, entering North America through Ellis Island. If a family vanishes from your research in the UK try going to www.ellisisland.org for post-1892 records. For earlier arrivals to North America – between 1830 and 1892 – try www.castlegarden.org

- **Births, deaths and marriages database** If you're having trouble tracing a relative because you lack information such as a maiden name or a place of birth, try typing www.freebmd.org.uk into your address bar. This website, Free BMD, lists birth, marriage and death certificates in England and Wales from 1837 to around 1911. Add a name or names to the **Search** box on this site and it will find names, locations and dates for each event, all of which you can view free of charge

- **Find fellow genealogists** Genes Reunited (www.genesreunited.co.uk) is a good way to discover distant relatives who may also be researching the same family tree as you. It's free to register, after which you can search other members' family trees for mutual relatives. If you find a match, simply send a message to the owner and they may let you see their entire tree. You'll have to subscribe (£10 for a year) in order to contact other members, but messages are sent securely through the site, so your email address isn't revealed

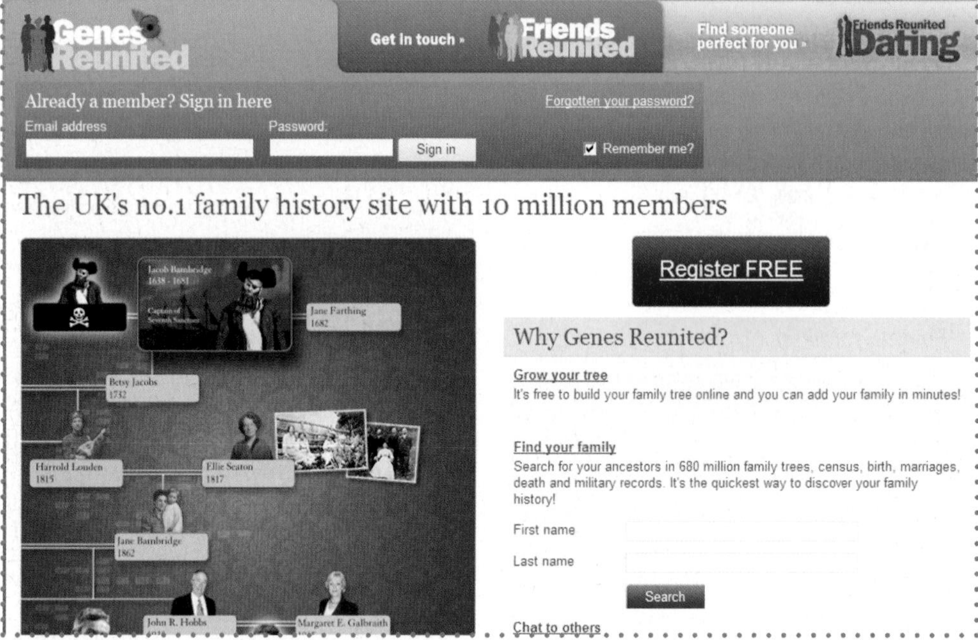

- **Advertise 'missing' ancestors** Many genealogy websites boast a community section, where members can post details about relatives for whom they're seeking information. Use websites where contacts between members are made through the site and email addresses remain private

- **Don't forget the old-fashioned way** Not all records are online (particularly those prior to 1837), so try visiting local records offices, churches, graveyards or libraries for more detail. Such trips can elevate your ancestors from being just names on a screen to real people

SHOPPING ONLINE

By reading and following all the steps in this chapter, you will get to grips with:

- **Choosing trusted shopping websites**
- **Using the internet to buy weekly groceries**
- **Ordering prescriptions and healthcare items online**

SHOP SAFELY ONLINE

Internet shopping means lots of choice, no queues and, because it's easier to shop around, you can often save money, too. However, do make sure you take some safety steps before you go ahead.

Important safety steps

- Before you buy, ensure you have a firewall switched on and anti-virus and anti-spyware software installed (see page 190 for more on security)
- Choose a reputable retailer such as a familiar high-street store, or use an online directory such as www.safebuy.org.uk or www.shopsafe.co.uk that lists only shops offering secure credit card transactions, with obvious delivery prices and clear returns policies.
- Secure web addresses start with the letters **https**, instead of **http**, and you should see a **padlock** symbol at the top of the page
- Find out how easy the website is to contact. Look for links called **Contact us** or **Help** to find the physical address and phone number. Call to make sure the line is working and someone picks up. If there's only an email address, send one to see how quickly they reply

Buy an item

Once you've spent some time browsing and have decided what to buy, it's time to go to the checkout.

1. Click the button marked **Add to shopping basket**

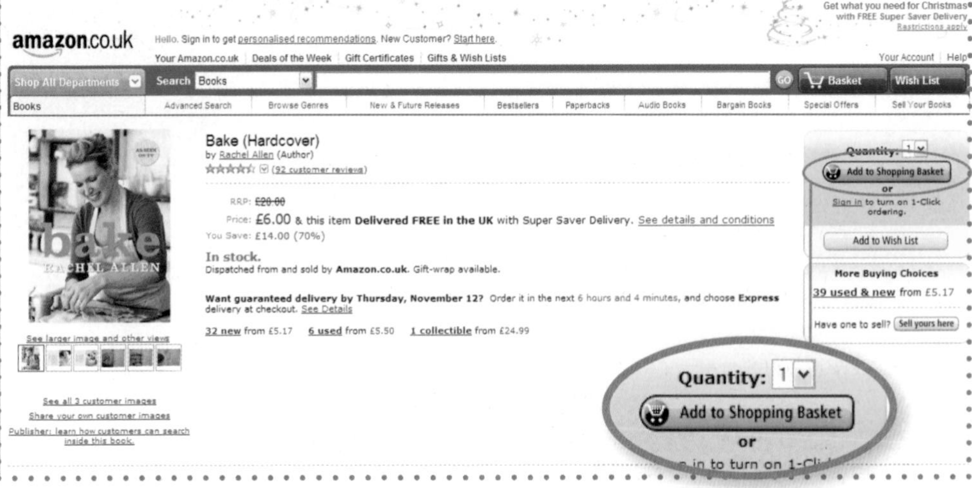

2. Many websites allow you to **View basket** so you can check what you've added, the total cost, and how many of each item you've ordered. Then you can either shop some more or make your payment

3. Once you're happy, click the **Proceed to checkout** button (or equivalent). If you haven't already registered, you'll be asked to now. This generally involves setting up a user name and password and entering your contact, delivery and payment details. Be aware that many online retailers will only deliver goods to the billing address of your credit card

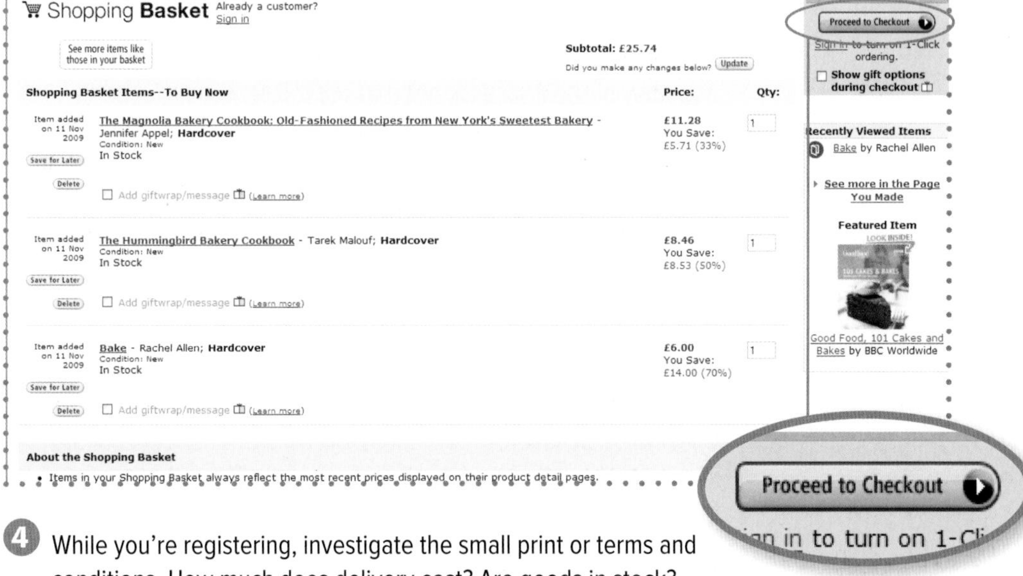

4. While you're registering, investigate the small print or terms and conditions. How much does delivery cost? Are goods in stock? Can you send items back if they're not what you expected?

5. If you're happy, enter your card details including the start and expiry date. Many websites now ask for the security code to ensure the person ordering has the card in front of them. This is on the signature strip on the back of your credit card; just enter the last 3 digits (4 if you use American Express)

6. Ensure you keep a record of the transaction and the order number. You should receive a receipt via email; if you have spam-filtering software (see page 65), this email may end up in your junk folder so do check it

Internet payments

If you use a credit card to pay for goods worth more than £100 (and up to £30,000), your card company is jointly liable with the company that you buy from for any problems. For smaller purchases, an e-cash system such as PayPal is often used (see page 152). These systems allow you to send or receive payments securely over the web without sharing your financial details or credit card number with anyone else.

Know your rights

Shopping online can be more convenient and cheaper than the high street, but it can be easy to make a mistake when ordering online shopping, and sometimes what you receive isn't what you expected. So what are your rights as a shopper?

If you buy online from a UK or EU-based retailer you have the same rights as if you'd bought from a shop. Under the Sale of Goods Act, items purchased must be of satisfactory quality, fit for purpose and as described when sold. If a retailer breaches any of these terms, you have the right to reject the goods within a reasonable time and get a full refund (see page 150 for more on returning goods bought online). Or you can demand that the retailer repairs or replaces the item. If you send goods back for any reason that is the fault of the supplier, you should not have to pay the postage.

Under the E Commerce Regulations, online shops must set out the stages you have to complete to place an order. You must also be given the chance to check your details before placing the order. If the online shop confirms acceptance of your order, you have a legally binding contract, but, if it simply acknowledges your order, you don't.

The E Commerce Regulations also state that the online shop has to give full details of who they are and provide a geographical address and an email address at which to contact them.

The online shop's terms and conditions should say who pays for returning goods. If they don't, they have to pay (see page 150).

Pay close attention to an online store's terms and conditions before you purchase. An example of an online shop's terms and conditions to watch out for is when they say that the price of your order will be fixed the day the goods are dispatched to you. This may mean that they may charge a higher price than when you placed the order, but they must still give your right to cancel under the Distance Selling Regulations (see below).

Cooling-off period

If you change your mind about the goods, or they don't arrive on time, the Distance Selling Regulations (DSR) give you a cooling-off period. This starts from the moment you place the order and ends 7 working days from the day after you receive the goods. During this period you can cancel without having to give a reason. Contact the seller and quote the Distance Selling Regulations to get a refund and arrange to send back the purchase. These regulations don't apply to items bought from foreign websites or to items such as unsealed CDs/DVDs, perishable items such as food and flowers and personalised goods.

EBAY – YOUR QUESTIONS ANSWERED

eBay is a website that allows you to buy and sell items – the online equivalent of the newspaper's classified pages. When you buy through eBay, you're not actually buying from eBay itself. It isn't a shop – instead eBay is a marketplace that allows buyers and sellers of goods – whether individual sellers or independent traders – to do business together. Moreover eBay is an auction site – so if you want an item you'll have to offer a better price than other interested buyers.

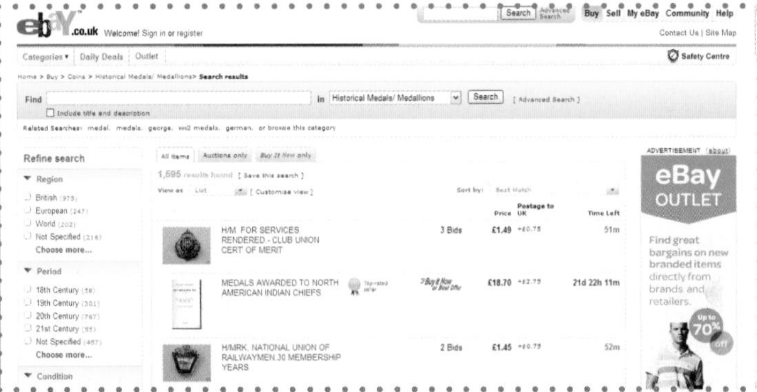

Set up an eBay account

Before you can start buying or selling goods on eBay, you'll need an account.

1. Type www.ebay.co.uk into the address bar of your web browser and press **Enter**

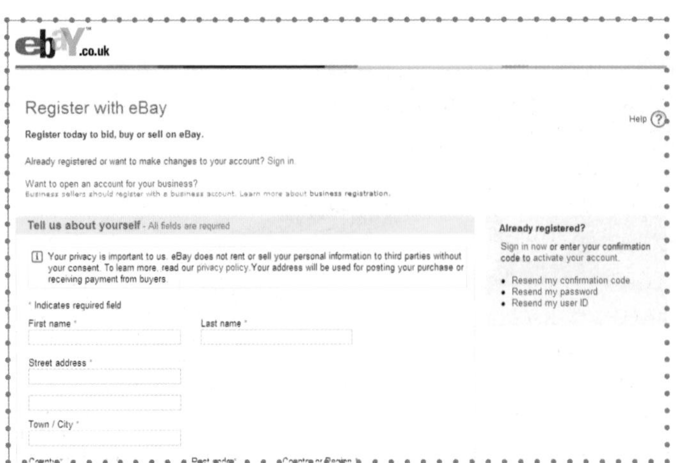

2. On the page that appears, click on **Register**
3. Enter your name, address and email address
4. Choose a username and password. You'll also need to enter your credit card details; this is a security check to confirm your identity

BUY ON EBAY

An eBay auction works like a normal auction – the highest bidder wins – but, in this case, it takes place over a few days and has a cut-off time.

1. Find the item that you want to bid on and click on it by searching using a keyword or by category

2. Enter the amount you want to bid and click on **Place Bid**

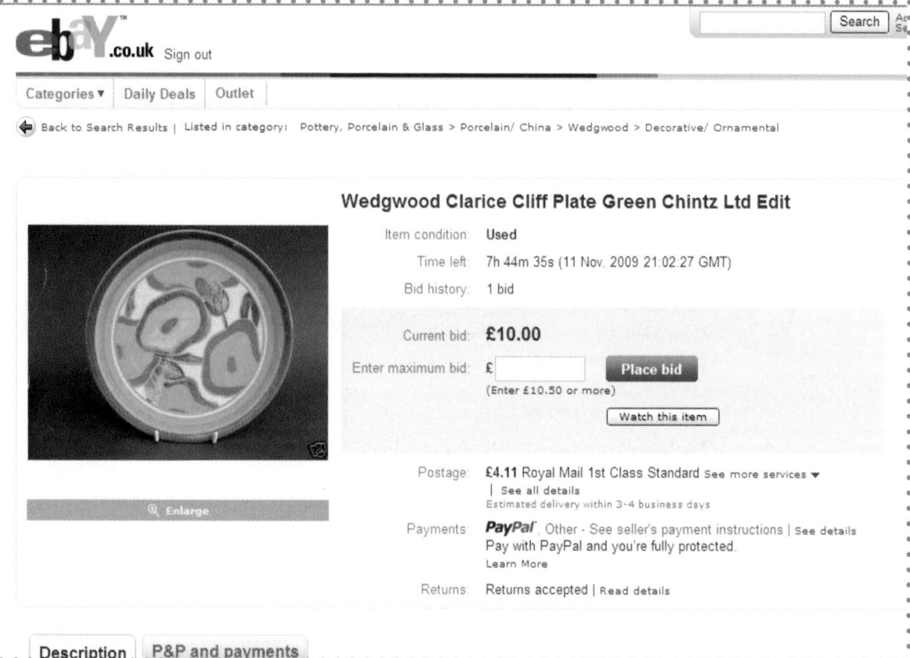

3. Ensure that your bid is higher than the current one then click **Confirm Bid** (by doing so, you agree to buy the item if you are successful)

4. Alternatively, you can enter the maximum that you are prepared to pay for the item and eBay's proxy bidding service will automatically bid incrementally on your behalf up to that amount

5. If your bid is the highest at the cut-off time then you've won the auction and will be told by email. It will contain details of the types of payment that the seller accepts: credit or debit card or PayPal, for example (for more on PayPal, see page 152)

BE CAREFUL

Don't pay via money transfer service Western Union even if asked by a seller. eBay has banned the use of these transactions on the website because money transfers leave no electronic paper trail or proof of payment.

SELL ON EBAY

To sell an item on eBay, you'll need to log on to the website and click the Sell button. Then you need to follow the on-screen instructions to fill in the details of your item. The better you do this, the more money someone is likely to bid. Here are a few simple tips you can use to make your auction stand out from the crowd.

- One of the first decisions you'll need to make is in which category to list your item. If you're unsure, type in a few key words about it and eBay will suggest a category for you. It's possible to list products in multiple categories to give them more exposure – but your listing fees will be doubled as a result (see **Costs**, page 137)

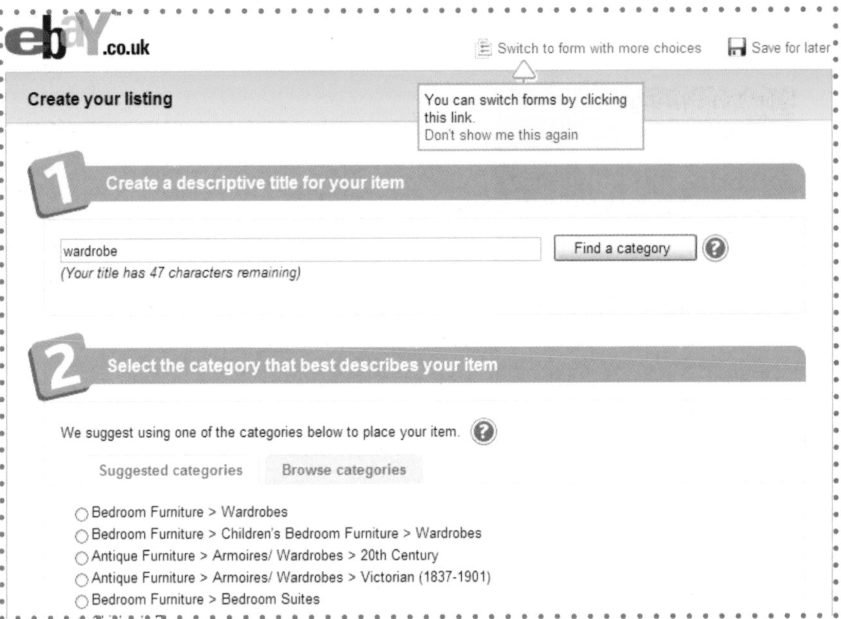

TRY THIS

eBay allows buyers to leave you feedback, which is added to your feedback rating. It's important to ensure that you have a good rating as buyers often check before choosing to bid. Selling a few smaller-value items is a quick way to increase your score.

- Each eBay listing has a one-line title – grab people's attention with a catchy one. Buyers will typically conduct title searches, and results will be listed according to relevance. The more information you provide, the more chance potential buyers will look at your item

- Include a photograph. Buyers want to be able to see what they're buying and it gives them a good indication of its condition. The first photograph is free, additional ones will cost more

- Keep descriptions (including the title) up-front and honest, while remaining positive and upbeat about the item
- Remember to get the brand/model names and spelling variations correct
- List all postage information and returns policies clearly
- Make sure your listing ends when traffic to eBay is busiest as it'll attract last-minute bids. Weekends and weekday evenings usually attract the most buyers
- Research how much items have sold for in the past by browsing 'completed items'
- Start the bidding at a low price – it will attract more people
- Respond to bidders' enquiries in a timely manner and build up a reputation selling smaller value items

TRY THIS

eBay has a community of users who discuss their top selling tips on the online forums. Check out your favourite sales categories at http://groups.ebay.co.uk or ask other members for advice at http://pages.ebay.co.uk/community/answercenter

Costs

eBay charges listing fees (the cost to insert your item; this depends on its starting price) and final value fees (a commission based on the price your item sells for). See http://pages.ebay.co.uk/help/sell/fees.html for the latest prices.

Never send out an item until you have received payment for it.

Postage and packaging

Post and packaging prices are paid for by the buyer but, as a seller, you need to list these charges up-front. Weigh your item along with all your packaging and make sure you've measured the package's exact dimensions, then consult the Royal Mail website (www.royalmail.com) to determine your shipping charge. Consider sending high-value items via a special delivery for insurance reasons.

Always keep a proof of postage for the item.

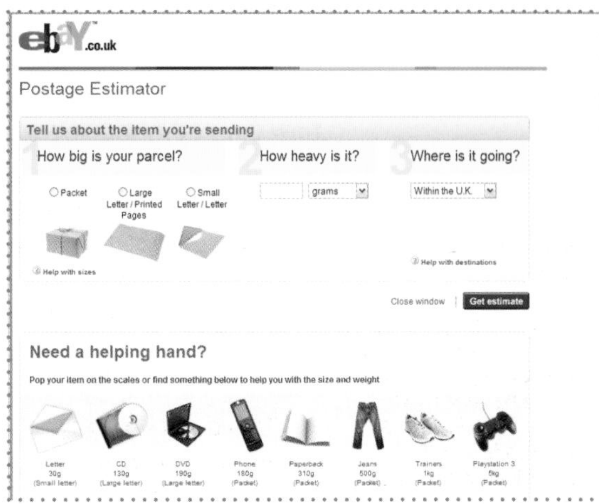

GENERAL TIPS FOR USING EBAY

How do I become a buyer or seller

You'll need to register first on the site before you can buy or sell. See page 134 for details of setting up an eBay account.

How do I find items to buy on eBay?

With so many goods on sale, it can be hard to find what you want on eBay. Make use of the Advanced search option and select the appropriate category as well as a keyword in order to narrow down results.

How can I be sure of the quality of goods?

Many items for sale via eBay are second-hand so the quality obviously varies. Read the item description carefully – in particular, details such as make, model and vintage, as well as any information about the condition. Look for a photograph of the item as well.

How can I be sure that the seller is legitimate?

Whenever you buy from an eBay seller you're invited to leave feedback about them, such as whether they delivered on time and whether goods were as advertised. All sellers have a Feedback Score and each starts outs with a feedback rating of zero. For every positive piece of feedback you give a seller, eBay adds one point; for every bit of negative feedback, they take away a point. The higher the feedback rating, the better.

Also look for a logo that denotes a so-called Powerseller. Powersellers must have traded on eBay for at least 90 days and had average monthly sales of £750 per month. They must also have an eBay Feedback Rating of 98% or more.

How does eBay bidding work?

An eBay auction works on the same principle as an auction in an auction house in that the highest bidder wins. Enter the maximum that you are prepared to pay for the item (ensuring it's more than the current maximum bid, of course). eBay's proxy bidding service means that the eBay system automatically bids incrementally on your behalf up to that amount. All bids have a cut-off date and time. If your bid is the highest on that date and time then you've won the auction.

What's a 'second chance' fraud?
Second Chance auctions are a legitimate part of the eBay system. Sometimes an auction winner decides that they no longer want the item or doesn't pay. If you're the second-highest bidder, the seller can offer you a 'second chance' to buy; an email will appear in the My Messages area of eBay and your personal inbox. Be aware, however, that hackers have sometimes taken advantage of this, sending out bogus emails to inboxes claiming to offer a bidder a second chance to buy an item. Clicking on the link within the email takes you to a site that looks like eBay, where you're asked to hand over your credit card details. A good way to keep an eye on your transactions is to log in and check your eBay messages to see whether the same message also appears there. If you're still unsure you can send a copy of the message to spoof@ebay.com.

How do I pay for an item?
If your bid is successful, you'll be told by an email, which will list the types of payment that the seller accepts: credit or debit card or PayPal for example. eBay's preferred payment method is PayPal – the electronic payment system it owns. PayPal transfers funds between buyers and sellers without them having to exchange bank details. See page 152 for how to set up a PayPal account.

What happens if it goes wrong?
As eBay is the middle-man in transactions between buyer and seller, it is not responsible if things go wrong. As such, if this happens, your first port of call is to contact the seller via the website.

If this fails, you can open an 'Item not received or significantly not as described' dispute from 10 to 60 days after the day the listing ended. eBay contacts the seller and the seller can choose whether to respond via eBay or to chat to you directly. If your concerns still aren't resolved, you can escalate this to a claim, which will be paid under eBay's standard protection scheme, which can reimburse you for up to £120.

If you've used PayPal to pay (see pages 135 and 152), you may be eligible for a full refund. Not everything is covered by PayPal Buyer Protection – check the seller information section of the site to see if the item you are buying qualifies for it – and you must register a claim with PayPal within 45 days of payment.

If you believe you have been the victim of fraud, you should report it to eBay, which will remove the seller from the site.

USE PRICE COMPARISON SITES

Comparison websites fall into two main categories: those that deal with retail products, and those that deal with financial and insurance services. Some of the very large comparison sites offer both.

Retail products

Price comparison websites such as Kelkoo, PriceRunner, NexTag, and Ciao let you compare products and prices from hundreds of retailers, side by side, helping you to choose the best deal. You can search these sites by typing in a product name, or browse through categories. One of the most popular features of price comparison websites is user reviews. To write a review or ask questions about a product, however, usually requires you to create an account.

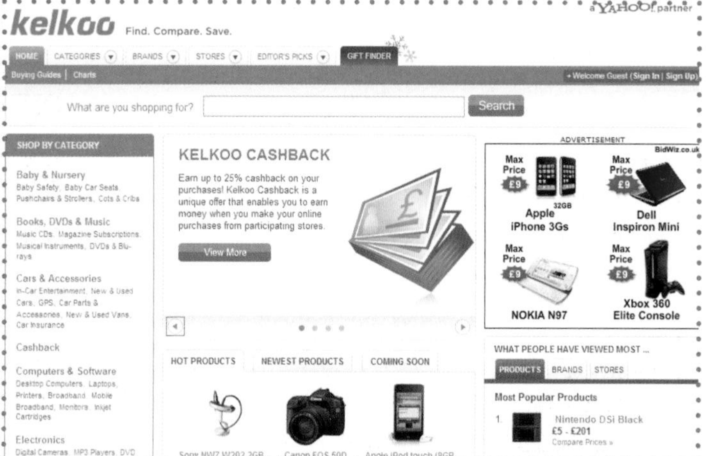

Once you decide you would like to buy a product from a particular retailer, click on the link or button that will take you through to that shop's website so that you can purchase the item directly. The retailer pays the price comparison site a referral fee when you click through. There's no cost to you as a user.

Be aware that price comparison sites don't compare prices from every shop online. Instead, they partner with a range of retailers.

Services, utilities and financial products

Sites such as www.moneysupermarket.com, www.gocompare.com and www.confused.com will help you compare financial and insurance products and services.

However, while they can be a quick and easy way to get a quote for insurance or a loan, they do have limitations. Product providers pay to be included so some deals may be promoted ahead of other products. The comparison sites earn a commission payment when a customer chooses to switch to or apply for a product through the website. With financial products such as loans, these commissions can be sizeable.

Get a quote for car insurance

1. Type www.moneysupermarket.com into the address bar of your browser

2. Click on **Car Insurance** from the list of options available

3. Click **Get a New Quote**

4. On the next screen fill in your car details and then click **Continue**

5. Fill in all your personal and address details and click **Continue**. Confirm and check your details again and click **Continue**

6. Now choose the level of cover you require and enter your email address and a password to create an account. Click **Get Results**

7. You'll see a list of insurance quotes that match your criteria. Once you've decided on a quote, click the **Go to site** button alongside the product to go to the provider's website. Here you can save your quote to return later or go ahead and purchase

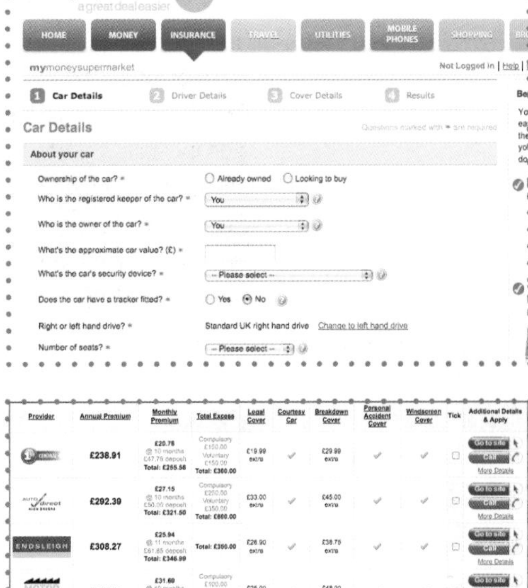

Get the best price for services

- Get quotes from several comparison websites and other places you trust before choosing a product

- Make sure any insurance policy you take out through a comparison site gets you the cover you request and require

- Avoid taking out insurance through a comparison website if you have a pre-existing medical condition

- Use quotes from comparison sites to haggle with your existing insurer as it may reduce your renewal quote

PROPERTY HUNTING ONLINE

If you're house hunting, the internet makes it easy to find the latest properties for sale anywhere in the world, and discover more about your chosen location. Many estate agents list the properties they have on their books on their own websites, although most also use the big selling and buying property sites, including www.zoopla.co.uk, www.propertyfinder.com and www.rightmove.co.uk. We've used RightMove for this example:

Search for a property

1. Type www.rightmove.co.uk into the address bar of your web browser and press **Enter**. You will see lots of ways to find property to rent and buy, including searching by map, looking at holiday homes, and guides to buying homes

2. In the large, central **Search** box, type in a postcode or town name, and click the **For Sale** button

3. The next screen will allow you to narrow your search so you can find a property within a specific area or price range, and with certain criteria such as number of bedrooms. If you want to see properties that are also under offer or reserved, tick the **Include Under Offer**, **Sold STC** and **Reserved properties box**

4. Click the **Find properties** button

TRY THIS

Use a website such as www.upmystreet.com to find out local information for the area you are interested in, including crime levels, schools, transport, council tax and entertainment.

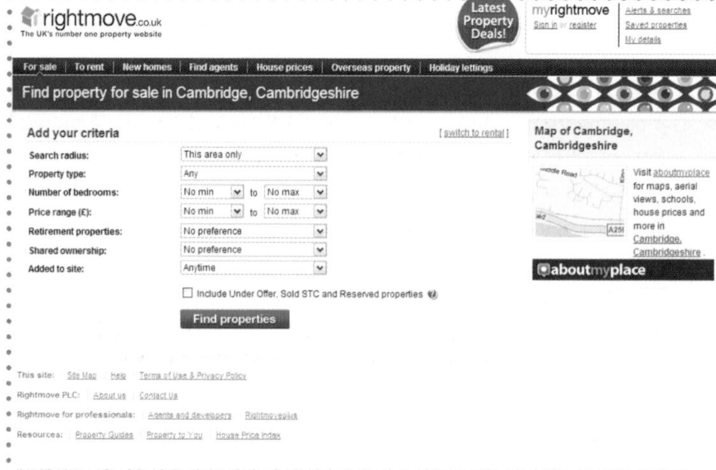

5. A series of properties will appear. In the upper-right corner, click **Lowest price first** to see properties in ascending price order. Options in the left-hand column allow you to narrow your search further. For example, you can choose **Detached houses** from the **Filter** your results box

6. Click on a picture of a property that you want to find more information about. The page that appears will allow you to click on more photos of the property, as well as to see a local map and the particulars of the property

7. Some properties will allow you to see the street in more detail. Click **Street View** in the centre of the page. The photo that appears can be controlled by clicking and dragging your mouse to pan around. Double-clicking on the photo will take you further along the street as if you are walking around the area. Close **Street View** by clicking the red circle with a white cross

8. To see a map and aerial photo of the property you are viewing, click **Local map**. In the map that appears, click **Aerial** or **Birds-eye** view to see a photo of the property from the sky. Use the + and – buttons to zoom into and out of the map

TRY THIS

There are lots of different property websites to try, including www.findaproperty.com, www.primelocation.com and www.propertyfinder.com.

Other options

1. To send property details to a friend or family member, click the **Send to friend** text at the top of the property details. Enter their email details and add yours so that you get a copy of the property details

2. To view a property or request details, click **Request details**. Enter your information and, if you do not want marketing offers emailed to you, ensure that you untick the marketing boxes on the page. The estate agent will then contact you to arrange a viewing, and send property details in the post to you

3. To find the average price of property in a certain area, click the **House prices** option at the top of the page. In the large **Search** box, type in a postcode or town name and click **Start search**. In the page that appears, click on a street name to see a list of properties that have sold in the last few years, including their address and sale price

BE CAREFUL

When you buy a product or register on a website, you'll often be asked whether you want to receive email or marketing materials from that company or other third-party companies in the future. Read the text carefully to check if you need to tick or un-tick the box so you can make the correct choice.

Shopping Online

TRY THIS

Speed up the time you spend grocery shopping online by making the most of the favourites or personal shopping features offered. If you click on this, you will find all the items you've ordered previously or items from a saved shopping list.

GROCERY SHOPPING ONLINE

You can now do the weekly food shop from the comfort of your own home and have it delivered at a time that suits you. You can save time by shopping from a list of favourite items you buy regularly, and keep within a budget by avoiding the temptations of shopping in store. Most big supermarkets offer this facility including Tesco, Sainsbury's and Asda. Ocado, the online arm of Waitrose, is one of the best known.

1. Type www.ocado.com into the address bar and press **Enter**

2. Before you start shopping you need to set up an account and check if the supermarket can deliver to your area. Click on **Register**. Keep the account type **Personal**. Enter your postcode

3. If the online store can deliver to your address, you will be asked to select your address, complete a form with your details and set a password. When you visit the site again, you can log in using your username – which is your email address – and this password

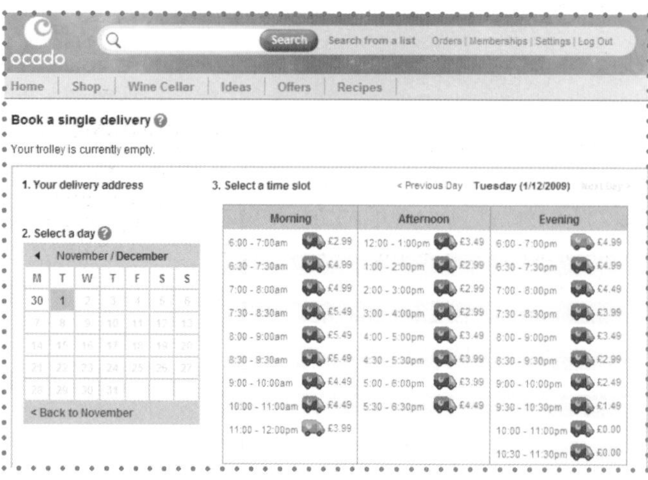

4. You can now start shopping. First book a delivery slot by clicking on the **Book a single delivery button** on the right-hand side of the screen. From the next screen, choose a date and then choose a time slot for the delivery. Then click **Confirm slot and continue**

5 To find groceries, you can either type the item name in the **Search bar** at the top of the page, or click through various categories. So, if you want to buy a pint of semi-skimmed milk, you can click **Food and Drink**, then **Fresh**, then **Milk Dairy and Eggs**, then **Milk Fresh** and finally **Semi-Skimmed** to bring up a shortlist of items to choose from

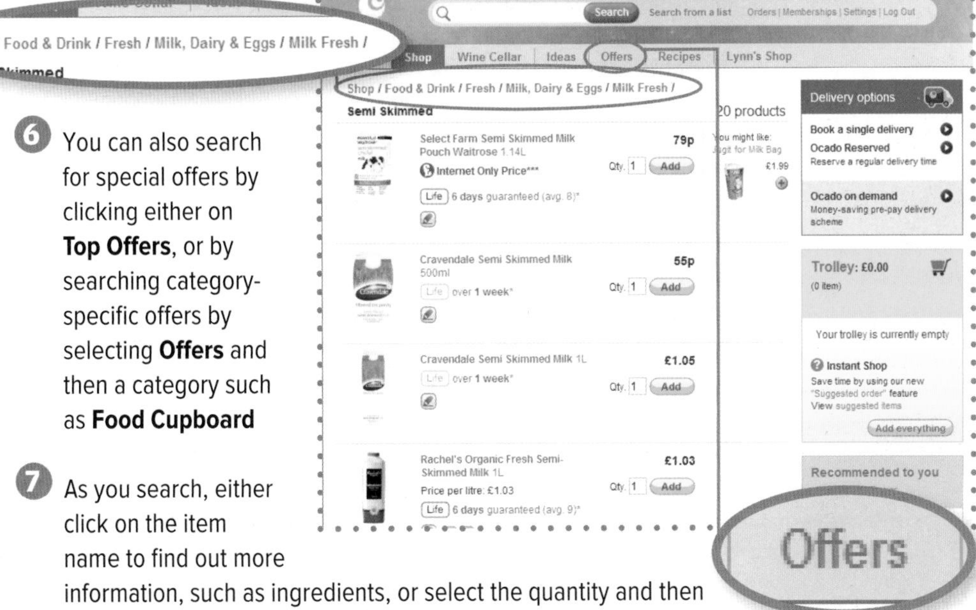

6 You can also search for special offers by clicking either on **Top Offers**, or by searching category-specific offers by selecting **Offers** and then a category such as **Food Cupboard**

7 As you search, either click on the item name to find out more information, such as ingredients, or select the quantity and then click **Add**, which will place the item into your basket

8 You can click on your **Trolley list** at any time to view the items in it in more detail. When you have finished shopping, click on **Checkout**. If you have money-off vouchers, these can be added on the next screen. Click **Continue**

9 You will be asked for your payment details, with the option to store them for future shopping. Add your card details and press **Continue**, which will take you to a summary page where you can double-check your order before confirming it. Make a note of the order number too and keep it for reference

TRY THIS

Search for recipes by meal type, cuisine, ingredients, dietary requirements and time to make – simply click on **Recipes**. Click on **Ideas** for seasonal items and offers.

BUY FROM ONLINE PHARMACIES

While using the internet should never replace a face-to-face meeting with a GP, online pharmacies do provide quick and easy access to healthcare information and services, particularly for the elderly, the disabled, those living in remote areas or working long hours. The main benefit of buying medicine online is the convenience of ordering prescriptions and prescription refills for pickup or delivery.

Dangers of buying medicine online

- It can be fake, unapproved, outdated or sub-standard, and have no quality control on purity of ingredients, storage and instructions
- Incorrect diagnosis – either by self-diagnosis or by a site's untrained and unqualified 'pharmacists'
- There's the possibility to obtain inappropriate medicine either for misuse or without regard for its interaction with other drugs
- Online pharmacies selling counterfeit medicine are often run by criminals; paying for medicine with your credit card and giving your home address for delivery may increase the risk of identity theft

Choosing a reputable online pharmacy

It's not always easy to tell the genuine pharmaceutical websites from the bogus ones. Follow these tips to help you find a safe online pharmacy.

- All retail pharmacies in Great Britain – including those online – must be registered with the Royal Pharmaceutical Society of Great Britain (RPSGB). Websites for legitimate internet pharmacies will display the RPSGB logo that clicks through to the RPSGB website
- Use a website with a contact address and telephone number in case of any problems – not just an email address
- Avoid websites offering to supply prescription-only medicines without a prescription
- Avoid online consultations that don't take a thorough medical history. Registered pharmacies are required to check a medicine is suitable for a patient before selling it

Order a prescription online with Boots

1. Go to www.boots.com and click on **My Account** at the top of the page to register. Enter your email address and click **Register for Boots.com**. Fill in your contact details, email, and create a username and password

2 After you've created your account, you'll be taken back to the home page. Click on **Pharmacy & Health** on the top menu bar. From the drop-down menu, click on **Prescriptions**

3 On the Prescription detail screen, enter the name of your prescription medicine, select the quantity and the prescription type – **NHS Chargeable**, **NHS Free** or **Prepay certificate** or **Private** – and press **Continue**

4 When you have finished adding items to your list, click **Yes**, **Continue to Patient Information Form**

5 Confirm whether the medicine is for you or someone else and then press **Continue**

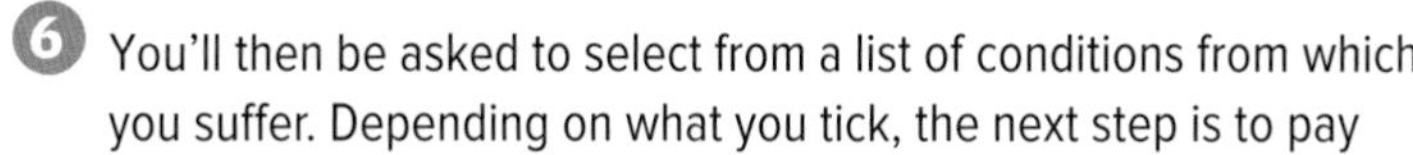

6 You'll then be asked to select from a list of conditions from which you suffer. Depending on what you tick, the next step is to pay

7 Then checkout your order, complete the delivery details and, if applicable, the payment details

8 You will need to post your prescription slip and, if applicable, NHS exemption or Prepay certificate to Boots. Once these have been received, your medication will be delivered

To order a repeat prescription

1 Register for Boots repeat prescription service either in store or online by clicking **Pharmacy & Health** on the home page and selecting **Prescriptions**. Click on **My Repeat Prescription** and then click on the link within the text

2 Fill in details of your GP's surgery and your NHS number

3 Once registered, you will receive a reminder email before your prescription is due. Click on the link in the email to confirm and reorder your prescription. The medicine will be requested from your GP and delivered directly to you

BUY SPECTACLES ONLINE

You can make big savings buying your next pair of spectacles online. Online retailers can offer cheaper eyewear because they don't have shop store or eye examination costs. High-street opticians, however, do offer personal customer service, prescription checks and will discuss your eyecare health and needs. So, even if you buy online, it's best to see a professional optician first, especially if it has been some time since your last visit or you suspect your eyesight has deteriorated.

Buy glasses online

First, you'll need to go to your local opticians and get an eye test. Ask the optician to include the pupillary distance measurement in your prescription. This is the distance between the centres of your pupils and it will help ensure that your new glasses fit. If you don't have this, you'll need a ruler and a mirror to do this yourself. Many online glasses retailers have instructions on how to do this.

1. Visit the website of the glasses retailer that you wish to buy from. You'll need your prescription. For example, type www.glassesdirect.co.uk into the address bar of your web browser and press **Enter**

2. In the left-hand panel, browse the range of frames by clicking on a category such as **New arrivals** or sort by frame shape. When you find frames you like, click on their name for more details

3. When you've chosen, click on the frames of your choice. On the next page click the colour option you want, if applicable. The frame dimensions are listed, as well as the lens options available. When ready, click the **Buy Now** button on the right-hand side of the screen

4. You will be asked how you will use the glasses you wish to purchase, such as solely for reading or for all day wear. Click **Select** for the option that applies and you'll be presented with a range of lens options. Click on the option that suits you

5. The next screen will ask about sun reactive and tinted lens options. You can select one of the options or skip this stage entirely if you wish

6. Then you will have the chance to purchase extras for your glasses such as cases and cleaning clothes. When you have chosen the extras you want (or none if you don't want extras), click the **Continue** button

7. Enter the details of your prescription – the site provides lots of step-by-step guidance on this process – and then click the box to confirm you have read the site's **Terms and Conditions**. Then click **Continue**

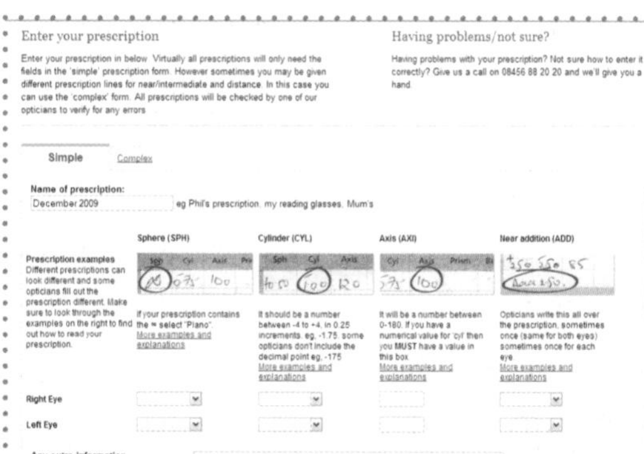

8. Check the details in your shopping basket carefully. When ready, click the button **Continue to Purchase**. Enter your contact address and payment details, and create a password for your account so you can track your order or re-use your prescription in the future. Press **Click Here to Submit Your Order**. Your new glasses should arrive within 10 to 14 days

Resolving problems with your glasses

As glasses are made to a certain prescription, your legal rights to a refund aren't as strong as they are with other products (see page 150). So check a site's returns policy before buying. With faults, however, legal rights still apply. If the glasses are not fit for purpose on arrival, you should return them within a reasonable time – usually by around three or four weeks. If they develop a fault later that's not normal wear and tear, the retailer must either repair or replace the glasses.

RETURN GOODS THAT HAVE BEEN BOUGHT ONLINE

As with any goods, you may decide that something you've bought online is not right for you. As soon as you know that what you ordered isn't what you want, let the online shop know. Check their terms and conditions to see if they say how you should do this: cancel by phone, confirm it by letter or email within the cooling-off period (see page 133).

Return the item as soon as possible. If the online shop's terms don't say who pays for returns, then they have to either arrange to collect the item, or refund the postage. Their requirements for how you return the goods should not be so expensive or involved that it would be cheaper and easier for you to keep the goods.

If online shopping is faulty

If there's a problem with the item, decide what you would like done about it. Do you want a refund, repair of replacement? If you want your money back, you have only a 'reasonable' time to 'reject' a faulty item and claim a refund.

What's reasonable depends on the item and the nature of the problem. As a general rule, three to four weeks is normal but, if the problem is immediately obvious, it may be less, so write to your online shop as soon as you become aware of it.

You don't have to reject the item outright. You can write to the online shop telling them you want a repair or replacement. However, legally, they can choose which of these they do.

Your right to cancel a service bought online

If you're buying a service, such as an upgrade of your mobile phone contract, you can cancel up to seven working days from the day after you agree the contract terms. But, if you have agreed that the service will start straight away, you give up these cancellation rights.

Claim your money back from your credit card company

If you get no response or the online shop refuses your request, you have two main options:

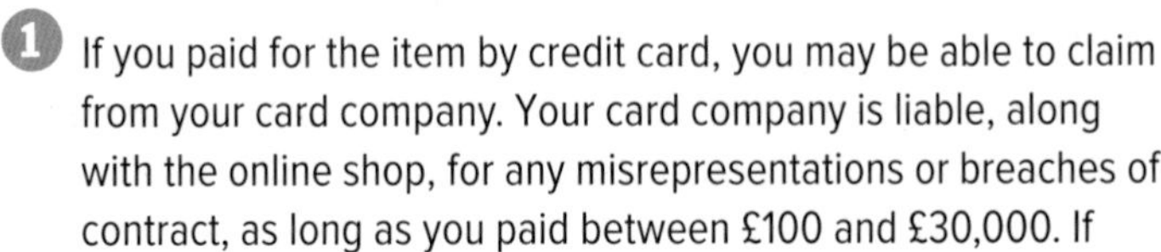

1. If you paid for the item by credit card, you may be able to claim from your card company. Your card company is liable, along with the online shop, for any misrepresentations or breaches of contract, as long as you paid between £100 and £30,000. If

you were given finance to buy the item, you may be able to claim from the credit provider in the same way

2 You could take the shop to the small claims court if you paid less than a certain amount (£5,000 in England and Wales, £3,000 in Scotland, or £2,000 in Northern Ireland). You must first send a final 'letter before action' saying you are giving the shop one last chance to settle and you will take them to court if they don't

Goods damaged during transit

Some disreputable sellers may claim this is the responsibility of the couriers and say that you need to deal directly with them. However, UK law says that the online shop is responsible for the quality and condition of the goods up until you receive them so it works the same as if a product is faulty (see previous page). If you have to sign for receipt of delivery, check the product thoroughly first.

Wrong online prices

You may see what appears to be a bargain price for an item on a website – a laptop for £9.99 – but, when you order, the online shop says it's a mistake and won't sell it for that price.

In the first instance, check the email response you got from the online shop when you placed your order. If they only acknowledged the order, then you have no contract to hold them to. If the order was accepted, it depends on whether you knew or ought to have known that the online shop had made a mistake with the price.

Ultimately, if the online store refuses to sell, a court will decide, but if an offer seems too good to be true (as in the case of a laptop for £9.99), the chances are that the online shop won't have to supply the goods. Of course, they will still have to refund your money.

Price rise after ordering

Some special price offers, particularly those by online supermarkets, have time limits. But be aware that these time limits often apply to the date of delivery rather than the date of order. The online shop's terms and conditions may say that your order is only accepted when they start taking the items you've ordered off the shelves, and you'll be charged the price of the goods at that time.

However, if you get caught out by this and are charged full price, you don't have to pay. Simply send the items back with the delivery driver.

SET UP A PAYPAL ACCOUNT

PayPal is an electronic payment system, owned by eBay, which transfers funds between buyers and sellers and provides a secure online account that stores your credit card or bank account details, but won't reveal these details to the person you're buying from or selling to.

The majority of eBay transactions are with PayPal. That way buyers are usually protected for the full amount (see page 139). Each listing will say whether the item is eligible for buyer protection; most tangible items are.

PayPal is also fast and free for buyers. As a seller you'll be charged a small transaction fee. After eBay has taken its cut, your received funds are transferred into your PayPal account, from where you can withdraw it to your bank account or credit it to your card.

BE CAREFUL

Watch out for scam emails claiming to be from PayPal and that ask for your account details. Always go directly to your PayPal account via the website – don't click on any links within emails.

Set up a PayPal account

1. Go to **www.paypal.com**

2. Click **Sign up**

3. Select your country from the drop-down list
4. Click **Get Started** under the **Personal section**
5. Enter your details on the form that appears
6. Click **Agree and Create Account**
7. You can now log into your account and manage your transactions

BE SOCIAL

By reading and following all the steps in this chapter, you will get to grips with:

- **Setting up a social networking page and finding old and new friends**
- **Viewing and sharing video and photos with others**
- **Creating simple blogs and websites**

SOCIAL NETWORKING EXPLAINED

The internet has changed the way we connect to friends and family and meet new people. It removes the need for face-to-face contact or for picking up a telephone – we can now get in touch instantly with others anywhere in the world.

At the heart of this change are social networks – the hundreds of websites that let you chat and interact with others online. Some people use them to keep in touch with friends and family; others to meet new friends with shared interests, hobbies or causes. Some sites are tailored for more specific users while larger, general sites such MySpace, Facebook and Twitter attract millions of users.

All about you

Most social network sites give you the chance to create a profile page, where you can tell others about yourself. You'll be asked for basic information such as your age and gender, and you can add details about your hobbies and interests, likes and dislikes, so that others can see if they have anything in common with you.

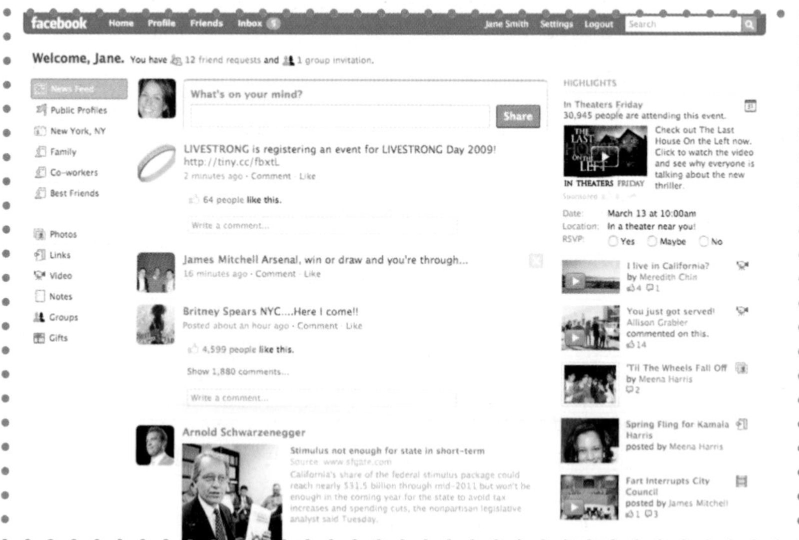

Social networks offer several ways to interact with others. You can send personal emails, you can leave messages or pictures on friends' message boards or join a group of people with a shared interest – say specific types of movie or Greenpeace. You can share photos and video clips with your friends, and even play games like Chess or Scrabble with them online.

Who is using social networks?

People of all ages use social networks. Your initial contact is likely to be with friends and family but, once you're established on a site, you may wish to make friends with new people – perhaps those that share similar interests or live in your area.

Access and join a social network site

You access a social network site via your web browser in the same way as you would visit any website. You don't need any specialist software to use these sites, although some of them will encourage you to download new applications or browser plug-ins (see page 42).

1. Go to the home page of the site you want to join, say Facebook, by typing www.facebook.com into the address bar
2. Click **Sign Up** or **Register** (this will differ depending on the site)
3. You'll need to enter some personal details to get started (the type of information you're required to give varies from website to website)
4. Once you've filled in your details, a confirmation email is usually sent to your email address. You must click on the link provided in this email to activate your account
5. You can now log in to your account to begin finding friends and adding information to your profile

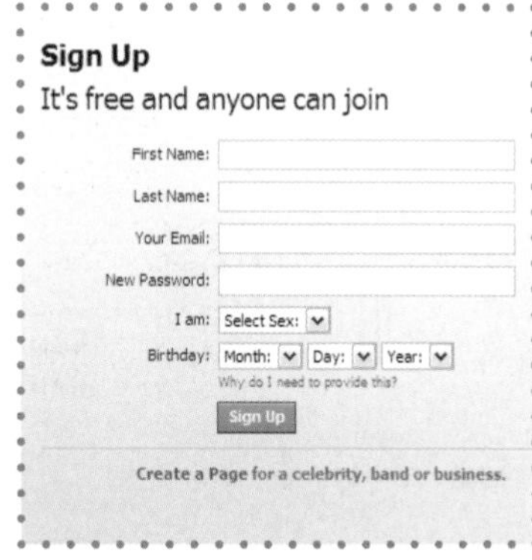

Find friends

You can search for a friend by entering their name into a Search box on the site. Alternatively, some social networking websites will search for people listed in your email address book and let you know if they're members of the site. See pages 160 and 161 for more on this.

Security

When you put personal details on the internet, you must consider where they will end up. If things go wrong (the site you're signed up with has a security breach, for example) your information could end up in the wrong hands. The social networking sites work hard to prevent this but see page 165 for tips on social networking security.

POPULAR SOCIAL NETWORKING SITES

BBC Talk – www.bbc.co.uk/communicate
A discussion board from the national broadcaster that lets you share your views on a variety of topics. Setup is simple and the lack of advertising is a definite plus, as is the familiarity and UK-centred approach. There's plenty to talk about and the website includes forums for your local region, or culture and sport. You won't find all the facilities you'd expect from a fully-fledged social network site but it's a great place to join a community.

Facebook – www.facebook.com
Facebook's popularity continues to grow worldwide. It's a site designed to help you find and keep in touch with friends. It is easy to navigate through the busy site and, once connected, to see what friends are doing. It offers various privacy settings on the site to protect users' information (see page 165).

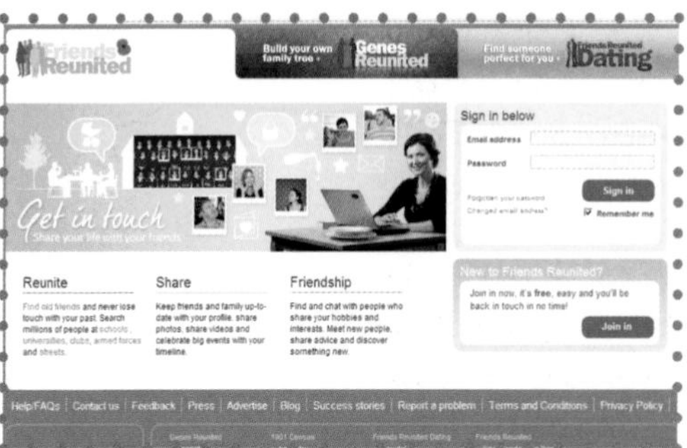

Flickr – www.flickr.com
Flickr is a photo-sharing website (see page 179) that has established a strong following among those keen to show off their photography skills. Free account holders can upload 100MB of photos to share, and can join in discussion groups and send messages to other users. It lacks sophisticated features, but is easy to use and allows you to restrict who can see your information.

Friends Reunited – www.friendsreunited.co.uk
Started in 1999 to help people track down old school friends, Friends Reunited has over 18 million users and has expanded to include school-based discussion groups and the additional ability to search by workplace, clubs and even the armed forces. The site used to charge for sending messages but now it's free. There aren't many fancy social networking features or advanced privacy features here. Once your profile is up, anyone can see it, but email addresses aren't revealed without your permission.

MySpace – www.myspace.com

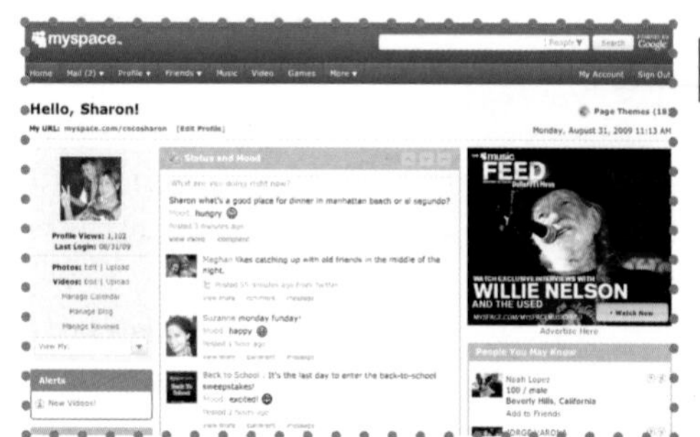

This widely used News International-owned site is also popular with celebrities, bands, comedians and filmmakers. It has been instrumental in launching the career of numerous new music artists. It offers lots of easy-to-use features including the ability to add video and photo, and customise your profile page.

Sagazone – www.sagazone.co.uk

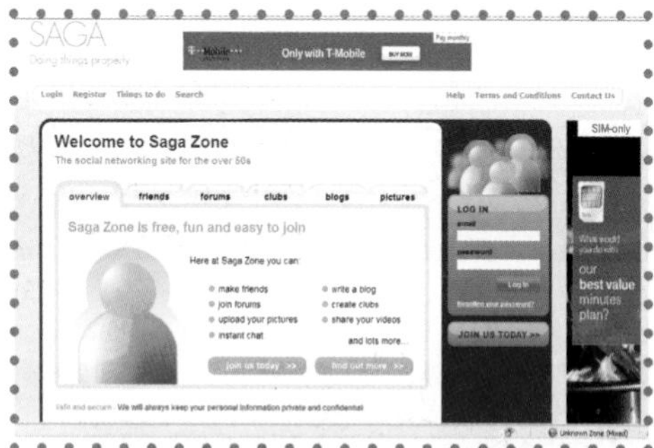

This is a social network site run by Saga Group and specifically aimed at the over-50s market. The site lacks many of the advanced features found on sites like Facebook, but its carefully chosen demographic means it attracts a large number of like-minded people. Signing up is a little convoluted but, overall, the site is simple and well-signposted.

Twitter – www.twitter.com

The newest way to stay up to date with friends is via Twitter – a site that allows its users to send and read text-based messages of up to 140 characters. These messages, known as Tweets, are displayed on your profile page and delivered to your friends, who are known as 'followers'. You can restrict delivery to certain people or, by default, allow open access. Tweets can be sent and received via the Twitter website, a text (SMS) on your phone or other external methods. While the service itself costs nothing to use, if you access it on your phone you may incur phone service provider fees.

Yahoo! Groups – http://groups.yahoo.com

Yahoo! Groups lacks many of the features people often associate with social networking groups. However, it lets you join or set up discussion groups on a range of topics. You need to register for a Yahoo! account first by visiting www.yahoo.co.uk and clicking on **Sign Up**. While you can't customise your profile and add features in the way you can on more sophisticated sites, Yahoo! Groups is an excellent starting point for anyone who's interested in trying out social networking for the first time.

SET UP A MYSPACE PAGE

One of the biggest and most popular social networking sites, MySpace, offers a quick way to socialise with others online.

Jargon buster

Captchas
Usually consisting of an image of a distorted word that you need to copy, these check that the user filling out a form is a human and not an automated program sending spam.

Create an account

1. Type www.myspace.com into the address bar and click **Enter.** Click **Sign Up**, which can be found at the far right of the Menu Bar along the top of the page.

2. This brings up a sign-up form, into which you need to enter a valid email address, password, name, date of birth and gender. Then click **Sign Up** again

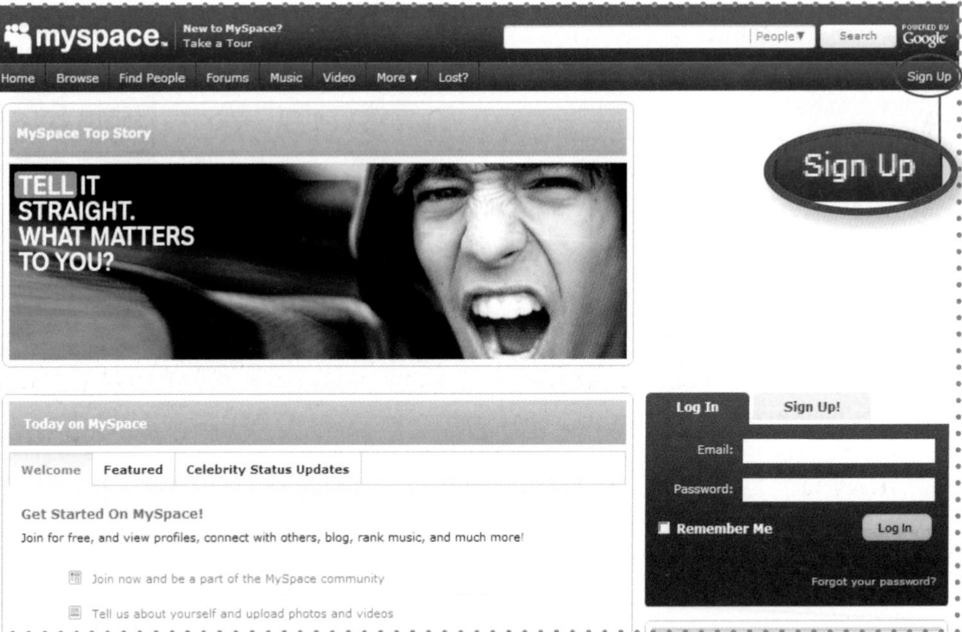

3. Type in the specific captcha in the box

4. An email will be sent to your email address with a link. Click on the link to confirm your account

5. Click on **Skip For Now** if you don't wish to invite others or add a profile photo at the moment. Both options are available in the future

Personalise your profile

Now you can get to work on your MySpace profile, which will let fellow 'myspacers' know who you are, what you like and who you'd like to meet.

1. When you are logged in, click on the **My Account** tab on the far right of the menu bar at the top of your new home page

2. Click the **Edit Profile** option that appears at the top right of the page, just under the menu bar

3. Under the About Me tab of the Edit Profile page, you will see two empty boxes, with headings **About Me** and **Who I'd like to Meet**. Under Interests, you'll see six empty boxes with headings including **Heroes**, **Music** and **Books**. Add information about yourself here. You can also add details of your schools and employment history

4. When finished, click **Save Changes** at the foot of the page

Privacy settings

1. At the top of the Edit Profile page, click on the **My Account** link

2. Here you can adjust your account settings. Clicking on **Privacy**, for example, allows you to set what others can view, filter those who can view it on the basis of age, or limit access to your profile to your friends only

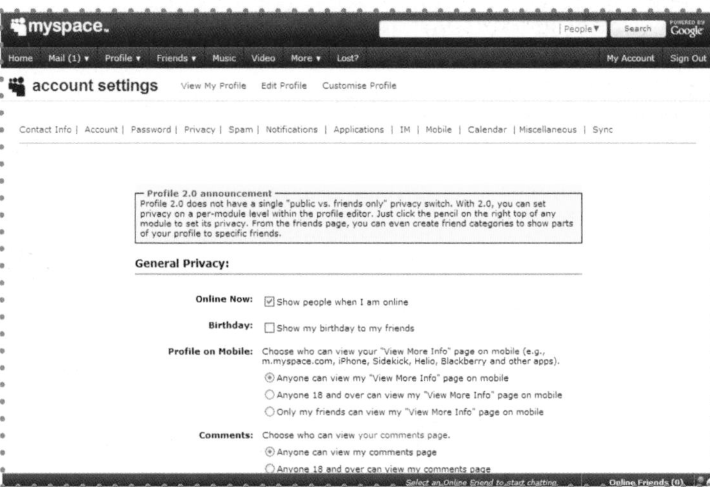

3. If you wish to upload images from a mobile device to MySpace, click on **Account Settings** and then the **Mobile** tab

Invite family and friends

One of the first things you'll want to do on MySpace is to invite any friends and family already using the site to list you as a friend.

1. Click on the **Friends** tab in the menu bar. From the drop-down menu choose **Invite Friends**. This lets you use your email's address book to search the site for people you already know

2. You can also search for users of MySpace who share your interests. Click on the **Friends** tab again and select **Browse**. A box will appear that lets you specify search criteria for other users based on gender, age and interests. Click on **Advanced** to add more search criteria

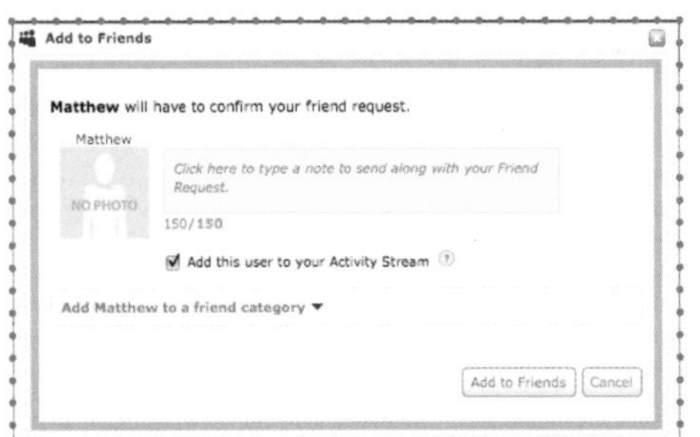

3. When you've found someone you would like as a friend, you need to send a friend request to that person. To do this, click **Add to Friends** next to their name and you'll see a box where you can add a personal message. Then click **Add to Friends**. Your request needs to be accepted by the other person before they appear on your friends list

4. To view requests from other people to be your friend, click on **Mail** (on the top menu bar) and then **Friend Requests**. Here you can see who has requested to be your friend and either **Approve**, **Deny** or mark as **Spam**

Add content to MySpace

Once people know you're on MySpace and are visiting your page, you'll want to start adding comments and pictures to your site.

1. Click on the **Profile** tab in the menu bar, and select one of the options available

2. Select **My Comments**. In the top right of the My Comments window you'll see the **Add Comments** link. Click this and, in the text box that appears, type your comment. Click **Submit**

3. On the menu bar, click **Mail**. From here you can compose a new message, view sent and saved mail, and edit your Address Book

SET UP A FACEBOOK ACCOUNT

Facebook is one of the biggest and most popular social networking sites and is a great way to keep in touch with friends and family.

1. To join Facebook, type www.facebook.com into the address bar of your web browser. Once the page is loaded, you should register. Registering means choosing a username and entering a valid email address. You'll need these each time you log in

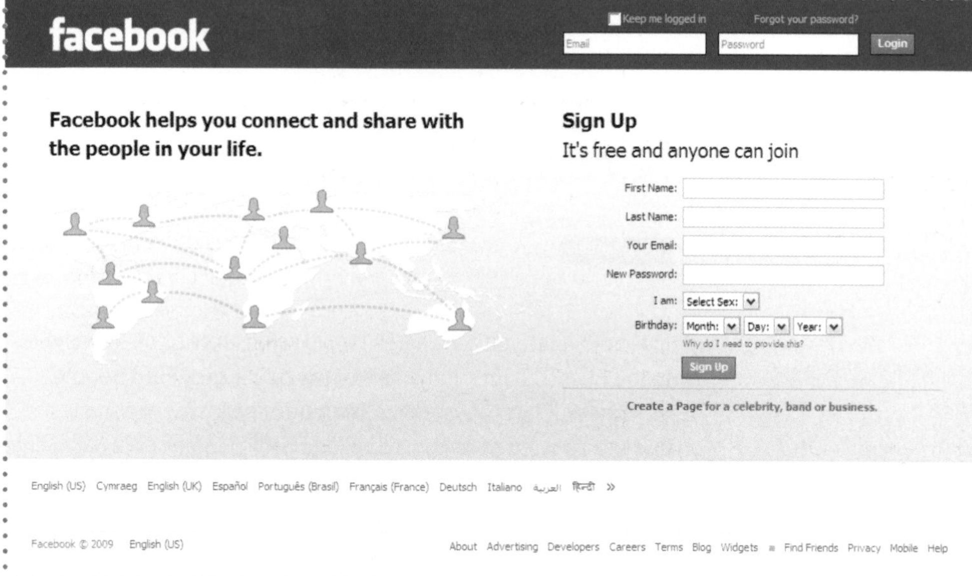

2. Complete your Facebook registration by clicking on the link sent by Facebook to your email

3. You will be asked to fill out your Profile information as well as uploading a photo or taking one with your webcam. You can skip both these stages if you wish. (See page 165 for tips on creating a safe profile on social networking sites)

4. If you've logged in using a webmail account (see page 60), Facebook will now invite you to locate friends on the site by entering your email address and password. It will search your email for names that appear in its own database and, if found, will then show their account details. Most of the popular webmail services can be searched, including Gmail, Hotmail and AOL

5. The Find Friends feature also lets you locate people with the email program you use on your PC. To do this, click **Upload Contact File** and then click **Choose File**. If you're unsure how to locate a contact file for the email program you use, click **How to create a contact file**. This lists 11 of the leading email programs. Click the name of the one you use to bring up a step-by-step guide

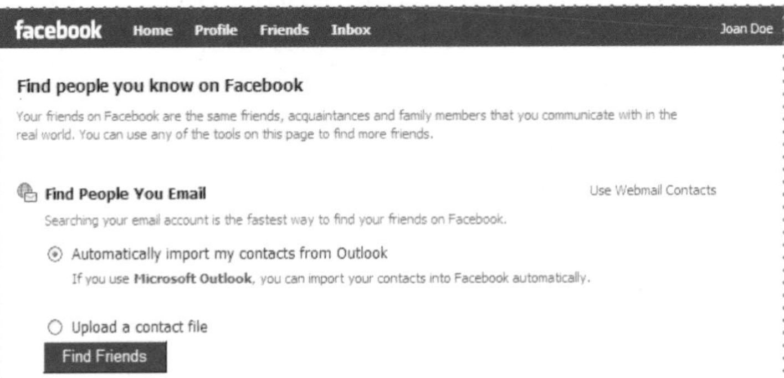

6. In Find Friends you can search for old school friends or co-workers. In the Friends panel at the foot of the page, click **Find people you know**. Click **Classmates Search** to search for classmates and then search by school or college name. To narrow down your results, choose a class year when searching

7. There is also a **Co-workers Search** button. Click this, enter a company name and hit **Search**

8. On Facebook, friends need to be confirmed by both people before they become 'official', and appear on your friends list

Search through the results

No matter how you search for friends, unless the person you're looking for has a very unusual name, you will need to sift through results.

1. Within your search results, you can search for people by name by typing names into the **Search** box at the top of the page

2. It's also worth trawling through search results manually for names or faces you may have forgotten. When you come across someone who you'd like to be a friend, click the **Add as Friend** link next to his or her name

TIPS FOR USING FACEBOOK

Edit your profile

1 Your Facebook profile shows who you are, with sections including **Personal Information**, **Contact Information**, **Education** and **Work**. Though there's no obligation to do so, filling these in will make it easier for other people to find you on Facebook. Click **Profile** in the menu bar and then the **Edit My Profile** link

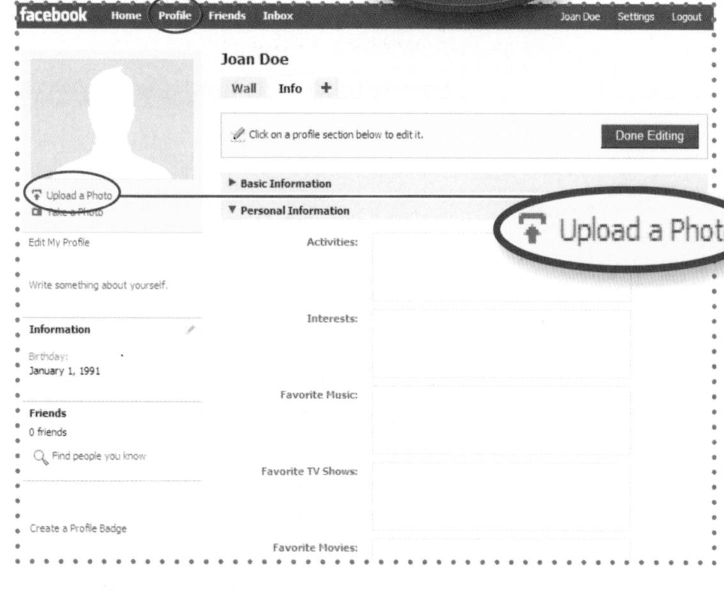

2 Adding a profile picture also makes it easier for friends to identify you, especially if you have a common name. To add a profile picture, click on **Profile** in the menu bar. Move your cursor over the picture box and click **Change Picture**, then click **Upload a Photo**. You can then browse for a picture on your computer in the normal way

Write something

1 On your Profile page, you can publish your status – how you're feeling, what you're up to – photos, notes and more using the 'publisher' feature. This comes in the form of a text box at the top of your page, below your name, just above the 'stream' of information

2 Clicking inside the text box also displays other types of content you can share

3 Once you've added content, click **Share**. Your posts will now show up on your Wall and on your friends' Home pages (see step 4 overleaf)

4 You have two streams. One is your Wall, which is in your profile area (click **Profile** on the menu bar) and the other is the News Feed on your Home page (click **Home** on the menu bar). These represent the ongoing, flowing conversations between you and your friends. The Wall is a space on each user's profile page that lets friends post messages (these can be seen by other friends), while the **News Feed** highlights information such as profile changes and birthdays and shows conversations taking place on friends' walls

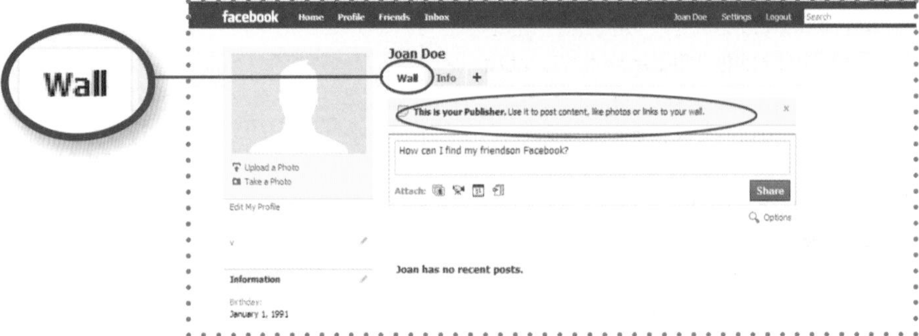

5 On the left-hand side of your Home page is a panel of 'filters' that allow you to determine what kind of content you see in your two streams at any given time. The options include **Public Profiles**, **Photos**, **Links** and **Videos**. Clicking a filter brings up options for publishing that sort of content yourself. For example, clicking on **Photos** will mean that you'll see all the photos recently posted by your friends, but not videos or links

TRY THIS

The right-hand side of your Facebook home page is the Highlights panel – a digest of photos, events and notes that the site thinks will interest you, based on your interests, posts and what your friends have been up to.

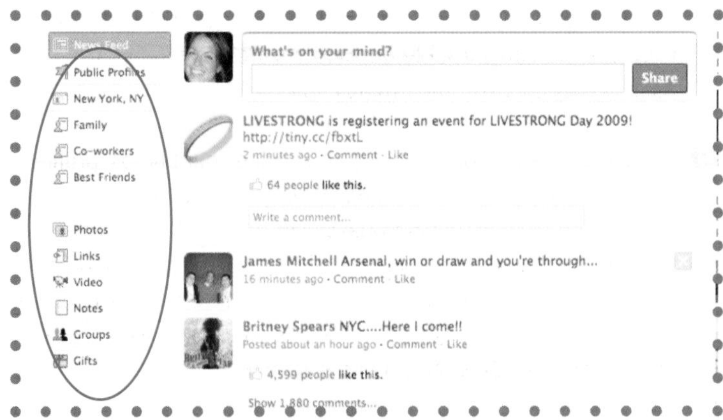

SOCIAL NETWORKING SAFETY AND PRIVACY

While most online personal safety and security advice is directed at children and young people, the general rules apply to social networking fans of all ages. Make good use of the privacy setting of whichever social networking site you use.

Set privacy settings on Facebook

1. Your Facebook profile information can, by default, be viewed by everyone online, which could compromise your privacy. Click the **Settings** tab located on the top-right of the screen, and select **Privacy Settings**

2. Click **Profile Information**. In the **Profile page**, use the pop-up menus alongside options such as **Personal Info** and **Photo Albums** to set who can see this information. Settings options include **Everyone**, **Friends Of Friends**, and **Only Friends**. The last setting – **Customize** – lets you name specific people who can see that information or even block people from seeing it. Click **Save Changes** once done

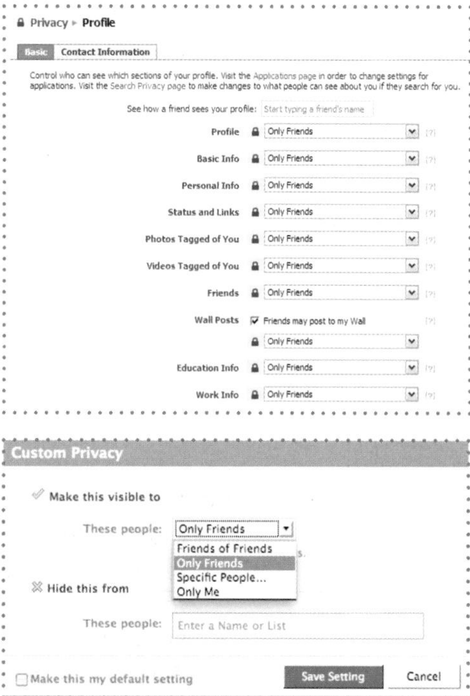

Set privacy settings on MySpace

1. To access and set your privacy settings in MySpace, log into your MySpace account. Click **My Account**, located on the top right of the screen, and select the **Privacy** option

2. You can set various options for who can see your photos, profile, information stream and comments using three settings. Change from **Anyone can view my updates** (for example) to **Only my friends** for the best security setting. You can also block people from seeing your profile from this page, and also choose if people can see if you're online by ticking the **Show people when I am online** box. Click **Save All Changes** when done

Delete your account

Most social networking sites let you deactivate an account. However, this does not delete your information or photos. To remove all information, you need to delete your account.

- To delete a profile on Facebook, go to www.facebook.com/help/contact.php?show_form=delete_account. Press **Submit** and follow the instructions. Your account will first be deactivated for two weeks. If you log in within that time, the deletion request will be cancelled

Delete My Account

If you do not think you will use Facebook again and would like your account deleted, we can take care of this for you. Keep in mind that you will not be able to reactivate your account or retrieve any of the content or information you have added. If you would like your account deleted, then click "Submit."

Submit   Cancel

- To delete an account fully on Myspace, log onto Myspace and click **My Account**. Click the **Account** link and then click **Cancel Account** in the Account Cancellation section. Select a reason for cancelling from the list and click the **Cancel My Account** button. Next, in the Confirm Account Cancellation section, click **Cancel My Account**. An email will be sent to you with a link. Click the link to delete the account. It can take up to 48 hours for the account to be fully cancelled

Privacy and security tips

- The Internet is a public space. Don't post anything online that you wouldn't be happy for everyone to see – now or at any time in the future. It can be very hard to delete information once posted

- Avoid posting your personal details – anything from phone numbers and home address to date of birth. Be careful posting details about upcoming holidays or times when your property might be vacant

- Be careful of clicking on links sent from strangers. Such requests may be links to viruses or other forms of malicious content

- Applications such as quizzes, polls and games can make your social networking experience more fun, but often, by signing up to these, you're giving the people who developed it permission to access the personal information contained in your profile. Check your privacy settings (see page 165) for ways to avoid this

SOCIAL NETWORKING ETIQUETTE

Your social life online will require some management and, as in the real world, the rules of social etiquette apply when dealing with other people. Here are some top tips for getting it right:

- Accumulating a huge number of 'friends' is common on social networking sites and it's easy to make new connections even with strangers. However, a good rule of thumb is that you should invite only people that you have some kind of link to, even if they're a friend of a friend of a friend
- If you accept friends from several generations, such as your children and grandchildren, be aware of the type of content you and your other adult friends post
- People know that, when they send an invite, you have the right to accept or reject their invitations. In real life it might be considered rude, but online etiquette allows you either to reply with a 'No, thank you' or not to reply at all
- Keep personal life and professional life separate. Use a business-focused networking site such as LinkedIn for work, and keep a Facebook account for your family and friends. If you only have a Facebook account, give different access settings to colleagues and family
- It's best to be honest but selective with personal information. Hiding your birth date from public view is acceptable, but don't use fake names, photos or lie about your personal life
- Don't post unfriendly comments about people or use your blog (see page 170) for a personal crusade against anyone
- Don't spam people – for example by constantly inviting uninterested friends on Facebook to play online games or try new software applications
- Don't tag friends in pictures that might harm their reputation or cost them their jobs

Jargon buster

Tagging
Process of adding descriptive keywords to a piece of information, such as a photo, video or web page, to aid in the search for it.

Jargon buster

Thread
A collection of related posts defined by a title and an initial post, which opens whatever dialogue or announcement the poster wished.

FORUMS EXPLAINED

A forum (also know as a message board) is an online discussion. Many websites have forums where visitors who share common interests can 'talk' to each other via messages. The most popular use of a forum is for users to ask questions, which other forum members then answer.

Forums range in complexity from site to site but all consist of a tree-like directory structure containing a set of topics (commonly called **threads**) and inside them **posts** (messages from users).

A thread can contain any number of posts, including multiple posts from the same members. Posts are commonly displayed with the newest at the top, and contain the user's details and the date and time the message was submitted.

Most forums have a list of rules detailing the guidelines. It's also worth reading the **Frequently Asked Questions** (FAQ) section of the site that will offer basic information for new members.

Jargon buster

Post
The term used for a message by a forum member, which is 'posted' onto the forum for others to read and respond to.

Before posting a message on a forum, you'll first need to register. Click on the **Register** or **Create an Account** button on the website of your choice and fill in your details as requested. Most forums require the following to register:

- Your name and your email address
- A username – this can be anything you want. Make sure it's easy to remember, as your username will be associated with you for as long as you're a member of the forum
- A password – choose a password you can remember easily but is hard for others to guess (see page 200 for more on passwords)
- A profile picture – many forums let users upload an image, also known as an 'avatar'. This doesn't have to be a photograph, any graphic or piece of clip art will do. (You can create your own in an image editor such as Adobe Photoshop Elements or search the internet for free avatars to download)

Create a new post of your own

1. Type the address of the forum website into your address bar. From the opening **Forum** page, select a topic or category that you wish comment on. A list of various separate discussions or threads will appear in that category area

2. Click **New Thread** or **New Topic** **a**t the top of the list to start a topic. You'll see a text box where you can type a message or question

3. Most forums let you preview your post before submitting it. If available, press the **Preview** button to do this. When you're satisfied, press **Submit** or **Post** to post your message

Reply to a post

1. If you want to join in a conversation, click the **Reply** link on the message

2. The text editor box will appear where you can type your reply. As before, press the **Preview** button, if available, to preview your response. When you're finished, click **Submit** or **Post message** to publish your response

Format your posts

Forums offer the chance for you to format posts or replies. This varies from making words bold or italic to adding 'emoticons' or 'smileys' – small graphic symbols used to show emotion. Forums often use a system whereby text representations of emoticons are rendered as a small image

CREATE A BLOG

A blog is a web-based diary or journal that's updated regularly. Generally, blogs are text, although you can add pictures, video and audio files, and links to other web pages or blogs. A blog can be about anything you want – from a personal account of your day to a commentary on news events. Some blogs have even achieved worldwide fame with thousands of followers visiting them daily.

Setting up a blog is easy. There's lots of blogging software available, and one of the most popular and free to use is Google Blogger.

Get started

1. To use Blogger, you must first create a free Google account. Click on **Create a Google Account** on the top-right corner of any Google page and enter a username and a password

2. Type www.blogger.com into the address bar of your web browser. Once the Blogger home page is loaded, enter your username and password (see Step 1), and click **Sign in**

3. Enter a display name (this will be what people will see) and click **Create a Blog**. On the next screen, click **Start Blogging**

4. You need to pick a title and web address (URL) for your blog. Type a name, such as 'My first blog' into the box next to the blog title

5. In the blog address (URL) box, type in a word. Click the **Check Availability** link to see if you can use that word in your blog URL address

6. You'll also be able to choose a template, which will determine how your blog will look when it's published. From the range of templates, you can click the **Preview template** link to see how your blog pages will look. Click a template name to use it for your blog design, then click **Continue**

Create the look of your blog

You can edit this default template at any stage to customise the look of your blog or simply change it to another template entirely by using Blogger's Dashboard.

1. Click **Dashboard** from the top right of the page. Click **Layout** to bring up the following editing options: **Page Elements**, **Fonts and Colours**, **Edit HTML** and **Pick New Template**

2. Click on each of these to choose from the list available

3. **Page Elements** may be of most interest at this stage, as it allows you to rearrange the elements of your Blogger site by dragging and dropping them around your site. You can also add new sections to your page. New sections include **About Me**, **Blog Archive** and **Followers** sections. These can be helpful to readers – the Blog Archive will, for example, allow visitors to see older blog posts that you have previously made

4. In **Page Elements** will be a range of gadgets you can add to your site, by clicking the **Add a Gadget** link. Gadgets can include the ability to search YouTube or view your Gmail inbox. There are thousands of gadgets to choose from, but clicking **Most Popular** will give you a good idea of what other bloggers find most useful

5. You can also choose **Monetize**, which helps you make money from your site by using Google AdSense – a form of advertising that pays you according to ads that appear

Customise your Blogger profile

1. Before you start blogging, you may want to add to your profile. Click the **Customize** link in the top right-hand corner of your Blogger home page, and then the top-right **Dashboard** link

2. Click the **Edit Profile** link, and fill in the fields on the **Profile** page. Click **Save Profile**. Return to the Dashboard by clicking on **Dashboard**

3. Click the **Create your Blog Now** button. You're now ready to add your first blog entry

Start writing

1. Click the **New Post** button and you'll be presented with a page that works in a similar way to a word-processing program, complete with all the usual text-formatting options. (For more on text formatting, see *Computing Made Easy for the Over 50s*)

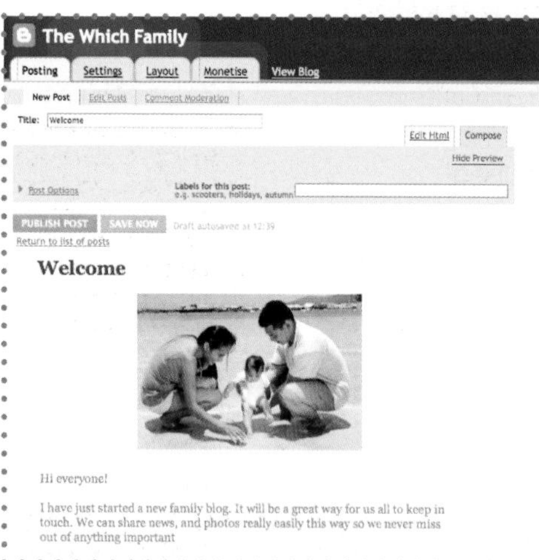

2. Each blog entry should have a title – enter a title for your entry in the **Title field**, and type your entry in the empty text field. Enhance text with the formatting options. You can also click the **Preview** link to see how any formatting will appear on the published page

3. When you're happy with your entry, click **Publish Post** at the foot of the page. You are now an official blogger

Promoting your blog

After taking the trouble to write a blog, most people want it to be viewed by as many people as possible, and there are Blogger settings designed to promote your efforts.

Make sure you 'ping'

You need your blog to 'ping' (ie make contact with) other sites, because this means it will be included in various 'recently updated' lists on the web as well as other blog-related services.

1. To do this, you need to enable two key settings. Click on **Dashboard**, then **Settings** then **Basic**

2. Click **Add your blog to our listings**. This determines whether or not the Blogger home page, Blogger Play, will link to your blog

3. Click **Let search engines find your blog?** This determines whether your blog will be included in Google Blog Search, and if it will ping Weblogs.com. If you select **No**, everyone can still view your blog, but search engines will be instructed not to list it in their search results

Feed reader software

Enabling your Blogger site to take advantage of 'feed reader' software is another good way to get your blog out there. A site feed means that it can be picked up and displayed on other websites and information aggregation tools, called aggregators.

These scan your site feed and automatically let your readers know when your blog has been updated. An example of such software is Google Reader, which you can use with your Google Account.

1. In your Google Account, go to **Settings** then **Site Feed**

2. You'll have one simple option of how much of your content you want to syndicate. Choosing **Full** will put the entire content of each post in your site feed; choosing **Short** includes only an excerpt from the beginning of each post. Choosing the **None** option turns your site feed off entirely

3. In **Advanced Mode** there are options for three different types of feeds. The first is for your blog posts, and is the same as the single option in **Basic Mode**. After that comes the comment feed that contains all comments made on all posts on your blog. Finally, there is the pre-post comment feed. With this option, each post will have its own site feed, containing only its own comments. Each option has the same **Full**, **Short** and **None** setting choices

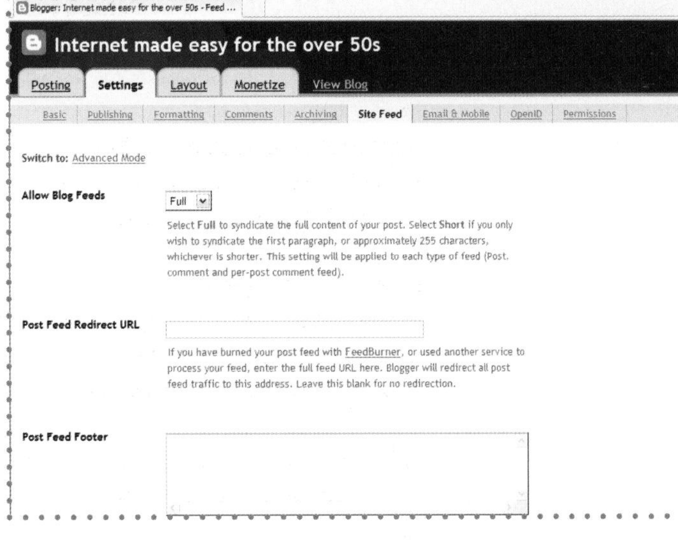

TRY THIS

More is not always better with blogs. Blog regularly but only when you have something interesting to say. Add personality to your blog by developing your own voice and having fun.

CREATE A BASIC WEBSITE

If you're involved in groups, clubs and social activities, a website is a good way to keep in touch with others, or with family members who live far away. Google Sites makes creating a website straightforward.

Register for Google Sites and get started

1. Before using Google Sites you must first create a Google Account. Click on **Create a Google Account** on the top-right corner of any Google page and enter a username and a password

2. When you've signed up, go to Google Sites by typing http://sites.google.com into the address bar of your web browser. Once the page has loaded, click the **Create Site** button

3. Choose a site name and give it a description. Choose a site theme from the list. Only three themes are visible but, if you click **More Themes**, a further 17 become available. When naming your site, choose a name that best reflects the content of the site. For instance, a site about photos of pets might be called 'My pet photos'

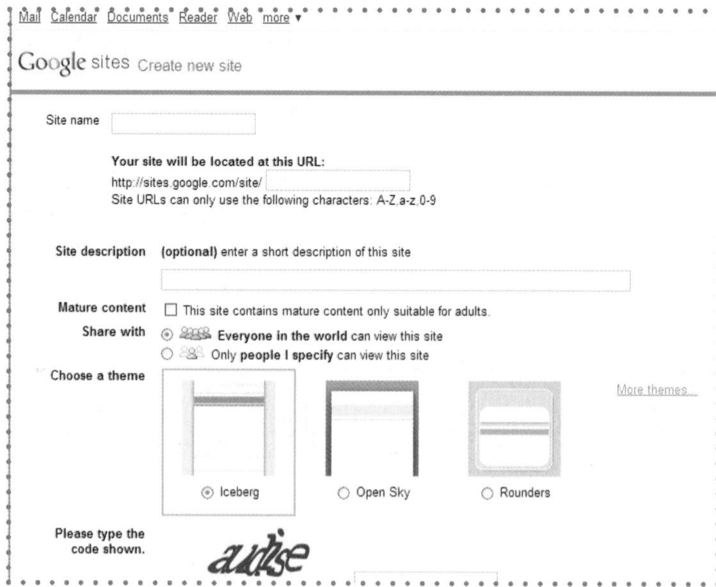

4. When you're happy with your selection, click **Create Site** at the bottom of the page

Create and edit a page

1 The page you'll now see has several buttons at the top right. Click **Create Page**. You'll be given four main page templates to choose from – **Web Page**, **Announcements, File Cabinet** and **List** (some themes may offer additional pages). A Web Page is an unstructured page where you can enter text, images and tables, and embed spreadsheets, presentations, videos and other content. An Announcement page is for posting chronological information, such as news or blog updates. File Cabinet pages let you manage documents from a hard drive and organise them into folders while List pages let you track lists of information easily

2 Once you have chosen a type, give it a Name and click **Create page**. You will then see this page with the page title filled in and ready for you to start entering text

3 To enter text, use the menu bar located at the top of the new page. This contains standard text formatting controls, such as bold, italic, underline, font, text colour and text highlighting. You can create bulleted or numbered lists, and link to other pages in your site, as well as attaching documents from your hard drive to the bottom of the page, and allowing other site users to comment on your pages. Once your text is entered, click **Save**

4 To edit a page at a later stage, such as to add a photo, click the **Edit Page** button located at the top right of the page. Position the mouse cursor where you want the image to appear and select **Insert**

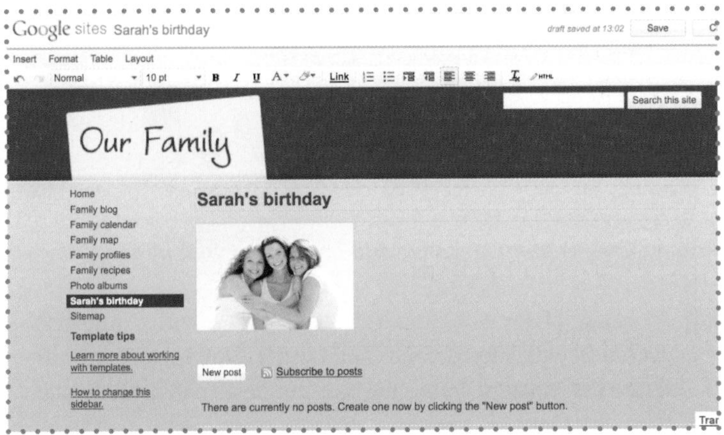

5 From the drop-down menu that appears, click on the object you wish to insert. When the embedded object is published, the page is updated automatically

6 You can change the overall look of your website in three main areas: **Themes**, **Site Elements** and **Colours and Fonts**

7 To change these elements, such as to choose a different template from the one you originally chose when setting up your site, click the **More Actions** button on the top right of the page. From the pop-up menu, choose **Manage Site**. From the left-hand sidebar, choose **Themes** (another name for the templates used when creating your site). Click a new theme, then click **Save changes**

8 Once you've chosen a new theme, you can change elements such as background colours and images using the **Colours and Fonts** tab within **Appearance**. Beware that, when changing themes, your previous changes will be discarded

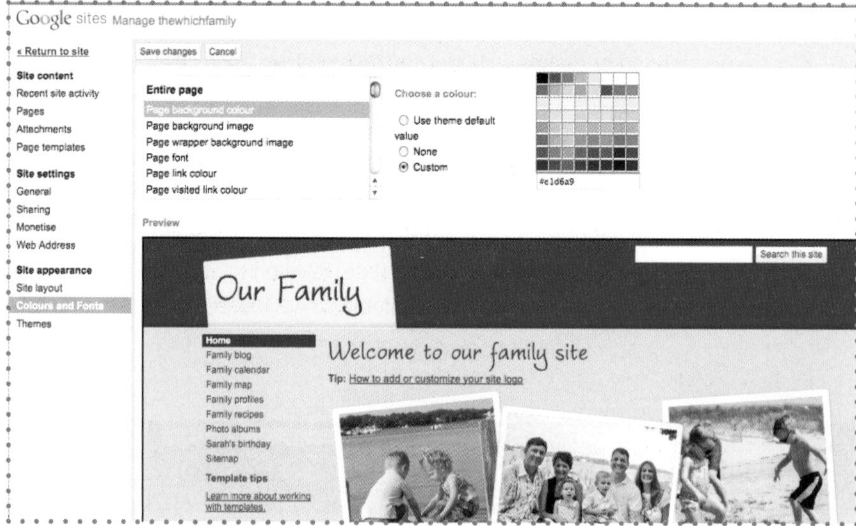

Adding links to other websites and organising your pages

1 A key part of any website is its links to other websites. Inserting links in Google Sites is done in **Edit** mode. Simply highlight the words that you wish your site visitors to be able to click on and then click **Link**

2. Now, enter the URL of the web page you wish to link to. This can be a page on your own website or on another website. Remember to provide the full URL including the http:// (for example, the Which? website full URL is http://www.which.co.uk)

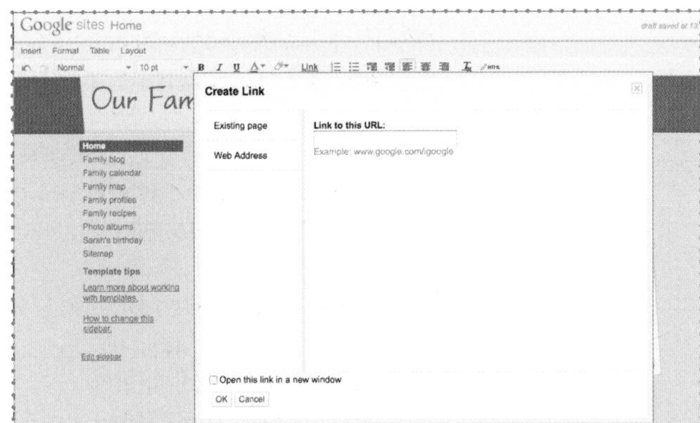

3. If your Google Site has pages with lots of information, you may wish to add a table of contents to a page. Tables of contents are created from the text headers on any given page, and are inserted using the Insert menu. To add a table of contents, click the **Insert** menu, and choose **Table of contents**. In the box that appears, select a width and click **Save**

Change your landing page

As your site grows, you may want to change your 'landing page' – this is the page that people see first when visiting your site.

1. Click on **More actions**, then **Manage site**

2. From the left-hand sidebar, click **General**. You'll see the option to designate a new landing page. Click on the **Change link** to change the page. If you make a change, click **Save Changes**

Delete things from your website

1. If you wish to delete pages, go to the menu bar and click the **More actions** button

2. Click **Delete page** from the menu. Confirm by clicking the **Delete** button. Note that this removes all subsidiary pages of that page and their attachments

HOW TO SHARE BOOKMARKS WITH DIGG

With so much to read and view online, social bookmarking sites are a great way to ensure you never miss out on the hottest content circulating the web. One of the biggest is Digg (www.digg.com). All its content is submitted and moderated by Digg users. Once an item is submitted, other people then Digg (vote) for what they like best.

Find interesting content on Digg

1. Digg is organised into groups of categories based on topics. These are found on the menu bar at the top of the home page and include **Technology**, **World & Business**, **Entertainment** and **Sport**

2. Click a category you're interested in and you'll see a list of top stories that you can search through, either by **Most Recent**, **Top in the Last 24 Hours**, **Top in the Last 7 days**, and so forth

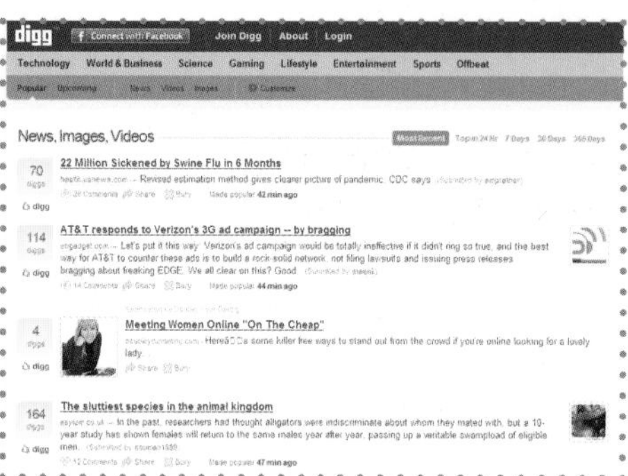

3. On the home page itself is a list of stories, images and videos across all the categories. There's also an **Upcoming** section for stories that haven't been voted on yet

4. Each story has a button that shows how many people have voted for it. If you've a Digg account (see below), you can add your vote by clicking **Digg** under this button

Submit a story to Digg

1. Once logged into your Digg account, click on **Submit New**

2. Paste the web address of the news story, image or video you'd like to submit, and indicate if it's a news story, video or image

3. On the next page, add a concise headline and description. Choose a thumbnail image if one is available and select the topic

4. Click **Submit Story**. You may be asked whether your item is a duplicate of something already submitted. If it isn't, then confirm your submission

SHARE PHOTOS USING FLICKR

You can share photos with lots of friends and family by creating an online gallery of photos and inviting people to view them. Online galleries include sites such as Flickr, and they save you the hassle of emailing photos to lots of people. You can upload photos and group them into albums. Once you have created a page of photos on a site such as Flickr, you can share access details to that page with others – and best of all, it's free.

TIP
When you log in to Flickr, click Your **Photostream** on the main page to see your pictures.

be social

Create a Flickr account

1. In order to use Flickr, you'll need to set up a free Yahoo! Account. To create a Yahoo! Account, type www.flickr.com into the address bar of your web browser and go to the Flickr web site. Click **Create Your Account** on the page that appears

2. This takes you to the Yahoo! sign-up page. Click **Sign Up** (which can be found on the bottom right-hand side of the page). Type in the personal information as requested, then click **Create My Account**

3. Go back to www.flickr.com, and log in to Flickr using your Yahoo! account details that you have just registered

4. Choose a screen name, and then click on **Create a new account**

Upload photographs

With the account registered, you can begin moving photos from your PC to Flickr to create a gallery – this is often referred to as 'uploading'.

1. On the welcome screen click **Upload your first photos** (whenever you return to the site from now on, just click **Upload Photos and Videos** in the top right of the screen once you've logged in)
2. Select **Choose photos and videos**. This will open a window that will enable you to browse your computer for your photos
3. Select a photograph and click **Open**
4. Your photo will appear on the Flickr web page
5. Select whether you want this picture to be private, whether you want your friends and family to be able to view it or whether to make it public and allow all Flickr users to see it
6. Click **Upload Photos and Videos**
7. Add a brief description of the photo and any tags by clicking on **Add a description**

8. Once you've done this click **Save** or, if you've uploaded more than one photo, **Save this batch**

TRY THIS

You can speed up this process by using 'Uploadr', an uploading tool provided by Flickr that will allow you to publish a group of photos directly from your computer. Find it at www.flickr.com/tools where you can download it to your PC.

Access to your photos

Once you've uploaded your photos, you can set up your own Flickr web address that you can give to friends who want to look at the photos.

1. When you're logged in on the Flickr website, click on the arrow next to **You** in the menu bar at the top

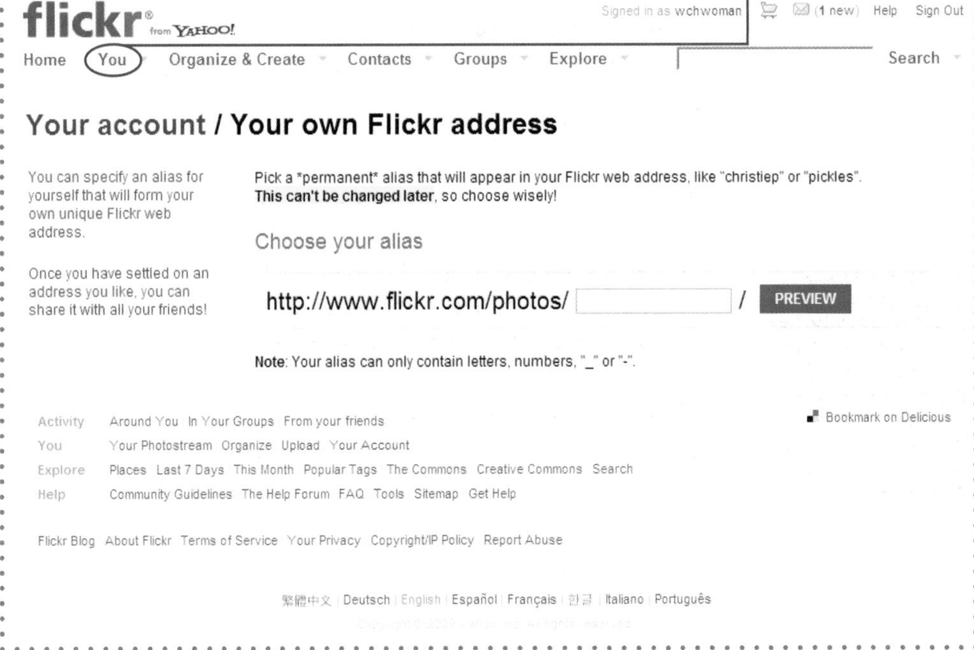

2. Click **Your Account**

3. Click **Create your own memorable Flickr web address!**

4. Complete your web address (make this up yourself) in the box that appears. Click **Preview**

5. Make sure that it's correct. Click **OK – Lock it in**

6. Now you can give your new address to friends to view your photos

WATCH A YOUTUBE VIDEO

It's easy to shoot video footage nowadays. Anyone with a camcorder, a digital camera with movie mode or the latest model of a mobile phone can capture special memories of family and friends, or even create a short movie. The hard part is when you want to share your videos with other people, as the files are usually too big to email. That's where the free video-sharing website YouTube (www.youtube.com) comes in.

You can search on the site and watch clips without logging in but, by creating an account, you can upload your own clip (see page 184), add comments about video clips that you have viewed and bookmark your favourites and give them star ratings out of five.

Search for a clip

1. Type www.youtube.com into the address bar of your web browser, and press **Enter**

2. Whenever a video is posted to YouTube, its owner assigns search terms (keywords) to it that help other people find it. Type in a few keywords that describe what you're looking for in the Search box in the top right of the YouTube home page and click **Search**

3. A list of clips matching your search criteria will appear

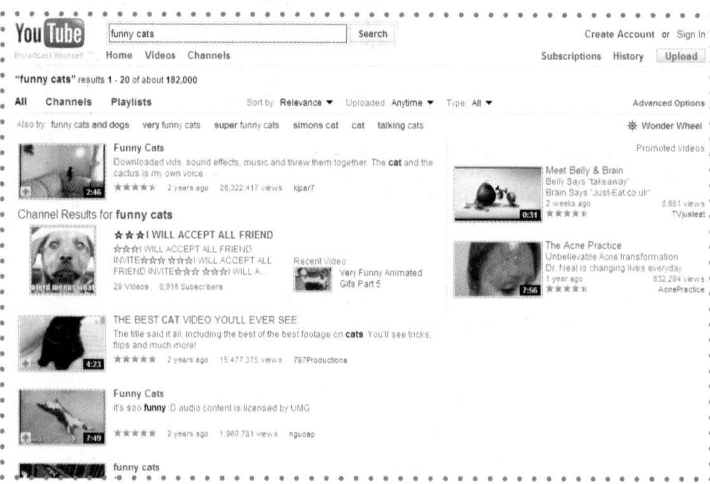

4. To refine your search, click any link in the **Search Modifiers** box that appears on the left

5 Alternatively, you can browse clips. Click on the blue **Videos** tab at the top of the page and it'll list the day's **Most Viewed** clips

6 To change the selection, click **More**. From the drop-down menu choose a link such as **Top Rated**. This will sort the videos according to their ratings

Watch a clip

1 To watch a video clip, click on the thumbnail image or title, which will take you to that clip's page. The video should load and play automatically in a box on the left-hand side of the screen

2 You may have to wait for a clip to load before you can watch it. This is illustrated by the red bar filling up. You can view a later part of the clip by clicking on the corresponding part of the red bar

TIP
To help you decide if you think a clip is worth watching, look at its YouTube rating.

3 Once loaded, you can click on the **Play/pause** and **Stop** buttons just underneath the picture

4 To increase the volume, click and drag the volume slider, which is located on the bar at the base of the video clip. It looks like a series of straight lines being emitted from a speaker

5 To blow up a clip so it can be viewed larger in 'full screen' mode, click the button at the bottom right corner of the video. Press **Esc** to return to small screen mode

UPLOAD A VIDEO TO YOUTUBE

You can upload your own video clips to the YouTube website and then let selected friends access your clips or – if you're feeling brave – share them with the whole planet.

Create an account

To post your own video clips you will need to sign up as a YouTube user.

1. Click the **Sign Up** link in the top-right corner of the YouTube screen

2. Fill out the form that appears, click to untick the box for the weekly email if you don't want it and then finish your registration by clicking on **Sign up**

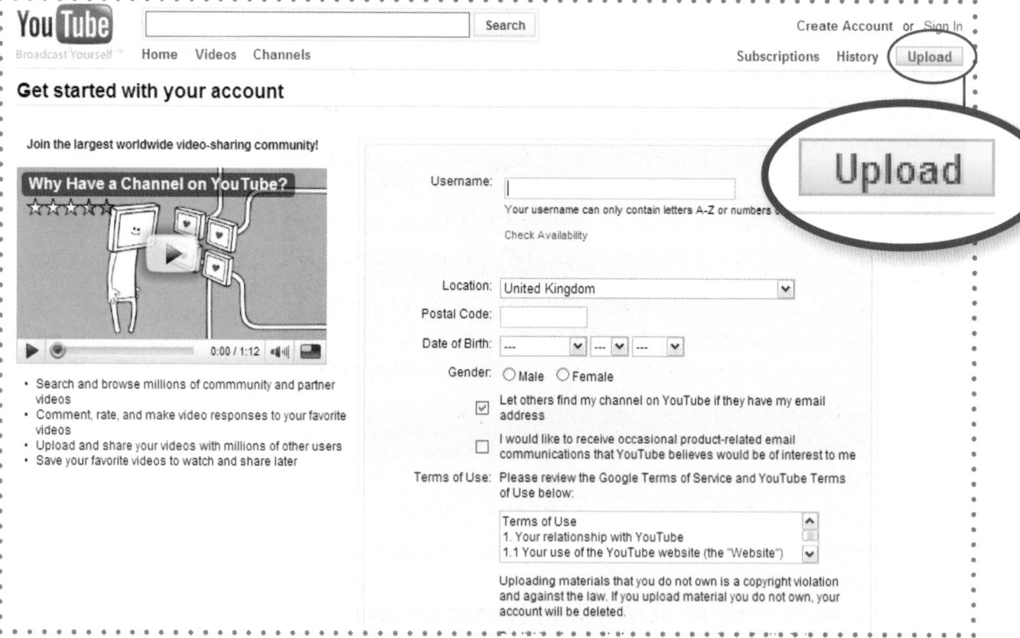

3. Click the **Upload** tab in the top right of your screen. Type your email address into the box and then click on **Send Email**

4. Now wait for an email from YouTube (this is the second email YouTube sends, the first is a welcome message). It may take a while to arrive. When it does, click on the link contained in it

Prepare and upload your clip

1. On the upload page, fill out the form with details about your video, including its title, a short description, a category and tags
2. Select your language from the drop-down list then click **Continue**
3. Click **Upload Video**. Locate the video clip you want to upload from your computer and click **Open**

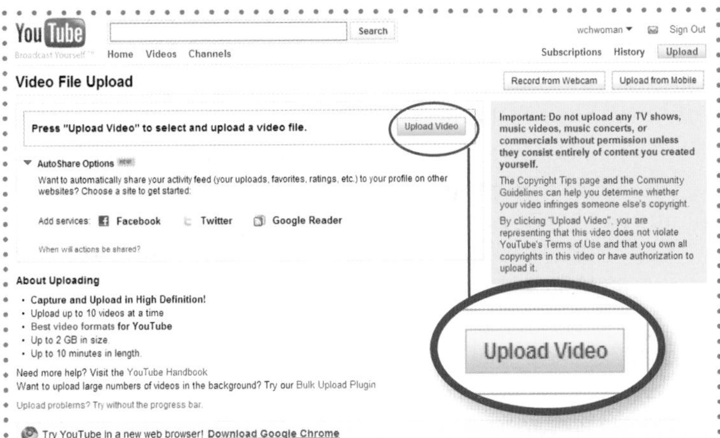

4. YouTube imposes a limit on the length of your clip (10 minutes) and its size (2GB). To edit video for size, or to a specific length, you'll need to use video editing software on your PC such as Adobe Premiere Elements and follow the instructions for that software

Keep it private

If you want only friends to view your clip, first you'll need to create a contacts list.

1. In YouTube, click **My Account** then **My Friends** and enter the email addresses of your contacts
2. Click **Private** and then your contact list
3. Finally, click **Upload Video** and a progress bar will appear as your clip is transferred to YouTube. Once it's loaded, click **Play**, sit back and enjoy

Jargon buster

Tags

Tags are keywords (such as 'holiday', 'France') that help others to find your video when they search YouTube.

TRY THIS

YouTube accepts video in a number of different formats, including AVI, MOV and MPG files. For the best results, read the site's guidelines on formats before you create your video clips. You can find these guidelines, plus more video tips, in the YouTube Handbook at www.youtube.com/t/yt_handbook_home

CONTRIBUTE TO THE INTERNET

A wiki is a piece of software (used by website owners) that allows users of the website to create and edit web page content using any web browser. These collaborative websites have been around since 1995 but the best known wiki is Wikipedia, a free online encyclopedia to which anyone can contribute information. With more than 3 million articles in English (it publishes in ten languages), Wikipedia is the one of the largest reference sites online and every day has hundreds of thousands of people making edits to pages or creating new articles. Anyone with Internet access can write and make changes to Wikipedia articles. You don't have to be a specialist in a given subject, nor do you have to give your real name when contributing, unless you choose to.

Edit an existing article

1. To add information to a Wikipedia article, you first need to find it. Go to http://en.wikipedia.org/wiki/Main_Page and use keywords in the left-hand **Search** box to find the article you want

2. With the article open on the page, click on the **Edit This Page** tab at the top. (Not all pages have this button. Some articles, such as those relating to current political events or people, are protected to avoid vandalism and can only be edited by Wikipedia appointed editors)

3. The article will open in a simple text editor with a number of buttons along the top. Here you can edit the existing text or add new material of your own. Text can be formatted using the various buttons along the top (holding your cursor over each button will show a description of what the button does)

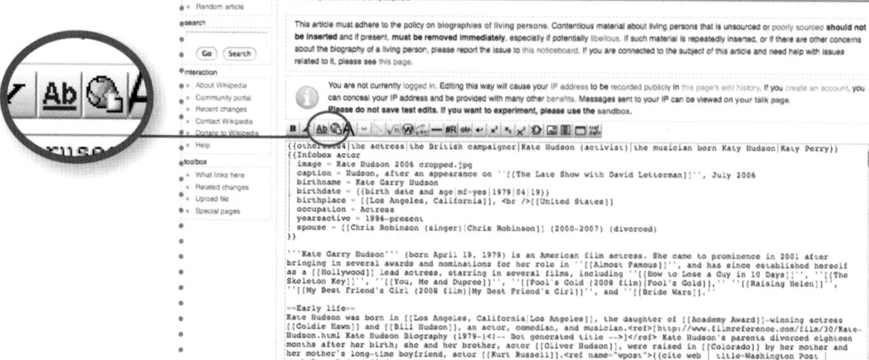

4. Links to both internal (within Wikipedia) and external (across the whole web) sites can be added pressing one of the two links buttons. You'll need to type in the URL of the site you wish to link to

5. Having made your edits, click **Show Preview**. This lets you see what the page will look like after you press **Save**

6. Alternatively, before saving, click **Show Changes**, which opens a window showing just the parts of the article that have been changed. The current article text is shown alongside so you can compare and check what you have changed or added

7. Before saving, it's considered polite to enter a brief explanation of your changes in the **Edit summary** box. Keep it short. For example, if you just made a spelling correction, you can enter 'typo'

8. When you're happy with your changes, click **Save Page**

Create a Wikipedia article

1. Before you can create a new article, you have to register and create an account on Wikipedia.

2. Once logged in, search Wikipedia to see if an article on your chosen subject already exists. If it doesn't, Wikipedia will respond **You may create the page "Dotted Tablecloths"** [insert your own search term here]. Click on the words you used to search and you'll see a text editor where you can create the article

3. It's best to create your article using the Article Wizard, so click on **Article Wizard** and follow the instructions. This is a six-step process that helps you check whether the subject or person you wish to write about has been previously covered, whether the subject matter is 'notable' or noteworthy enough for inclusion and whether your source information is original and copyright free

4. When you've completed this process, you can choose to create a new article by either posting it live or in draft form on your own userspace. Either option takes you to a page of instructions and the same text editor as used when editing articles. Here you can write your article and then click **Save Page**

CREATE AND SEND AN ECARD

An ecard is an online version of a traditional greetings card or postcard that's sent via email. There are ecards for every occasion and using them can save you money and time in buying and posting expensive paper cards. Most ecards offer animation, music and allow you to write a personal message. There are numerous websites offering ecards – the majority of which are free to use. Here's how to use the www.regards.com website.

Create an ecard

1. Type www.regards.com into the address bar of your web browser, and press **Enter**. From the list on the left-hand side of the Regards.com home page, select an ecard category. Lots of different categories are available including **Birthday**, **Love & Romance** and **Thank You**, many with sub-categories, so it's quick to narrow down your selection.

2. From the cards in your chosen category, choose an ecard. You can preview the card before you fill it out by clicking on it

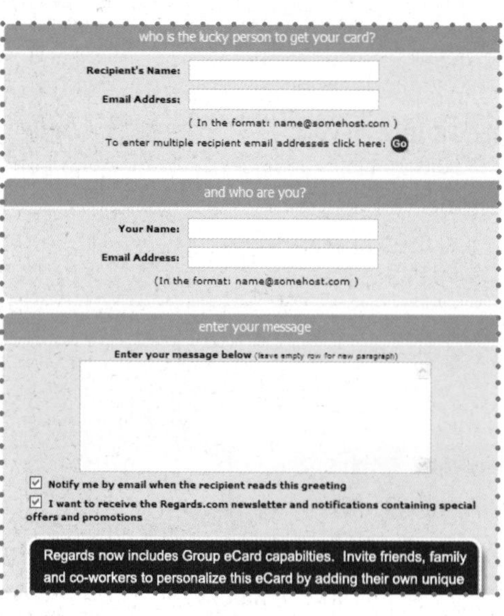

3. Enter the recipient's name and email address. If you want to send this ecard to multiple individuals, click the **Go** button. Separate each email with a comma. Enter your name and email address

4. In the large box under the information, type your message. Clicking **Notify Me By Email** will send a message to your email inbox when the recipient views the ecard

5. Click the **Continue With This eCard Coming From Just Me** button

6. You can preview the ecard one last time. Choose the date to send the ecard. Use the arrows to change the month, day and year. Click the **Send eCard Now** button

PROTECT YOURSELF

By reading and following all the steps in this chapter, you will get to grips with:

- **Security threats to watch out for**
- **Scanning your PC for viruses and spyware**
- **Protecting yourself online**

SECURITY ONLINE

There are numerous security threats online that could potentially damage your computer or jeopardise your personal information. With the proper precautions, however, there's no need to worry. Taking sensible steps while browsing the internet and making sure your security settings are switched to maximum can make your online experience a carefree one. There are different types of security threats.

Phishing

What is it?

An email that appears to be from an official organisation or business such as a bank, but is actually a sophisticated fake. It is designed to trick you into parting with personal information.

Potential risk

Phishing emails can be convincing. They look like they come from an official body (see page 203). Clicking on links in the email, and then entering passwords or financial details could mean that you hand over the keys to your bank account to criminals.

Spam

What is it?

Spam is unsolicited junk email, often purporting to sell you things like medication and sent out in bulk by automated web robots.

Potential risk

Spam can clog up networks and make sending and receiving email annoying. Many phishing emails are spam.

Spyware

What is it?

Software that installs itself on your computer without your knowledge.

Potential risk

Once installed, spyware can get in the way of the ordinary operation of your computer. It can cause your computer to flash up warnings and messages, change your computer settings or cripple its functions. Worse still, some spyware literally spies on your activities, collects personal information and passes it to criminals over the internet.

Trojan

What is it?

A computer program that gets through your computer's defences disguised as something else – like the Trojan horse of legend.

Potential risk

Running the disguised program could install dangerous software on your PC, allowing hackers to access or delete your data via the internet.

Worm

What is it?

A computer program designed to make copies of itself, which it sends to other computers.

Potential risk

As well as slowing down networks, worms can sometimes contain software that might damage your PC or open a back door to hackers.

SECURE YOUR COMPUTER

To protect your computer from attack you need to have several different types of security software installed on your PC and kept up to date. To protect your computer fully you need to install:

A Firewall This is a piece of software that sits between your PC and the Internet, protecting your computer from incoming attacks from hackers or malware such as viruses. It is vital that your firewall is switched on.

Anti-virus software This protects against a number of different types of threat, including Trojans and worms. Some anti-virus software will include anti-spyware tools.

Anti-spyware software This protects your computer from spyware (malicious software that downloads to your computer without your knowledge). Spyware can monitor your activity and collect information about you.

SECURE YOUR WIRELESS CONNECTION

If you connect to the internet via a wireless connection, you need to ensure that your network is secured. Otherwise anyone within range of the network (such as neighbours) who has a wireless-enabled device could use your internet connection or possibly gain access to your PC.

To secure your network, you need to enable encryption when installing it. There are two main kinds of encryption: WEP (Wired Equivalent Privacy) or WPA (Wi-Fi Protected Access). Both use a system that prevents any wireless device that doesn't have the correct authentication key, such as a password, from accessing the network. WPA is newer and stronger as it scrambles the encryption key, further protecting it, but check the product details of all the devices (PCs, iPhones etc) that you wish to connect to your wireless home internet to make sure they can use it before choosing this option.

1 The first step is to turn on encryption on your wireless router. Click on the **Start menu** and select **Control Panel** and then **Wireless Network Setup Wizard**

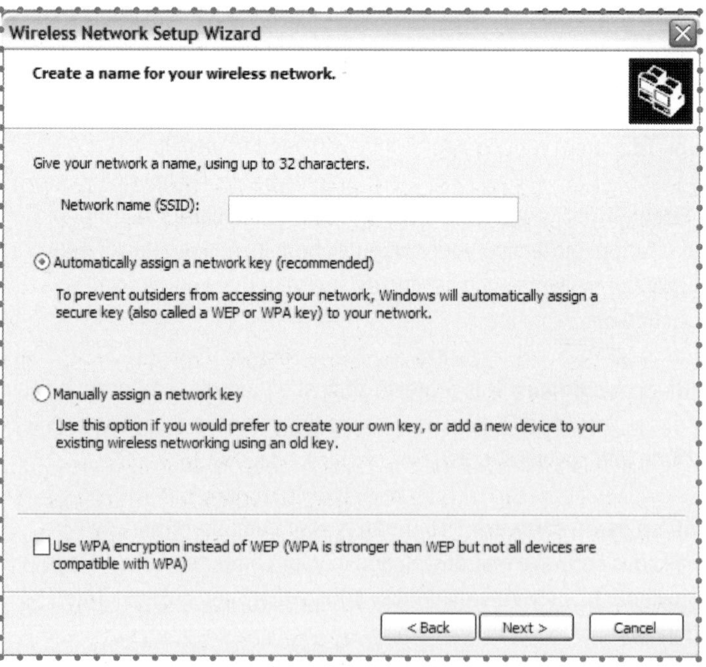

2 Follow the instructions in the box and make a note of the authorisation key you'll be given. Type this in when asked during the setup for each of your wireless devices

Jargon buster

Encryption

Encryption is a security measure that transforms data or information into code. This code needs to be converted back into its original form to be able to be read.

BROWSER SAFETY

Web browsers such as Internet Explorer and Firefox make it easy for us to find our way around the internet. However, all web browsers continually collect personal information about what you do and where you go online.

Not only do browsers keep records of the web pages that you visit in their history files, they use cookies – small text files that store information about you, such as login details and passwords. When you visit a website, a cookie is sent to your computer. The next time you visit that particular site, its cookie is sent back to the web server so that the site can be personalised in some way for you. For example, returning to an online shopping site, which you have registered with, you'll see 'Hello John Doe [insert your own name here]' rather than a generic 'Hello new customer'.

While cookies and history files have their uses, they can expose your personal information to identity thieves. Armed with a few choice facts about you, an identity thief might be able to open a bank account in your name or, worse, access your bank or credit card account. A criminal could run up debts, apply for benefits or even attempt to obtain a passport or driver's licence in your name. Fortunately, there's plenty you can do to protect yourself.

Delete your browser history

If you're using a public PC (in a library or cybercafé, say) it's wise to clear your browser history when you've finished surfing the web.

In Internet Explorer

1. Go to **Tools**, then **Delete Browsing History**. From the pop-up box, tick the items that you wish to delete
2. If you do not want to delete data for websites that you have bookmarked, ensure that **Preserve Favorites** is ticked. Press **Delete** when done

In Firefox

1. Go to **Tools** and then **Options**. Select the **Privacy** tab
2. Make sure the box next to **Clear history when Firefox closes** is ticked

Delete cookies

To keep your virtual paper trail clean, delete your cookies, especially at the end of any public computer session.

In Internet Explorer

1. Go to **Tools** and then **Delete Browsing History**
2. Ensure the box that says **Cookies** is ticked and then click **Delete**

In Firefox

1. Go to **Tools, Options** and select the **Privacy** tab
2. Click on the **Show Cookies** button. In the pop-up box you can either identify particular cookies to be deleted or remove all cookies

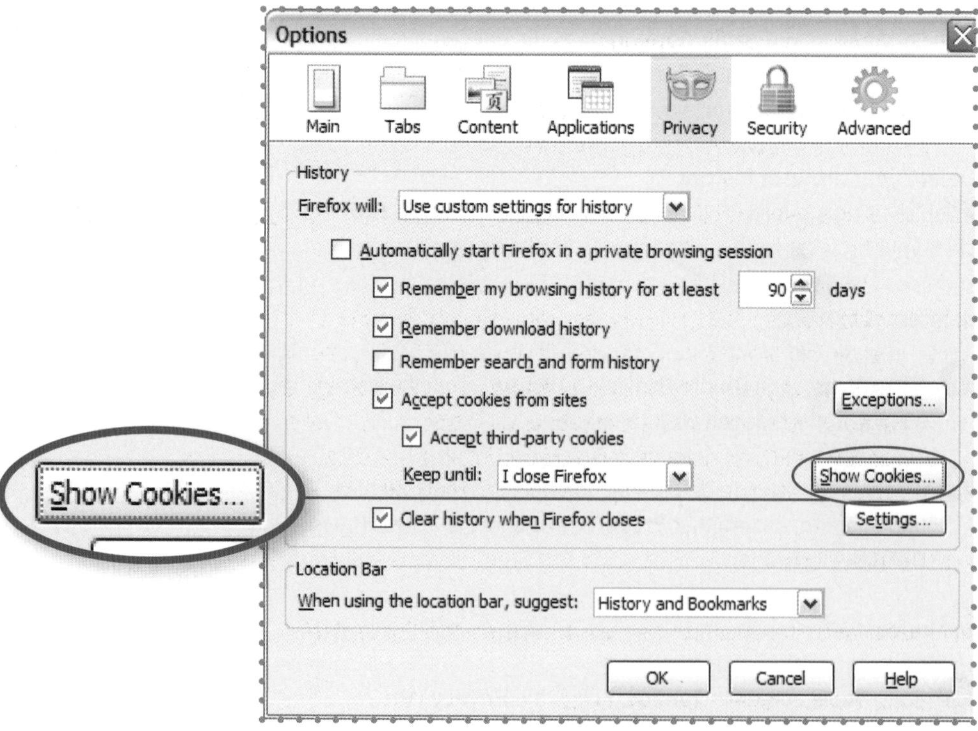

Block pop-ups

Pop-ups are small windows that open automatically when you visit certain web pages. Many are just annoying or confusing, but they can also contain malicious code or phishing scams. Both Internet Explorer and Firefox have built-in pop-up blockers. Bear in mind, though, that some sites use legitimate pop-ups, so you may have to allow pop-ups for some individual sites manually.

In Internet Explorer

1. Go to **Tools** and then **Pop-up Blocker**. Click **Turn On Pop-up Blocker**
2. Click **Pop-Up Blocker Settings** to add an allowed website

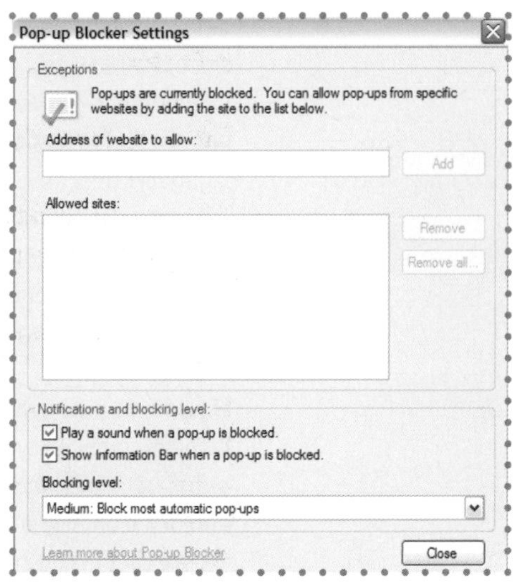

In Firefox

1. Go to **Tools** and click on **Options**
2. Click **Content** from the menu at the top of the box and tick **Block pop-up windows**
3. Click **Exceptions** to add an allowed website

Switch off the autocomplete function

Autocomplete is a feature that allows some browsers to 'remember' what you enter into online forms. It's useful if you frequently log into the same sites or fill out your postal address or telephone number in online forms, but it also represents a threat to your privacy, since anyone who has access to your PC can automatically find out details from online forms. For shared PCs (see page 196), it's wise to turn this off.

In Internet Explorer

1. Go to **Tools** and click **Internet Options**. Select the **Content** tab
2. Under **Autocomplete**, click **Settings**
3. Remove the ticks next to **Forms** and **User names and passwords on forms**

In Firefox

1. Go to **Tools** and click **Options**
2. Under the Privacy tab, untick the box next to **Remember search and form history**

Is it safe to save login details?

Some websites and services give you the option to save your login details. This makes it convenient if you often use the same computer, since it means you don't have to type your username and password in every time you want to access the site or service. Saving such information to a shared PC is a security risk, particularly on a public computer (this includes a computer in your office).

Some sites, Windows Live Mail (Hotmail) for example, offer an option to save just your email address. This is appropriate for home use but, if you're using a public PC, ensure that the **Always ask for my email address and password** box (or equivalent) is checked.

How do I know when a web page is secure?

A secure website will be prefaced **https://** rather than the usual **http://** – the extra 's' standing for 'secure'. In Internet Explorer and Firefox, a padlock icon also appears in the address bar every time you arrive at a secure page. You can check the security certificate for a web page to make sure it's genuine to.

In Internet Explorer

1. Go to **Page** and click **Security Report**
2. Click **View certificates**. Under the details, you should be able to check that the certificate was issued to the correct site and whether or not it is valid

In Firefox

1. Go to **Tools** and click **Page info**
2. Click **Security** then click **View**

RESTRICT ACCESS TO YOUR COMPUTER

If more than one person will be using your computer, it's best set up a separate user account for each. Each person will then be able to keep the settings for the desktop, documents and other files the way they prefer, and security settings can be protected from being viewed or changed.

Restrict user accounts

When you first set up your computer, Windows creates an **Administrator** account. This is an access-all-areas pass to your computer. Someone logged in as Administrator can install programs and make advanced changes, so avoid using this setting as it leaves you more open to security breaches.

Instead, Microsoft Windows lets you set up separate user accounts. Known as 'Standard accounts' in Windows Vista ('Limited accounts' in Windows XP), these account settings grant access to the computer, but they include limits. When the user is logged into the account, Windows knows which folders or files they may open, how they like their screen to look and what changes they're permitted to make to the computer. If they try to make a change they're not permitted to make, they'll be asked for the Administrator password.

So, if everyone in your household logs in with a limited user account, the risk to your PC is minimised.

Instructions for Windows XP

Create a new user account

1. Click **Start** and then **Control Panel**, then **User Accounts** and **Create a new account**

2. You'll be asked to give the account a name. Type one in and click **Next**

3. You'll be given the option of selecting an account type. The two account types available are **Computer Administrator** and **Limited**. Click in the circle beside **Limited**, **Create Account**. Your new user account has now been created. You can create more accounts by simply repeating this process

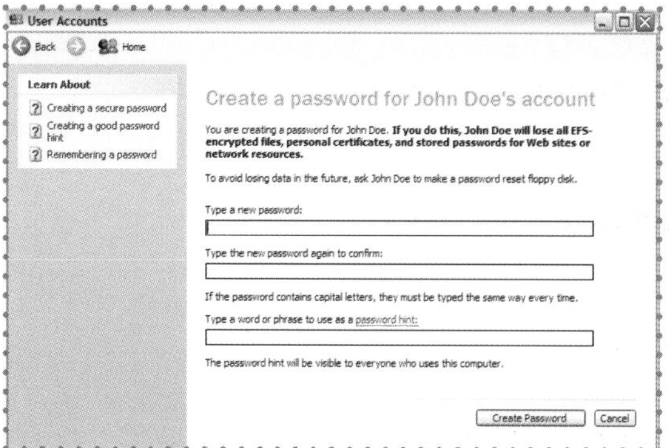

Create a password

Now your account is set up, there are several ways you can amend it, such as making it more secure by password protecting it. From the User Accounts screen, click on the account for which you want to add a password and then click on **Create a password**. Follow the instructions. Add a password hint in case you forget it.

Change the picture icon

Every user account in Microsoft Windows XP is allocated a picture icon to make it easy to identify on the login screen. If you don't like the icon that has been allocated to your new account, you can choose a different picture. From the User Accounts screen, click on the account you want to change then on **Change the picture**. Click on a new picture from the selection onscreen. Click **Change Picture**.

Instructions for Windows Vista

Create a new user account

1. Click the Windows icon (bottom left-hand corner of the screen), then click **Control Panel** and **User Accounts and family safety**
2. Click **Add or remove user accounts**. Click on **Create a new account**
3. You'll be asked to name the account and choose an account type. Type in a name for your account and select Standard user, then **Create Account**. Your new account has now been created

Change your password

1. From the **Choose the account you would like to change** screen, click on your new account and then **Create a password**
2. Type your password in the **New password** box and again in the **Confirm new password** box
3. Add a password hint to serve as a reminder should you forget your password

Change the picture
Windows Vista allocates a picture icon to each user account. You can change this if you like.

1. From the **Choose the account you would like to change** screen, click on your new account
2. From the list, select **Change the picture**
3. There are a number of default images to choose from or click **Browse** to look for an image on your PC. Click the picture that you want and then click **Change Picture**

Set up parental controls
You can also use Vista's Parental Controls to further limit how someone uses your PC.

1. Select the new account from the **Choose the account you would like to change** screen
2. Click **Set up Parental Controls** and select the account you want to restrict
3. Under **Windows Settings**, select the things you'd like to control from the options
4. When you've made your choices, click the circle beside **On** to enforce current settings. Click **OK**

Instructions for Windows 7

1. Click the **Start** icon, and then click **Control Panel**
2. Click **User Accounts** and then click **Manage another account**
3. Click **Create a new account**. On the new screen give the account a name and choose either standard account or an administrator. Then click **Create Account**
4. To set a password, click on the account name and then **Create a password**. You can also change the picture icon here

CREATE A STRONG PASSWORD

Good passwords are the key to keeping your personal data safe. Many people use things like their mother's maiden name and their date of birth, but you might be surprised to learn just how easy it is to find out information like this – from public records, for example.

It can be difficult to remember multiple passwords, but, if you can, use a three-tiered password system, where you have different levels of password for different types of website:

Low security: such as signing up for a newsletter
Medium security: for webmail and instant messenger services
High security: for anything where your personal finance is involved

For a high security password, a series of randomly generated letters and numbers is best. If you need something to help you remember your password, try creating it from something such as the first letter of each word in a line from a favourite song.

If you can't remember different passwords

You might consider using a password manager, which will remember all your passwords for you. That way, all you need is to remember is one single 'master' password. (However, if you can manage without a password manager then do, since they can make it easier to gain access to your data.)

Windows Vista has a password manager that uses your user login as the master password. Mozilla Firefox also lets you store passwords.

On Windows Vista

1. Go to **Start** and then **Control Panel**
2. Click **User Accounts and Family Safety** and click **User Accounts**
3. Click **Manage your network passwords** in the left-hand task pane
4. Click **Add** in the new box. **Under Log on to**, type the address of the site you want to sign into and then enter your username and password underneath
5. Put a tick next to a website or program credential and click **OK**

On Firefox

1. Go to **Tools**, click **Options** and then click **Security**
2. Put a tick next to **Remember passwords for me**
3. Put a tick next to **Use a master password**

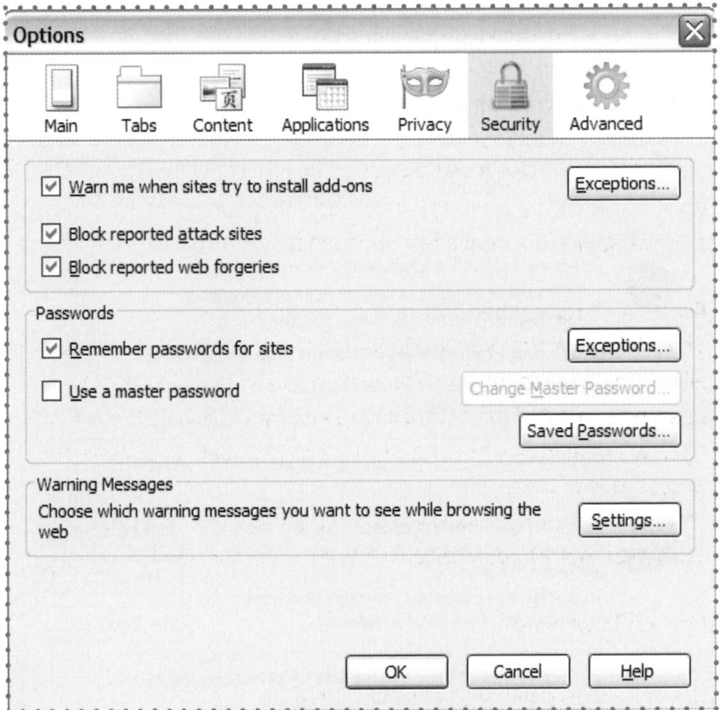

4. In the window that appears, enter your password twice and click **OK** and **OK** again

ENCRYPT EMAIL

It's generally best to avoid sending sensitive personal information such as your bank or credit card details via email. However, if you need to get information to somebody halfway round the world in a hurry, it's possible to encrypt data to help to keep it safe. The email program Outlook Express includes an encryption feature (with Outlook Express open, click **Tools** then **Options**; click **Security**). However, it's fiddly to use and requires your recipients' digital identities to be verified before you can exchange encrypted emails with them.

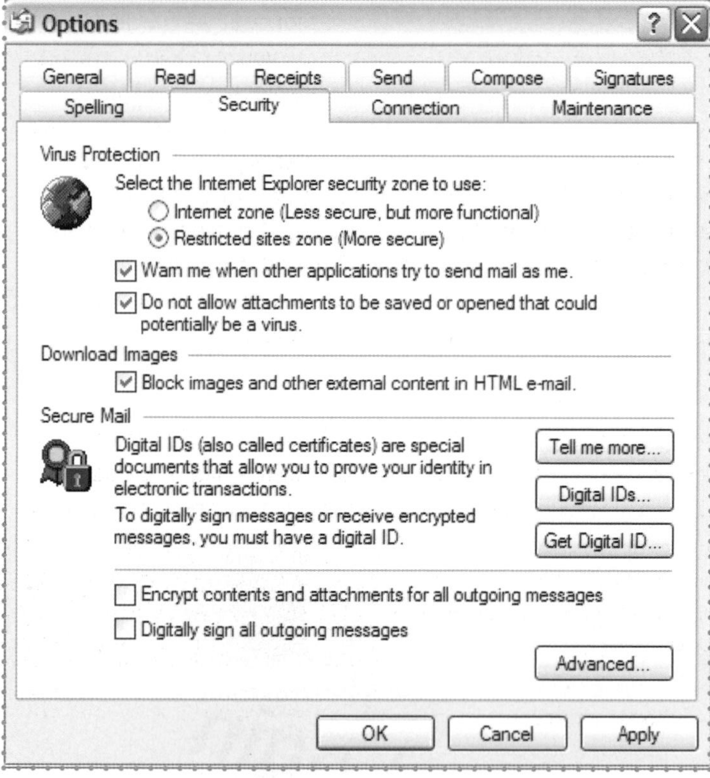

You can use other programs, such as Winzip (www.winzip.com) or WinRAR (www.rarlab.com), instead. You could also consider including the sensitive information in a separate encrypted Word document attachment rather than in the email itself.

Remember that the person you're emailing the encrypted file to will need to know the password in order to decrypt it at the other end. Under no circumstances should you put the password in the email, as this would defeat the purpose of sending them an encrypted email.

AVOID PHISHING SCAMS

Phishing is the name given to online scams where unwitting victims are hooked into handing over personal information by email – bank account details, passwords, credit card numbers and the like – by criminals who sell this data or use it themselves to commit fraud.

Phishing scams frequently take the form of a hoax spam email that looks like it came from an official source, such as your bank or building society. Sometimes they contain a threat such as your account is in danger of being closed down for, ironically, security reasons. Other popular scams involve the promise of winning competitions you haven't entered, or the chance to make money on a business deal.

A phishing email (see page 205) may ask you to email back personal account details or click on a link within the message. The link takes you to a fake website that looks like the real thing. Entering personal information in such a web page directly places your details into the hands of identity thieves. Banks and building societies NEVER send emails requesting sensitive account details. If in doubt, pick up the phone and check directly with them. The best thing is to delete suspicious emails and avoid suspicious sites. Also make use of the anti-phishing filters provided by your web browsers.

Phishing filters

Most web browsers have built-in tools for spotting fake sites and potentially dangerous web pages. Most phishing filters compare the site you're visiting against a list of known hoax pages and then warn you if it looks like the web address you're visiting might be fraudulent. To turn on your phishing filter:

In Internet Explorer

1. Go to **Tools**
2. Click **SmartScreen Filter**
3. Make sure there's a dot next to **Turn on SmartScreen Filter** (recommended) and click **OK**

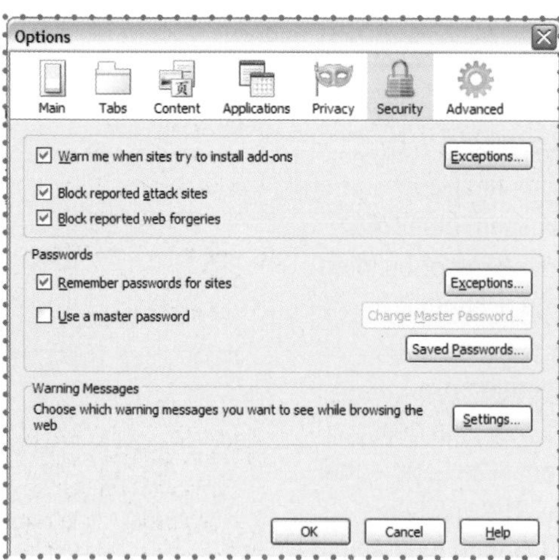

In Firefox

The phishing filter is turned on by default in Firefox 3 so, unless your security preferences have been changed, you're likely to be already using them.

1. To check they're on click on **Tools**, then select **Options**
2. Click **Security**
3. Make sure the boxes next to **Block reported attack sites** and **Block reported web forgeries** are ticked

Reporting potential hoax websites

In Internet Explorer

1. While on a suspect web page, click **Tools**
2. Click **SmartScreen Filter**
3. Click **Report Unsafe Website**
4. A new window will open showing the address of the site. Tick next to **I think this is a phishing website**
5. Type the characters that you can see in the box at the bottom
6. Click **Submit**

In Firefox

1. With the web page open, go to **Help**
2. Click **Report Web Forgery**
3. This will bring up a web page where you can report the suspected site
4. Add a comment if you want to and click **Submit Report**

HOW TO SPOT A PHISHING SCAM

Logos
These might look like the real thing, but logos are easily copied online and should never be viewed as a guarantee of authenticity.

which? bank*

Dear Valued Customer

We recently have determined that different computers have logged into your Which? Bank account, and multiple password failures were present before the logons.

In this manner for your security, your specified access account has been locked and needs to be reactivated, in order for it to remain active, please Use the link below to proceed and unlock your account.

So we want you to use this oppurtunity to upgrade your account to our new security with the Which? Bank.

https://www.mybank.which/index.asp?

I am convinced that Which? Bank will be a leading UK bank focused on giving you great service and value-for-money products.

Yours sincerely

Chairman, Which? Bank

This message was sent to you as a Which? Bank customer, to inform you regarding important information about your account.

The small print
This might look genuine but it could easily have been copied from a genuine email so it is not a guarantee of authenticity.

Impersonal
The email might be addressed to 'Dear valued customer' or 'valued client'. Your bank will not email you in this way.

Scare tactics
To frighten you into taking action, an email or website might tell you that someone has tried to access your bank account fraudulently and that you must log in now to verify your personal details otherwise your account will be closed.

Spelling/grammar
The email or website might have spelling mistakes, poor syntax (overuse of capital letters, for example) or the wording may be overcomplicated.

Link
They will send you a link to the fraudulent web page. This may look suspicious in itself or it may even appear to be exactly the same address as the genuine login page, yet will redirect you to the fake site. Never click on an emailed link.

*This email and the use of a Which? Bank logo is for illustrative purposes only.

AVOID VIRUSES AND SPYWARE

Viruses are computer programs designed to 'infect' your system, usually causing it to crash, either immediately or at a later date.

You can pick up viruses from files downloaded from the internet, but the most insidious type arrive in your email inbox and can be activated even if you delete the email without opening it or any infected attachment.

Are viruses a threat to my privacy?
Yes. Adware, spyware and other malicious software (malware) from online sources can invade your privacy and, in some cases, monitor keystrokes, hijack your email or use your identity to send out spam.

Does Windows have anti-virus software?
Neither Vista nor XP come with anti-virus protection. You'll need to use a third-party product. Anti-virus software works by scanning your system for viruses, either all the time or on-demand, searching for viruses, or programs that look like them. If it finds a virus, it will usually remove it and repair the damage, or offer to delete the offending file. Windows 7 users can download Microsoft Security Essentials for free from www.microsoft.com/Security_Essentials/. This guards against viruses, spyware and other malicious software.

How do I know my anti-virus software is on?
Most anti-virus programs put an icon in the taskbar (bottom right) to show that they're switched on. You can also check by going to **Windows Security Center**. Click **Start** and then click **Control Panel**. Double-click **Security Center**. The box that appears shows if the following are on:

- A software firewall
- An up-to-date antivirus program
- Automatic Updates

How can I tell if my computer has a virus?
If your computer becomes slow or unresponsive or if you find that programs you use all the time are behaving in an unusual way, then your computer may have been infected by a virus.

How many anti-virus programs should I run?
You need to run only one anti-virus program. You should also run a firewall and an anti-spyware program.

What's the difference between anti-spyware and anti-virus software?
Anti-virus software protects you against viruses that arrive via email messages or infected files. Anti-spyware programs check for and eliminate other types of malicious software within a program you have chosen to install.

How do I scan for viruses?
Generally the Scan option should be accessible from the main program page of your anti-virus software. Check your anti-virus programs settings for a scheduling option that lets you run a weekly automated scan.

How often should I update my anti-virus software?
Update your anti-virus program daily. The best anti-virus programs can be set to look for and retrieve updates automatically. In other cases, you may see a message pop up to alert you when updates are available.

Set up a firewall

Anti-virus and anti-spyware protection is an absolute must on your home PC. Similarly, a firewall will help to prevent anything from getting onto your computer.

Windows Vista users have a built-in firewall and will find that adware and spyware are dealt with by the operating system's Security Center. XP users who have kept their machines up to date can use the firewall that comes with the Service Pack 2 update.

You can also use Microsoft's Windows Defender. Formerly Microsoft AntiSpyware, Windows Defender is a software product that detects, removes or quarantines spyware. The product is installed and enabled by default in Windows Vista but Windows XP users can download it free of charge from www.microsoft.com. The new Microsoft Security Essentials (MSE) can be used instead, but you will need to disable or uninstall Windows Defender before using MSE.

1. To access Windows Defender from Windows Vista, click the **Start** button

2. Point to **Control Panel** and then click on the **Windows Defender** link on the left-hand side of the **Security Center**

3. Alternatively, you can type **Windows Defender** into the Search box provided

Set up an automatic scan

1. To set your computer to run an automatic, daily scan, click **Tools** then **Option**

2. Using the drop-down arrows select a daily scan and your preferred time for the scan to run

3. You can tell Defender what to do when it finds, for instance, high alert items, again using the drop-down menus

4. Click **Save** and **Continue**

Run a manual scan

1. Alternatively, you can run a manual scan. As before, click the **Start** button and scroll to **Control Panel**

2. Select **Security Center** and click on **Windows Defender** in the left-hand panel

3. Click **Scan** and Defender will look for spyware. The scan may take a few minutes. You can then ignore, remove or quarantine files

Other security tools

There's a wide range of anti-virus software and tools available but securing you computer against viruses needn't be expensive. There are some excellent free security tools available to download. Software manufacturers who offer security products for free tend to specialise on one particular area, so you'll typically need to download and install separate anti-virus, anti-spam, anti-spyware and firewall programs to make up your own 'pick and mix' security suite.

Keep it up to date

Security software is only as good as its last update. With new virus and spyware threats constantly emerging, software manufacturers issue regular security updates. Many programs let you set up automatic updates – look for this under the Settings menu.

INSTALL AND SET UP AVG 9.0

The new, free AVG 9.0 software from AVG Technologies includes basic, yet effective, anti-virus and anti-spyware tools. Previous versions have earned Best Buy status in Which? Computing security tests. Because AVG doesn't cost a penny, it's only meant for personal use. There's no formal technical support but it's easy both to install and to use.

Download the installation file

1. Enter http://free.avg.com into the address bar of your web browser, and click **Get it now** in the section where it says AVG Anti-Virus Free Edition. This is the version you need (make sure you aren't incorrectly downloading a trial version of their fully featured software that you'll need to pay for later).

2. Click the link that says **Download** under the column headed AVG Anti-Virus Free Edition

3. On the following page, click the left-hand column that is headed **Get AVG Anti-Virus Free Edition 9.0**

4. This will take you to CNet Download.com partner site. Once there, click **Download Now** and the file should save to your desktop

Install the program

1. Close all open applications and then double-click the AVG file you downloaded (it will be located in your Downloads folder, which is found by clicking **Start** and then **My Documents**). Start installing it by pressing **Run**

2. For security reasons, you may receive a warning at this point (or you may need to use your computer's Administrator username and password) but it's safe to continue

3. To install the program, follow the easy steps, choosing **Install only basic free protection** when you're asked to choose an installation type

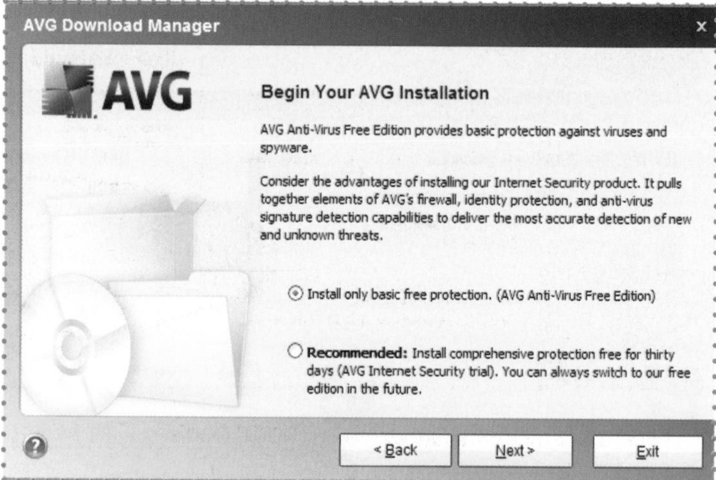

4. Click **Next** and the remainder of the software will download from the internet and install

5. Towards the end of the process you can, if you wish, choose not to add the **AVG Security Toolbar** to your web browser by unticking the box (most browsers have a similar toolbar built in so it's safe to omit this feature). At the end of the installation process click **OK**

Configure the software

1 Once AVG has successfully installed, choose **Optimize scanning now (recommended)** as this will speed up future scans

2 Once finished, launch AVG Free 9.0 from the **Start** menu, choosing **AVG Free User Interface**

3 Everything should have a green tick and a reassuring **You are protected** message in green

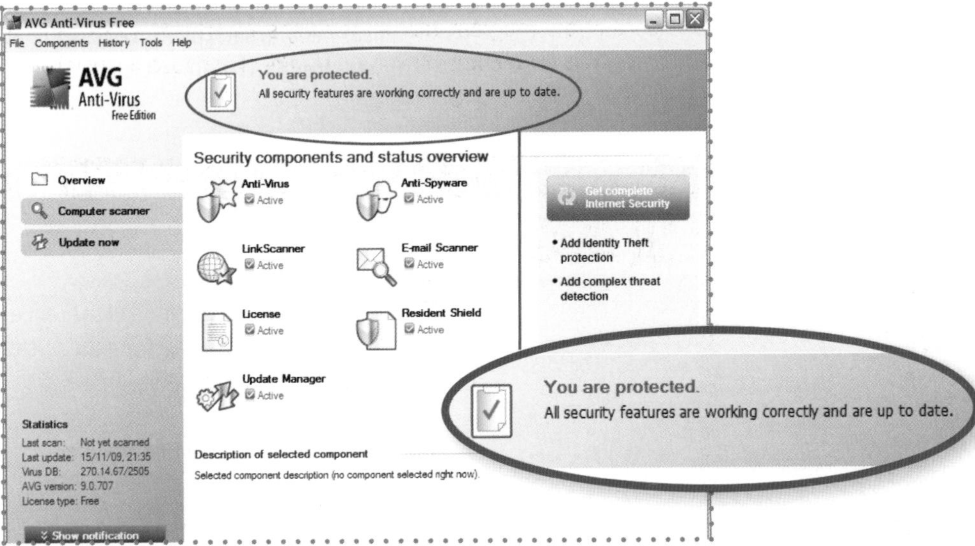

4 Click the **Computer scanner** tab, then **Scan whole computer**. This will examine the entire computer hard drive to check for any resident viruses or spyware – be aware that this scan can take a while to run. If it finds any infected files, AVG will remove and repair them

Schedule scans

1. Click the **Computer scanner** tab and then click **Manage Scheduled Scans**. The screen that appears shows a list of scheduled scans

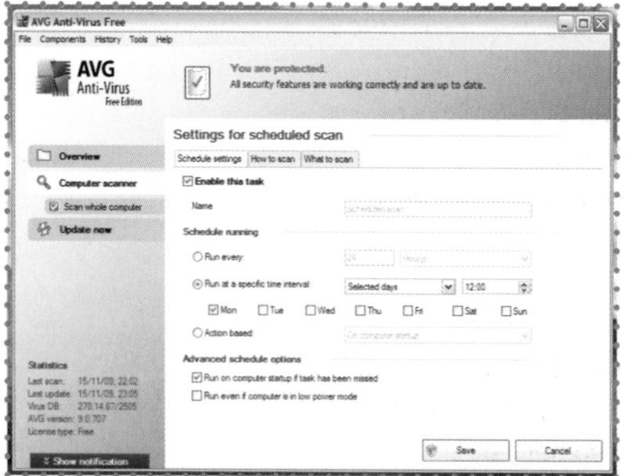

2. To change timings, click the **Edit scan schedule** button. Tick the **Enable this task** option

3. In the Schedule settings section, choose a time interval such as **Run at a specific time interval**. The default is midday once per week

4. Tick the **Run on computer startup if task has been missed**

Update software

AVG will automatically update at least once a day to keep you protected from the latest threats. To change the default:

1. Double click **Update Manager** from the **Overview** tab

2. Ensure **Start automatic updates** is ticked, and set a time such as 5pm every day

Keep protected

Every day from now on, AVG will automatically do an update, and scan your PC once a week. Because you've downloaded a free version, AVG will occasionally encourage you to upgrade to a more complete version, but this won't be free. You can ignore these messages – the basic, free version of AVG, combined with the other security software elements mentioned earlier, does an effective enough job.

YOUR INTERNET LEGAL QUESTIONS ANSWERED

Do I need a TV licence to watch TV online?

At the moment, you don't need a licence to watch online TV purely on demand. You do, however, need a TV licence if you're watching live TV online through any receiving device in the home, including a computer. For example, if you just watch a BBC show that was broadcast four days ago, you do not need a licence, but if you watch BBC News or Sport as it happens you do. However, you do not need a separate TV licence for online TV viewing – it is covered by your main TV licence.

What is copyright?

Copyright protects intellectual property – whether it's a piece of writing, a photograph, music, a film or a painting. It is normally owned by the creator(s) of the work, such as the author, composer, singer, artist, photographer and so on. Only a copyright holder can give permission for their work to be copied, given, rented, performed or broadcast to the public or adapted in any way.

What is a Creative Commons licence?

This licence keeps copyright firmly with the content creator, but does allow more generous use of the content according to a set of criteria set by the author. It means that content has 'some rights reserved', but might allow you to make personal back-ups or even pass content freely onto others. Be sure to check the terms and conditions of each licence.

Can I download music, video and images freely from the internet?

It is illegal to download anything that's protected by copyright – unless you're paying for it or have permission from the content creator to view or use it.

Can I download music from the internet if I already own the CD?

Even if you've already bought the latest album or single of your favourite band or singer, it's unlawful to download their music from the internet without paying for that download.

I've bought a song online. Can I share it with friends and family?

Just because you've bought a copy of a copyright work does not give you permission to use it as you wish. For example, buying a copy of a book, CD or film does not necessarily give you the right to make copies

Jargon buster

DRM

Digital Rights Management (DRM) is an anti-piracy technique used mainly by music companies to control what you can and cannot do with the files that you download, including the ability to play files on multiple devices. Many music sites now offer MP3 files without DRM restrictions.

(even for private use), or to play or show them in public. It means that you cannot pass it onto others.

How can I be sure that a download site is legal?
If you're using a site that's backed by the music industry – such as Apple iTunes, Amazon, Tesco and HMV among others – you usually have to pay to download music, games, films and so forth. If you use an 'unofficial' site, you're exchanging files with another computer over the internet – which is known as 'peer-to-peer' file-sharing – and usually there's no charge. This type of downloading is illegal because unofficial sites generally breach copyright laws.

What will happen if I download illegally?
Internet Service Providers (ISPs) can now take action against their customers who use their internet line to download or share copyright material, including music, games and films. Any user suspected of downloading illegal files may be sent a warning letter for the first offence, have their internet connection suspended if they're caught again, and have their internet connection cancelled if they're caught for a third time.

What are my rights to change my ISP?
Before starting any switching process, you should talk to your current provider. If you switch broadband provider before the end of any minimum contract term, you may have to pay a hefty cancellation fee. Under broadband switching regulation, the following rules apply:

- It is the responsibility of all broadband providers to ensure that technical and operational problems do not hinder consumers' ability to switch between broadband suppliers
- Where the MAC process applies (see page 23), your broadband ISP must issue your MAC code within five days of your request and is not allowed to charge you for access to it
- You may have to pay a broadband cancellation fee if you switch within your contract term, but broadband providers can't withhold MACs if you don't pay the broadband cancellation fee
- Your broadband MAC must remain valid for 30 days and, if it runs out, you can request another MAC for free

JARGON BUSTER

Jargon Buster

ADSL (Asymmetric digital subscriber line) A way of sending data over a copper wire telephone line.

Adware Software that tracks your web use to determine your interests and deliver relevant adverts.

Anti-spyware Software that prevents and/or removes spyware.

Anti-virus Software that scans for viruses and removes them from your computer.

Application A type of program that's used by a person, as opposed to a program that's used by a computer.

Attachment A computer file that is sent along with an email message. It can be any type of software file, and can be opened by the receiver if the appropriate software to view the file attachment is installed or available.

Blog A regularly updated online diary or journal.

Bookmarks A collection of favourite websites visited and saved by the user. Also called Favorites.

Broadband A method of connecting to the Internet via cable or ADSL (see above). Much faster than a dial-up connection.

Browser The software that enables you to view web pages. Often these contain phishing filters.

Browser History A folder, stored by the browser, which contains details of recently visited websites.

Cache The way web browsers store recently accessed pages, images, and other data so they can be displayed rapidly the next time they're requested.

Captcha A series of letters and numbers that are scrambled in such as way that only a human can read them when filling in a form, rather than an automated system.

Case sensitive Most search tools are not case sensitive or only respond to initial capitals, as in proper names. If in doubt, it's best to type lower case (no capitals) because lower case will always retrieve upper case letters too.

Chatroom Virtual environments that allow users to share information.

Cookie A piece of information sent to a user's web browser by a website. The web browser then returns that information to the website. This is how some websites 'remember' your previous visits.

Dial-up An internet connection via a normal phone line, which is slow compared to broadband.

Digital Rights Management (DRM) Special software that limits the number of copies you can make of a particular piece of music.

Domain name A unique name that identifies a website.

Dongle A small device that connects to a computer's USB port. In this context, it enables you to connect to the internet.

Download To transfer data from a remote computer to your own over the internet.

Email client A computer program that manages emails. Emails are stored on your computer, and you only need to be connected to the internet to send and receive them.

Ethernet A means of connecting computers together using cables – a common method for networking computers.

File extension The letters that appear after a file name. They show what type of document it is.

Firewall Software (or hardware) that blocks unwanted communication from, and often to, the internet.

Flaming Hostile and insulting interaction between internet users. Flaming usually occurs in the social context of a forum.

Forum An online message board.

FTP (File Transfer Protocol) Ability to transfer entire files rapidly from one computer to another, intact, for viewing or other purposes.

Hyperlink See **Link**

Icon A small picture that represents an object or program.

Instant messaging A form of communication allowing two or more people to hold a conversation in real time by typed messages over the internet.

ISP (Internet Service Provider) An ISP is the company that enables and services your connection to the internet.

Link Short for hyperlink, a link can be either text or an image that lets you jump straight to another web page when you click on it.

Log in/out To log in or sign in is to provide a username and password to identify yourself to a website. To log out or sign out is to notify the site that you're no longer using it, which will deny you access to the functions until you log in again.

Login name See **Username**

Malware Malicious software. A generic term for any program that is harmful to your computer, for example, a virus.

Mbps (Megabits per second) A measure of the speed of data transfer, often used when talking about the speed of broadband.

Media aggregator Software that regularly checks specified websites for updated content, such as the latest instalment of a podcast.

Microfilter A device that attaches to your telephone socket and enables you to make voice calls and use broadband at the same time via ADSL.

Modem A device that allows a computer to send information over a telephone line. You need a modem to connect to the internet.

MP3 The standard file format for digital music. The attraction of the format is that it is not tied to any one manufacturer in the way that AAC (Apple) and WMA (Microsoft) are.

PDF A file that captures all the graphics, fonts and formatting of a document, regardless of the application in which it was created.

Phishing A type of email scam where you're tricked into giving away personal details by being directed to a spoof website that resembles the site of an official organisation (a bank, for example).

Podcast Regularly updated audio or video content, such as a radio show, that can be downloaded from the internet.

Podcatcher Software that lets you subscribe to podcasts. It can automatically download new episodes as they become available.

Pop-up A small window that appears over an item (word or picture) on your computer screen to give additional information.

POP3 (Post Office Protocol) A way of allowing an email server (a computer dedicated to delivering email) to 'post' emails to your computer.

PowerPoint Part of Microsoft's Office suite of programs. It allows you to create slideshow presentations.

Router A device that routes data between computers and other devices. Routers can connect computers to each other or connect a computer to the internet.

RSS (Really Simple Syndication) A way of sharing information about new content, such as news headlines and podcasts, to other websites and software.

Screen name See **Username**

SMTP (Simple Mail Transfer Protocol) A standard internet protocol allowing an email program on your computer to deliver outgoing emails to an online email server (such as a webmail service).

Social networking A way for people to socialise online, typically via a website, such as Facebook or Bebo.

Software A general term for programs used to operate computers and related devices.

Spam filter Software or a system that helps to keep spam – unsolicited junk email – out of your email inbox.

Spyware Software that secretly installs on your computer and is able to track your internet behaviour and send details to a third party.

Tagging Process of adding descriptive keywords to a piece of information, such as a photo, video or web page, to aid in the search for it.

Taskbar The bar running across the bottom of your screen, from where you can open programs and access the main Windows functions.

Trojan A computer virus that disguises itself as an innocent program to entice people to install it. Trojans can allow third parties complete access to your computer remotely.

Upload Process of sending files from your computer to the internet.

URL (Uniform Resource Locator) A website's 'address'.

Username Also called a login name, screen name, or login. A unique name used to identify a person online.

Virus A malevolent program that spreads from computer to computer within another program or file.

Voice over Internet Protocol (VoIP) Term used to describe making phone calls over the internet rather than via a standard phone network.

Web browser See **Browser**

Webcam A video camera attached to or integrated into your computer.

Webmail Email accounts accessed through your web browser. Email is not stored locally on your computer.

Web page Each website on the internet usually has more than one page. These are referred to as web pages. Each web page has a unique address that you type in to go directly to that page.

Wiki A wiki is a type of website that allows users to create, edit, and organise web pages easily.

World Wide Web Frequently shortened to just the web or WWW, the World Wide Web refers to the billions of websites that are hosted on servers all over the world and are accessible via web browsers all over the world. These form a 'web' of the billions of web pages that link to one another.

Worm Similar to a virus, except a worm doesn't need to attach itself to a document and can simply spread via the internet.

XML (eXtensible Markup Language) The standard computer code RSS is based on.

Index

Index

Index

ABOUT THE CONSULTANT EDITOR LYNN WRIGHT
Lynn Wright is an editor and journalist with 20 years' experience in writing about computing, technology and digital photography.

HAVING PROBLEMS WITH YOUR COMPUTER?

A few years ago **Which? Computing** launched an online Helpdesk service. The team has a combined experience of over forty years and promises to answer questions within five working days.

To date, the team has answered tens of thousands of queries from readers, and there's no PC problem they won't tackle.

As a reader of **Internet Made Easy for the Over 50s**, you can now access this indispensable service absolutely free.

To submit a question for the Helpdesk*, simply go to **www.which.co.uk/computinghelpdesk**

Enter your query and, where it asks for a membership number, simply enter the code that can be found on page 6.

*This service is only available online

For more information about Which? Computing magazine and membership, go to www.which.co.uk or call the Which? Helpline 01992 822800.